Climate Responsive Design

Climate Responsive Design

A study of buildings in moderate
and hot humid climates

Richard Hyde

London and New York

First published 2000
by E & FN Spon
11 New Fetter Lane, London EC4P 4EE

Simultaneously published in the USA and Canada
by E & FN Spon

29 West 35th Street, New York, NY 10001

E & FN Spon is an imprint of the Taylor & Francis Group

Printed and bound in Great Britain by
St Edmundsbury Press, Bury St Edmunds, Suffolk

The publisher makes no representation, express or implied, with regard to the
accuracy of the information contained in this book and cannot accept any legal
responsibility or liability for any errors or omissions that may be made.

Publisher's Note
This book has been designed and typeset by the author

British Library Cataloguing in Publication Data
A catalogue record for this book is available from the British Library

Library of Congress Cataloging in Publication Data
A catalogue record for this book has been requested

ISBN 0-419-20970-0

Contents

Contributors

Michael Docherty, BArch, MArch, Lecturer, Department of Architecture
University of Queensland
Professor Peter Woods, B Arch, PhD, School of Architecture, Universiti of
Malaya

Foreword

Students in schools of architecture in tropical countries often seem hell bent on mentally dragging their project sites several thousand miles north or south. The result is designs that in their construction, fenestration, massing and planning ape environmentally defensive models sitting in benign temperate climates. I wish I could say the same is not true for many practising architects in tropical countries. Textbooks on environmental design have often tended to treat warm climates as an interesting side issue to the main stream of climatic architecture. Warm climates are not a marginal concern to the increasing portion of the world population living in the tropics, where a great amount of construction activity in the world will have to take place in the next century.

This book makes frequent reference to the work of Maxwell Fry and Jane Drew, and in many ways it is resonant with their observations of forty years ago. Recognition, that it is always the site and the climate that provides both the opportunities and problems for design in tropical countries, is the starting point. The other realities of programme, aspiration and economics are not ignored, this is always a practical book, but the climatic and context imperatives remain foremost. Descriptions of site and microclimate evidence the sensibilities of architects designing with the sun on their back, knowing the essential need for shade, understanding the violence and subtleties of the various warm climates. The book helps to dispel some of the gross generalizations and myths about tropical climates, identifying design strategies that work for one but are ineffective in another. The necessary architectural physics is introduced as is required, and the relevance is thus made clear. It is impossible to design with a serious regard for the environment without understanding these principles. The case studies are also introduced to illuminate, rather than promote, hence the choice ranges from the mundane and common place to some of the best examples of responsive design in the tropical region.

By far the most significant feature of this book is the extensive use of the building section to explain the climate modification, the idea that the edge between inside and outside is where all the action is. This has to be a large step forward if designers can be persuaded to consider both the plan and section in the microclimate of the site. Climate responsive design is at least three-dimensional, frequently four.

Peter Woods
Universiti Malaya, Kuala Lumpur, 1998

Preface

The inspiration for this work has come from the many fine buildings that have been visited over the last three years and the enthusiastic interaction with the many building designers, clients and users of these buildings. It is also evident that there is an emerging design culture which focuses on the environmental design of buildings. The thrust of this design direction is to utilize concepts that minimize environmental impacts of buildings through selecting an appropriate response to the climate.

The intentions are therefore to provide a description of buildings which can be defined as climate responsive design, that is those that have used a climate-based design process and climate response concepts as major generators of the architecture. Furthermore, the framework departs from the traditional discussion climate and architecture which normally starts with an analysis of climates and finally examines the synthesis of climate and building form. In this case a more practise-based approach is taken which examines specific design issues, strategies, architectural elements and built examples. The foci is on moderate and hot humid climate types. The benefit of this framework is that the resulting climate response can be seen in a more holistic context thus providing a better understanding of design synthesis in the architecture.

Therefore, it is not an exhaustive review of the architectural science theory and practice, there are many excellent texts available for that purpose and readers are directed to these for further amplification of the scientific basis for this knowledge.

It should also be noted that this is a primer for design use and that wider generalizations based on the cases may not be appropriate to specific to different design problems. Therefore, since climate responsive design is microclimate, function and context specific, designers should carefully examine the application of the concepts used in this text to the particular problem in hand. It is intended that the following discussion is an illustration of strategies applicable in climate responsive design rather than a textbook of solutions. A careful consideration and analysis of the utilization of these strategies in specific projects in hand is advisable. It is hoped that the buildings discussed here will inspire and encourage responsible environmental design practice and thus minimize negative building impacts for users and the broader environment.

Richard Hyde

Acknowledgements

The author would like to thank the many people who have contributed to the text. It is impossible to list all those involved with the production. Important support has come from the following organizations.

The Australian Research Council for funding the research projects from which evidence of the effectiveness of climate responsive design is used.

The University of Queensland Special Studies Program for the teaching relief to make this manuscript possible.

The Department of Architecture, The University of Queensland, for assistance in the production of the manuscript.

Special thanks should be given to Professor Emeritus Henry Cowan, for reviewing the manuscript and his many constructive comments. Also thanks to Professor Peter Woods for his advice on the text and assistance with issues of content.

Caroline Mallinder and Rebecca Casey from E&FN Spon, without whose continued support for this project it would not have been possible.

The many colleagues who have contributed advice and in particular Helmut Ranch who worked on the electronic camera ready form of the manuscript and Paul Raynis who edited the text.

Design Issues

PART 1

Introduction

CHAPTER 1

Climate is clearly one of the prime factors in culture, and therefore built form. It is the mainspring for all the sensual qualities that add up to a vital tropical architecture, Tan Hock Beng.[1]

1.1 Definition

Climate responsive design is based on the way a building form and structure moderates the climate for human good and well-being. Any cursory exploration of this concept reveals that there is a strong form determinant aspect to the relationship. The pragmatic and physical parameters associated with this aspect of architectural design are constants that transcend time and are regulated by the laws of science, in particular the laws of thermodynamics.

Yet the pragmatics are also balanced by a desire to respond to the poetic aspects of climate. Many architects seek to use the building as an implement, not just to moderate climate, but to enhance and expose the senses to the spectrum of thermal and visual delight. Warm climates have a potential far beyond that found in more temperate and cool climates. Unlike cool climates where the sense of enclosure requires a defensive strategy, the warm climate

1.1 *In this tropical Queenslander house, the form determinants of climate are found; the elevated floors, lightweight construction and the windows open to the microclimate of the site for ventilation*

buildings open and filter the climate in a multitude of ways. Thus the architecture responds to climate as one further vehicle for extending people's experience of the building. These intangible aspects of architecture provide an additional palette of aesthetic and creative concepts. The harnessing of these concepts in architectural design requires careful consideration. This comes from both the timing of the consideration of climatic issues in the design process and the procedure by which it is synthesized with the range of issues that present themselves in the design problem.

Climate responsive design, by definition follows the latter course, and requires of the architect both analytical and synthesis skills to optimize the relationship between the site, climate and briefing requirements. In addition, those buildings which use climate as a form determinant in both the pragmatic and poetic sense result in climate responsive architecture.

1.2 Moderate and hot humid climates

Global climatic parameters

If climate responsive design uses climate as a form determinate then the first issue to be addressed is defining the nature of warm climates. Climate can be defined as the broad meteorological conditions pertaining to a region. Warm climates are near to the Equator, receive high levels of solar radiation and therefore are in heat surplus for a large proportion of the year. The higher temperatures allow the air to hold more moisture and therefore have greater relative humidity.

The seasonal variation increases further from the Equator and therefore climates nearer to it have little seasonal change and stable temperatures with large variations in rainfall during the year (some have one or two monsoons). Further away from it greater seasonal variation occurs with cooler winters which can present an under-heating problem. This global heating pattern is modified by differences in land and ocean effects.

Land dominated climates such as the interior of Australia have larger diurnal ranges in temperatures and low rainfall whilst ocean dominated areas have smaller diurnal ranges and higher rainfall. Yet in spite of these modifying effects, the first major difference between warm and cold climates is the amount of solar radiation that is received, thus a classification by temperature and humidity is used. Three climate types are defined – hot humid, hot dry and moderate. These classifications are purely descriptive and provide a convenient nomenclature in the text. This is not to say that more climates cannot be defined, but for clarity three suffice.

This classification defines the the global climatic parameters in which the building is located. The significance of the classification from the design point of view is that some designers see these parameters as physical constraints; others as a challenge and use them to establish contrast in the building. For example, the physical characteristics of climate can be defined and related to thermal comfort which gives the design basis of selecting climate modifica-

tion strategies in a building. These basic climate modification strategies involve the use of airflow, solar gain, evaporative cooling and thermal mass.
The more challenging design problems are where there is an inherent conflict
between the design objectives and climatic factors. For example, it may be
that the best views from the building face west so the constraint of trying to
reduce high solar gain can be contrasted with the need to respect the view.
This presents the designer with a particular challenging climate design problem. A discussion of the physical determinants of climates, climate modification strategies and the resulting design challenges forms the first part of
Chapter 2.

Building context and microclimate

Yet even with these basic strategies, the question arises of how to integrate
them within the building and building context. It is useful to focus on how
this can be addressed by comparing the building response with that of buildings in cooler climates where there is a heat deficit. Invariably in these cooler
climates the designer looks for a solution inside the building. For example,
Frank Lloyd Wright designed many of his houses with the fireplace in the
conceptual centre of the building. In practice this serves to heat the house
efficiently; other strategies can be used such as the use of insulation and
mass for the walls and roof, a reduction in the window size can also be used.
The overall effect of these strategies is to reduce heat loss. In warm climates
this pattern is not followed; the methods of reducing heat gain come from
without, in particular from the use of the site and its immediate microclimate. The main passive method of cooling is ventilation, therefore the building requires careful design, as well as site planning for an optimum orientation. The avoidance of heat gain can also be effected at the site level through
shading from the landscape. Thus the building context becomes a major
factor in the climate response of the building. The second part of Chapter 2
examines the relationship between building, site and context. This discussion leads to a broader focus of climate responsive design and to the approach taken in design and its relationship to the evolving field of environmental design.

1.3 Climate responsive and environmental sustainable design

The increasing concern for environmental impacts of buildings and the quality
of their internal environments has raised the debate as to the role architects should
play in the environmental design of buildings. In particular, attention is drawn to
the case for the 'Green' building. The Green perspective makes the environmental issues related to building design of prime importance. Indeed some
have challenged the concern for aesthetics from the Green perspective.
    The Vales have examined the relationship between the goals of design

1.2 *The site and climate is the view from the windows of the resort shown to the right. Research into users perceptions of climate in tropical resorts questions the need for the use of active and highly defensive building skin aims to connect the building to site and climate*

and the use resources, suggesting the following: 'Monumental architecture, from its beginnings, is associated with a profligate attitude to resources.' Their main argument is that 'true architecture' has failed to link resources with design and consequently with environmental impact. Thus they maintain that the first major axiom of Green design is concerned with resource utilization. There is also concern for the profligate use of resources for purely conceptual and aesthetic purposes, and more focus on architecture that is more holistically orientated to its environmental role. In this view, the designer is concerned for the 'the web' that makes up the building as well as the object quality of building.[2]

Clearly this represents a paradigm of thinking concerning design and requires a philosophical and ethical commitment from the designer. This ethical position has been endorsed by many architects and follows the lead of professional bodies. These bodies have developed policies and guidelines to reduce negative environmental impacts. For example, the Royal Australian Institute of Architects has developed the following environmental principles:

1. Maintain and, where it has been disturbed, restore biodiversity
2. Minimize the consumption of resources, especially non-renewable resources
3. Minimize pollution of soil, air and water
4. Maximize the health, safety and comfort of building users
5. Increase awareness of environmental issues[2]

Individual architects need to implement these principles within the following framework:

– holistic consideration of negative environmental impacts that arise in the construction of the building and its infrastructure

1.3 The skin as a separator to create an artificial climate inside the building, separates users from the environment they have come to enjoy, climate responsive building design exploits this potential

- make design recommendations, which minimize the negative environmental effects of building and buildings

As can be seen, principle 2 is concerned with resource utilization and is further defined with regard to climate:

1. Use of renewable resources in preference to finite resources

2. Encourage the reduction of power consumption by, for example, maximizing passive thermal comfort and enabling users to make efficient use of building appliances[3]

Climate responsive design is therefore an integral part of the environmental framework that is being developed to reduce environmental impacts and provide for human well-being. One main feature is to use passive climate control systems rather than rely on active energy systems that consume non-renewable resources. Traditionally designed building, the models for which predate the power revolution, are also a useful basis for examining the relation between building and climate. As has been seen, the use of climate responsive design is a subset of the wider issues of environmental design, therefore the philosophy of climate design has as its foundation the holistic orientation of environmental design. Hence it is appropriate to consider in particular the nature of traditional buildings and their environments. These buildings encapsulate thousands of years of unconscious research into the relationship between building and climate and represent more holistic models for the development of a climate responsive architecture. These traditional models can be examined as precedents, which inform the architecture, rather than to

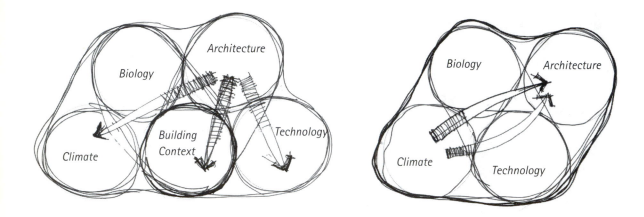

1.4 Bioclimatic and climate responsive design. In bioclimatic design the procedure is to start with an analysis of the climate and then move to design synthesis. Climate responsive design is focused on the synthesis and the selection of climate responsive strategies to meet design objectives

provide a set of ready-made solutions. Analytical studies of the traditional buildings offer an understanding of the relationship between culture, climate and building form. Indeed the historical aspects of traditional architecture are founded in the concerns for a regional architecture.

Regional architecture is defined as the architecture of the place, with the form and character generated out of the culture, climate and the region. This is a particular problem for the developing nations of the world such as Southeast Asia, where the tide of industrialization and westernization has swept away the traditional architecture. This has caused a questioning of the lack of identity and historical linkages in the architecture,[4] thus Tan Hock Beng suggests:

'Many architects working in the region today have forgotten how to design bearing in mind the climate and landscape. They are now caught in the homogenizing forces of mass media and are repeating the built mediocrities of international fashion. Each commission is seen as a vehicle for egoistic self-expression while little importance is attached to memory and continuity.'[5]

Yet the problem is that the context in which these buildings have been built has changed. Factors such as the urbanization of the city, the development of technology and the reduction in availability of resources bring into question the use of traditional models as set-piece solutions.

The 'man-made universal climate' and the natural climate

The self-evident feature of traditional architecture is that it uses the natural climate. The modification of climate is through the building form, fabric and landscape. The recent use of plant and equipment in buildings to modify climate has led to the problem of the man-made climate – the ability to use air-conditioning to modify climate to 25 degrees C and 50 per cent humidity creates an internal climate which can be replicated around the world, indeed it can be constructed in outer space. Hence it is not only man-made but also

1.5 *Left and middle: a church in Cairns, Australia using a buffering strategy of the veranda to protect the building skin from heat gain and also provide a semi-outdoor space:*
right: the church makes use of the strategy of single skin construction of timber studs and weatherboards leading to a skin-cooled building that has a quick response to the hot humid climate, also the construction easily dissipates the occasional high casual heat gains from the occupants

universal. Designers can now reach for the energy solution to climate modification with ease, passing on running costs to consumers and designing buildings without concern for place. Examples of this approach can be found in many places, one case is found in some of the holiday resorts built in northern tropical Queensland. The practice is to use air-conditioning plant and equipment to regulate comfort. In addition, highly defensive skins with large amounts of mass and solar glass are used to reduce energy consumption. The use of the universal climate in this context is a lost opportunity for climate responsive architecture. First, the architectural consequence of this is that building form and fabric creates a barrier to the exterior and the connection to climate is lost. Second, a further consequence of this is to separate the visitors from the place they have come to experience, clearly defeating the purpose of the building.

The design of these resorts is based on the assumption that visitor's expectations regarding the thermal comfort of the internal environment are for the 'universal climate'. Yet research has shown that visitors expectations may be very different and that acceptable comfort levels can be provided by passive means.[6] This suggests that there is the potential to use more passive means and avoid design conditions where the building is clearly out of place within its context. Indeed, the building separates the visitor from the context which he or she has come to experience and enjoy. The argument here is not that air-conditioning as a method of climate control is less appropriate than natural climates, rather that the designer has to consider more holistically the strategies used for environmental control given a particular building function, design and context.

1.6 *The landscape of water and vegetation, when combined with the need for shelter as found at the Kuranda railway station in Cairns, Australia, draw on both tangible and intangible aspects of climate response*

Bioclimatic design and strategic design

It is clear from this case that the designer has to consider quite clearly the over-arching design decisions regarding the building context. These centre on the requirements of the brief, the site and the climate that form the point of departure and direction of the project. These decisions are particularly important in large non-domestic buildings where the size of the environmental intervention is both extensive and costly. A way of articulating decision making in the design process is to suggest that these are large complex buildings requiring careful application of appropriate environmental strategies.

Strategies are basic directions that can be taken with regard to optimum climatic performance of the building. Thus optimum orientation is a key strategy in warm climates which may suggest that buildings should be positioned so that they receive the cooling breezes in summer. Thus the strategy has a particular planning implication for the designer. It also has tactical consequences for the building fabric; the fenestration should be designed to accord with the climatic conditions. There is also a responsibility for the user to appreciate this strategy and use the building skin to make the most of summer breezes. Finally, the effectiveness and efficiency of strategies and tactics can be examined in terms of both tangible and intangible design consequences.

In theory there is a level of clarity and rationality in this approach, but it belies a complexity that exists in the way buildings are designed. It is a simplistic assumption to think that a climate design is just a collection of strategies; rather it is a synthesis of a range of factors that are both within and outside the domain of climate responsive design. The argument for the strategic framework is embedded in the following case:

'In hot weather, when the external temperature is high, too much heat may enter the space. If this heat can be absorbed by the fabric of the building, the peak air temperature during the day will be less. If night time ventilation is possible, the heat absorbed by the fabric can be lost at night when temperatures are lower. But if buildings are lightweight and sealed, they are likely to overheat and a need for air-conditioning will result.'[7]

If this strategy is unpacked into its constituent arguments, it can be seen to have a number of prerequisites, a range of architectural science concepts and certain limitations.

First, the term 'hot weather' should be examined. This is a general description and therefore requires qualification of the type of climate within the classification of warm climates, moderate, hot dry and hot humid.

Second, the building 'fabric' is used to modify climate by way of the thermal flywheel effect. This uses high-mass materials for heat storage thus providing a passive heating and cooling system. This is not a simple strategy to use particularly in warm climates which have little diurnal range of temperature. Thus there are a number of factors that make this strategy effective. Furthermore, a cursory examination of buildings in warm climates, tells us that this strategy is by no means globally used. For example a traditional church in Cairns, Australia, in an area with a hot humid climate, uses a large volume of space and a lightweight timber single-skin construction. The thermal loads are received from the external environment and the internal high casual gains caused by the congregation at weekly mass. Ventilation and skin cooling dissipate the heat loads from the latter.

Third, the reference to lightweight sealed buildings that are problematic and need air-conditioning. This assertion can equally be levelled at sealed heavyweight buildings. Therefore a range of questions related to the relative effectiveness of microclimate, fabric and use of air-conditioning plant should be considered in the assessment of building strategies. In addition to the physical attributes of these strategies, there are also other considerations.

Intangible and tangible qualities

Further examples of buildings found in these hot humid climates reflect the intangible qualities that come from response of buildings to the climates: the minimal use of shelter and the connection with the lush landscape.

These aspects reflect the quality of place with regard to the need for a climate responsive design approach. Kuranda railway station in Cairns is a useful example. A light steel structure is used to provide the needs for shelter. This is then used as an armature for a myriad of plants that enjoy the shade. This transforms the building in terms of experience from a utilitarian structure to an integration of building and microclimate. Indeed it takes advantage of the microclimate created by the building to develop the landscape. These landscaping elements soften the light and glare and provide an environment that is something quite unexpected. Thus whilst there are a number of tangible factors that explain the scientific basis of climatic responsive architecture there are also a number of qualitative aspects that contribute to the experience of the building.

The second part of Chapter 2 examines the issues concerned with the climate responsive design from the standpoint of environmental design and traditional architecture and how the principles from these sources can feed a strategic approach to climate responsive design.

Finally, the tangible and intangible measures that are available to designers as a way of assisting with the evaluation of these strategies are discussed in subsequent chapters on building strategies.

1.4 Design issues and building elements

The examination and reflection of climate design follows a strategic framework. The first two chapters discuss the broad design issues related to climate types and building form. These constitute the first part of the text. The remaining part is concerned with the strategies used for the design elements. This starts with a discussion of structural systems for warm climate buildings. Little work has been carried out on the use of different types of structural system for climatic advantage, although there has been considerable assessment of the use of materials for thermal performance.

The next chapter examines the effect of climate on building design and construction arguing for strategies that avoid labour intensive systems, use a top-down construction system with early roof completion to protect building workers and the fabric of the building from climatic effects. The issue of health and safety in the building work place is of increasing concern, and the

1.7 *A colonial house in Singapore uses a veranda strategy as a buffer zone for climate modification. The design methodology of placing strategies in context in this way gives a holistic understanding of climative responsive design*

systems that provide protection from the extremes of climate are advantageous. The analysis of the building process identifies the roof as a dominant element in the warm climate building.

The roof provides the imagery, which is articulated in many cultures, and this is hardly surprising as it is a highly defensive mechanism in the climatic control system of the building. The types of roof are discussed in relation to climate types and the section of the building. As will be seen in Chapter 6 , the importance of the building section in conjunction with the roof demonstrates the climate control features in the building, in particular ventilation, solar access and lighting.

The section of the building comprises walls and floors but different strategies apply to the external walls than to the internal walls. Therefore the external wall is examined separately in Chapter 7. The relationship between external wall and plan depth is discussed here from the point of view of the differing zones for climate control. The problem with the external wall is complex due to differing and competing performance requirements. There is the need to maximize transparency for light and ventilation yet also the need for closure and shading to prevent solar gain. Strategies for accommodating these conflicting requirements are discussed specific to orientation. An argument is also made for classifying buildings according to exterior or interior dominance. The exterior dominant buildings are those that rely more on exterior factors for their climate control whilst the interior dominant buildings use internal factors such as the moderating influence of fabric within the walls and floors.

Floors and internal walls are examined in the Chapter 8. The floors in warm climate buildings are conceptually seen as platforms that are juxtaposed in space for climatic advantages such as accessing ventilation and shade. The combination of floor and wall can also act as a thermal moderator if built of mass construction such as concrete or masonry. Therefore, this chapter examines the role of the floor in interior dominant buildings where the mass of the interior construction is used to assist with controlling internal temperatures. The principles of mass charging and decharging are considered.

Various additional strategies are found in the design of warm climate buildings for providing transition spaces between the building from the climate. This involves adding semi-outdoor areas such as verandas and courtyards to the basic building form. The use of these strategies is examined in Chapters 9 and 10. These spaces are important forms of buffer zoning providing privacy and varying degrees of shading to the building and glare control. In larger complex buildings these form ducts and re-entrant spaces for ventilation. The airflow around this open type of space is important so as to maintain the climate control function. In particular the use of types of solar driven chimney are discussed. The efficiency of these systems is questioned as it relies extensively on natural forces and is therefore unpredictable. Thus, whilst these systems may be practicable on a small scale, the effectiveness of using these systems on large buildings is debatable. Thus, these external spaces provide a useful microclimate that moderates the climatic extremes of the site and also orchestrates the moderating effects of climate to provide the optimum response from the building.

1.5 Case studies

The method used in discussing the respective strategies is through a series of case studies. In all chapters these are used to identify and explain the strategies identified. Each case is examined selectively, depending on the issues in the chapter. The range of cases is based on both traditional and modern buildings; the traditional buildings demonstrate that the climate response has been optimized over time whilst the modern buildings help examine the way the traditional approaches have been adapted to the modern context. In this way the use of strategies can be seen in the context in which they are applied. This reinforces the notion that climate responsive design comes not from a potpourri of strategies but from a synthesis of a number of underlying concepts on which these strategies are based. The effective practice of climate responsive architecture lies in the generation and evaluation of strategies applicable to the particular building context.

The selection of these case studies and the scope of the book focuses on examples from mainly the hot humid and moderate climates. This is due to the fact that a large part of the population inhabits these less arid areas. The hot arid climates are less populated as they sustain little agriculture and people live in these areas mainly for the extraction of mineral resources.

1.6 References

1. Tan Hock Beng, *Tropical Architecture and Interiors*, Page One Books, 1994, p.13.
2. B. Vale, and R. Vale, *Green Architecture*, Thames and Hudson, 1996, p. 5.
3. K. Harman, *The Environmental Design Guide*, Royal Institute of Australian Architects, 1995, General 1, pp. 1–3.
4. R. Powell, *Architecture and Identity*, Exploring Architecture in Islamic Cultures 1, The Aga Khan Award for Architecture, Concept Media, 1983.
5. Tan Hock Beng, op. cit., pp. 14–15.
6 Z. Bromberic, 'Passive climate control for tourist facilities in the coastal tropics,' unpublished thesis, Department of Architecture, The University of Queensland, 1995.
7 M. Fordam, ed., *Environmental Design*, E&F Spon, 1996, p. 4.

Warm climates and the building context

'But we repeat, we are on the edge of knowledge only and much more must be known, not only of the facts themselves: of climate, animals and insect life, materials and behaviour of materials – but of their correlation in a widening and complicating civilization', Fry and Drew.[1]

2.1 Introduction

The underlying principle behind climate responsive design is the understanding of the climatic parameters in which the building is situated. Climate by definition is related to the atmospheric conditions of temperature, humidity, wind, vegetation and light specific to a geographical location. Three levels of climate conditions can be found. First are the global conditions of the region created by the dominant geographical features of land, sea, sun and air. Next, these are modified by local conditions dependent on dominant features of water, topography, vegetation and built environment. Finally, there are the site conditions and building context, which are an interaction of local conditions and the building. These factors modify climate at a macro- and micro level. This description of climate belies a continuously changing set of conditions where the only certainty is that today will not be the same as yesterday. Thus the weather, that momentary state of atmospheric conditions, is so difficult to predict. Yet the designer has to examine patterns in the climate that are discernible and use these as basic parameters for design. Not

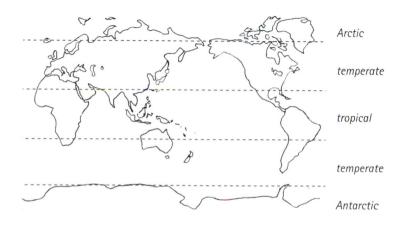

Arctic

temperate

tropical

temperate

Antarctic

2.1 Global climate zones: Arctic, Antarctic, temperate and tropical zones

only the macroclimate but also the microclimate associated with the site has to be taken into account.

In the last chapter the importance of the site as a predeterminant in climatic design is argued, in this chapter the parameters of climate will be examined. A review of the nature of warm climatic conditions is discussed, followed by the identification of appropriate climate modification strategies based on bioclimatic principles. This is followed by a discussion of issues related to the site and building context.

2.2 The nature of warm climates

Natural forces of land, sun, sea and air drive the global conditions of climate. In principle it is solar energy that provides the energy to create the world's weather systems. The angle of incidence of the sun to the earth is particularly important as it controls the amount of solar radiation and therefore the temperature of the atmosphere at a particular point on the surface of the globe. Four main areas are found, the Arctic, Antarctic, temperate and tropical areas. In the tropics, the angle of incidence of the sun is 90 degrees, whilst at the poles it is zero. The amount of solar irradiance is therefore greatest at the equator and least at the poles. The heat differential creates pressure differences and airflow across the surface of the globe, thus the cold air at the poles is at higher pressure, descends and moves out to the hotter rising air at the tropics. Moderating effects occur with the differential heating of land and sea as well as the rotation of the earth. During winter months the land will cool, causing high pressure systems. In summer it heats up causing areas of air to rise giving creating low pressure systems. The warm climates are those which lie from the equator to the tropics of Capricorn and Cancer, although this is not an exclusive categorization as some climates outside this area have characteristics of both the tropics and the temperate areas.

There is some debate about the best way to classify climates, whether by temperature and humidity or by other factors such as vegetation and altitude. Lippsmeier, for example, classifies climate by a wide range of factors and identifies five main climate zones as follows:[2]

- subtropics
- hot arid zone
- savanna zones
- monsoon zones
- hot humid zones

In addition, he defines two secondary zones, a mountainous zone where altitude affects climate and a maritime zone where ocean effects dominate the climate. Szokolay, on the other hand, relates climate mainly to human comfort. Four main factors are important for thermal comfort: air temperature, humidity, air movement, solar radiation.[3] Four main climate types are defined:[4]

Table 2.1 Stages in climate investigations, after Lippsmeier[6]

Stage 1: Climatic meteorological data collection	Stage 2: Bioclimatic comparative analysis	Stage 3: Selection of climate modification strategies
Solar radiation Sunshine Temperature Humidity Rainfall Wind velocity and direction	Assessment of the climate data in relation to thermal comfort	Cooling strategies through dehumidification, evaporation, airflow and mass. Heating through mass and solar gain

- cool
- moderate
- hot dry
- hot humid

This classification by Szokolay is particularly useful as it can be related to building design and therefore utilized in this study. Warm climates are those that form the last three types – moderate, hot dry and hot humid.

2.3   Climate investigation

'It is the designers task to analyse climatic information and present it in a form that allows him to identify features that are beneficial and harmful.'[5]

The work of Olgay suggests a way of assessing harmful and beneficial features of climate through an analytical investigation of climate that can proceed through a series of steps. He called this form of investigation and interpretation of climate factors 'bioclimatic design'. It follows clearly the analysis and synthesis model of design which starts from the general analysis of climate and moves to specific issues of design synthesis.[7] Further discussion of the strengths and weaknesses of this approach are given in the next chapter. Broadly though, the advice given to designers is to follow a linear form of enquiry. This involves an interpretation of the climate data of a particular location in relation to the biological conditions of human comfort in that location. Thus, the first issue to be resolved is the relationship between human physiology to the climate conditions.

Stage 1: Information on seasonal and daily climatic data

The first step involves investigation of the macroclimatic conditions of the zone in which the building is located (see Table 2.1). The first stage is to collect broad meteorological data on the macro aspects of climate in which the building is located. The important data are humidity and the dry-bulb temperature recorded for a typical year. Minimum and maximum tempera-

2.2 *Bioclimatic chart showing climate modification strategies for extending the comfort zone by the use of air-flow for over-heating and radiation for under-heating periods*

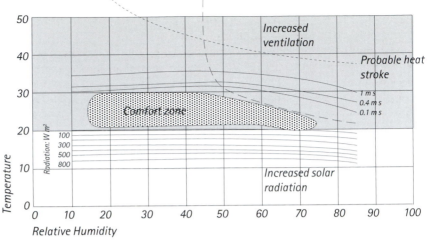

tures on a monthly basis should be used. The reason for this is that the bioclimatic chart uses this data to assess comfort conditions. Data is available from a number of sources including computer programs.[8]

Stage 2: The bioclimatic chart

An examination of the bioclimatic chart reveals particular important information for the designer. The first is descriptive, that is it describes a set of temperatures and humidity at which it is thought humans feel comfortable.[9] Thus the climate data for a particular location, as defined in Stage 1, can be compared to the zone of comfort defined by the bioclimatic chart. A level of fit can be assessed through examining the data in terms of the times of the year or day when the climate exceeds or is below the comfort zone. A close assessment of climate is the first level of interpretation required for the designer to gain an awareness of the climatic parameters.

The second important value of the bioclimatic chart is its predictive role. Where the climate data suggests that the climate does not fit within the comfort zone a number of strategies are suggested to extend the zone. These can be called climate modification strategies since other factors can be used to moderate the conditions of temperature and humidity.

Stage 3: Climate modification strategies

For warm climates the temperatures usually range above 20 degrees C. Thus the major climate condition is the concern for over-heating with temperatures above the comfort zone. A further complication is the concern for relative humidity which reduces the upper limit of acceptable temperatures to 22-23 degrees C. In under-heating conditions the effect of humidity in not so pronounced. The strategies for extending the comforts zone using both person and building related factors are as follows:

1. Over-heating:
- use of airflow, this improves the efficiency of cooling the body also re-moves heat from inside the building
- the use of building mass as a thermal flywheel, this can be used to store coolth periods of low temperatures and used to cool air during the hotter periods
- evaporative cooling, the use of the latent change of water absorbs heat and thus can cool the air thereby reducing temperatures
- dehumifying, the use of the building or plant to reduce moisture in the air.

2. Under-heating:
- building mass can be used as a thermal flywheel in the reverse of the above by storing heat during periods of higher temperatures and using this to heat air during cooler periods
- solar gain can be used to increase the efficiency of heating the body by direct solar heat thus, although the air temperature may be low, heat from the sun provides additional heat to provide comfort.

To establish which strategies are most or least effective for a particular climate it is necessary to overlay the data from the first stage with the data in the bioclimatic chart. This form of comparative analysis is available from a number of sources, but of particular interest are a number of computer programs such as DA Sketch Pad and ARCHIPAK[10] which can carry out an analysis of climate from this bioclimatic perspective. The application of this approach can be seen by examining locations that come from the three main climate zones – moderate, hot dry and hot humid. The interesting outcome from this analysis is the debate about the relative effectiveness of each strategy and the practicality of integrating the strategies into the building design.

2.5 The moderate climate

These types of climate have characteristics of both the tropical region and the temperate region and are therefore some times called composite climates. These climates are located far from the Equator and usually occur in large land masses. There are marked seasonal changes mostly and rainfall can have the characteristics of the monsoon with pronounced wet and dry seasons. An example of a moderate climate is Brisbane, Australia: first the broad climatic pattern is discussed followed by the particular characterisitcs of the climate.

Seasonal pattern

The seasonal pattern varies considerably with rainfall, solar gain and wind flow. In summer the land mass will heat up creating rising air and low pressure. In winter the land will cool down, causing high pressure from denser air. The

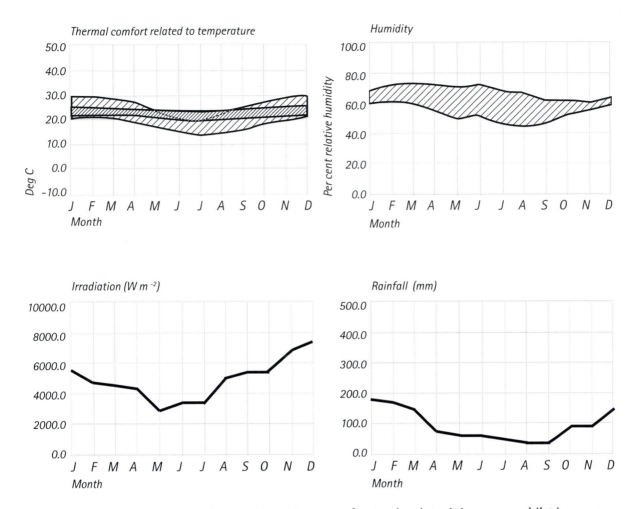

2.3 *Seasonal pattern for the moderate climate of Brisbane, Australia*

 Comfort zone

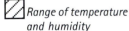 Range of temperature and humidity

sea temperature acts as a moderator; in winter it is warmer whilst in summer it is cooler. The effect on temperatures and humidity depends on whether the air is moving across the sea or the land. Onshore sea breezes in summer can bring cooling and more humid air to the land, whilst land breezes can bring dryer, hotter air. In addition, pronounced wet seasons and dry seasons bring different amounts of cloud cover and thus availability of solar radiation for heating and problems of cooling in summer.

Brisbane has a coastal location and the climate responds in a similar way to this pattern. In winter the land mass of central Austalia can dominate the climate giving cool dry winters. The summers are hot and humid influenced by monsoonal and ocean conditions of the tropical north of Australia. High levels of solar irradiance are found most of the year, 3000-8000 W m-². The cloudy conditions in summer moderate solar radiation whilst the clear sky conditions in winter facilitate solar radiation in winter. Temperatures are low in winter (15-20 degrees C) with low humidity (45-70 per cent relative humidity), whilst summers have high temperatures (20-30 degrees C) and high humidity (60-75 per cent relative humidity). Cooling sea breezes are found in

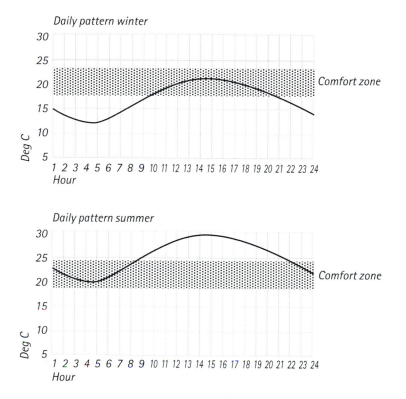

Daily pattern winter

Comfort zone

Deg C

Hour

Daily pattern summer

Comfort zone

Deg C

Hour

2.4 *Daily temperature pattern for Brisbane in relation to the Comfort zone. Note in winter the rapid rise in temperatures in the morning due to solar gain. In summer, the comfort zone is exceeded during the day but is achieved during the night*

summer. The predominant pattern seems to indicate an under-heating climate but the high levels of solar radiation in winter moderate this effect giving higher mean radiant temperatures.

Daily pattern

The daily pattern of climate change is also important. This varies through the seasons. In winter Brisbane has cool nights and clear sunny days. Thus whilst night temperatures are low, 3-10 degrees C, the daily temperatures quickly rise to 20 degrees C. In summer there is more rain and cloud cover which moderates the diurnal range of temperature. The reduction of sunshine and thus solar radiation lowers air temperatures. The mean daytime temperature is 29 degrees C with night temperatures at 21 degrees C. This gives a diurnal range of approximately 8 degrees C. Relative humidity is in the range of 70 per cent relative humidity in summer.

Moderate bioclimatic chart and climate modification strategies

If this data is related to the bioclimatic chart, it can be seen that the temperatures are in excess of the comfort zone for 27 per cent of the year. Excess humidity is also a problem, exceeding the comfort zone for 59 per cent of the

2.5 *The bioclimatic chart and climate modification strategies for the moderate climate using Brisbane as an example. The dark shaded area shows the temperature range for the climate above and below the Comfort zone. The Comfort zone can be extended by using the following strategies in the building:*
Temperatures above the Comfort zone by mass and/or ventilation, those below, by mass and/or passive solar heating

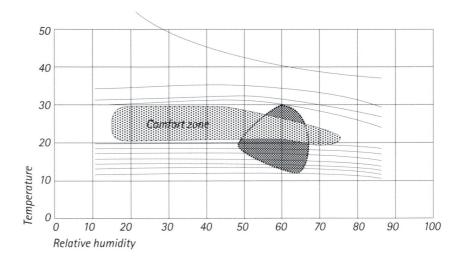

Temperature

0   10   20   30   40   50   60   70   80   90   100

Relative humidity

▨ Comfort zone

▧ Modification to the Comfort zone by the climate responsive building strategies

year. The evidence from this data is that there is primarily a heating problem, yet the hot humid summers are often perceived as the main concern. This is due to the high humidity and high temperatures that exceed the mean temperature, sometimes up to 40 degrees C.

First, for the summer therefore the strategy of using evaporative cooling of air is likely to be the least effective of the cooling strategies. Mass and air are thus the alternative main strategies. The over-heating can be addressed by using mass as a heat sink to moderate internal temperature in conjunction with air. The relatively large diurnal range of temperature, with low night time temperature means that the building is cooled down at night. This coolth is stored in the structure for absorbing heat during the day, thereby cooling the internal air (see Chapter 8). This strategy, called the 'flywheel effect', relies on cooling ventilation at night and little during the heat of the day (this would bring in hotter outside air). In winter the under-heating problem can also be addressed by the use solar radiation for passive heating and also the use of building mass to store heat, the reverse of the summer use pattern. Thus given the climate conditions of the moderate climates, both mass and airflow are alternative strategies that can be used selectively or in combination to effect climate moderation in the building. The interesting feature of this approach is that there are limits to each strategy. Without airflow of 1.5 m s^{-1} the strategy is ineffective, similarly with the mass there needs to be diurnal changes in temperatures for it to be effective.

2.6 The hot humid climate

The hot humid climate is found close to the Equator and extends to15 degrees latitude, north and south. This climate is the complete antithesis to the moderate climate. The dominant feature is lack of seasonal variations in temperature. Cairns, Australia, is an example of this climate and is characterized by high humidity and relatively high temperatures although it does not have the extremes of temperature and humidity as are found in the moderate climate, that is the lower winter temperatures and high peak summer temperatures.

Seasonal pattern

The seasonal pattern for hot humid climate is dominated by periods of high rainfall. This is created by monsoon activity from the position of the tropical convergence zone. This is where moist air from the tropics meets cooler temperate air creating heavy rainfall called monsoons. In Cairns this occurs in the summer months of January through to March, with a dry season at other times of the year. The force of this front creates other dramatic weather patterns such as cyclones and typhoons. Thus summer temperatures are high (21-32 degrees C) with high humidity (60-80 per cent relative humidity). The drier winter weather comes from southerly air streams and gives moderate

2.6 *Seasonal pattern for the hot humid climate using Cairns as an example*

Comfort zone

Range of temperature and humidity

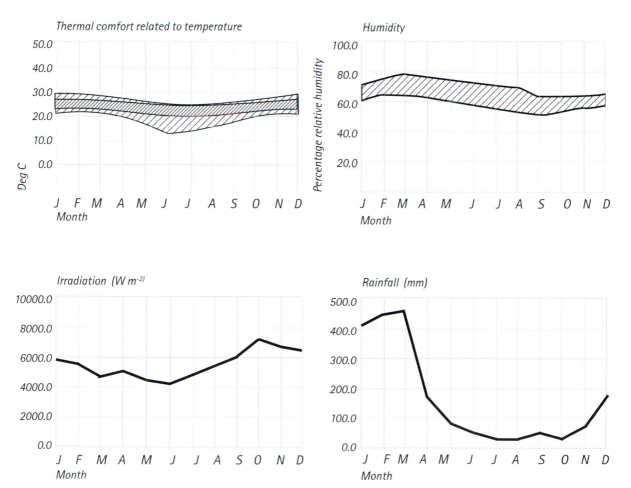

2.7 *Daily temperature pattern for Cairns in relation to the Comfort zone. Note in winter the rapid rise in temperatures in the morning due to solar gain. In summer, the comfort zone is exceeded during the day but is achieved during the night*

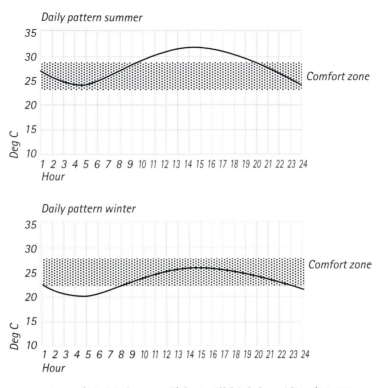

temperatures (15-28 degrees C) but still high humidity (58-75 per cent relative humidity).

Other hot humid climates such as Singapore may have two monsoons, with a shorter drier period. Clear sky conditions are usually less prevalent than in the moderate climates due to cloud cover and humidity in the atmosphere.

Daily pattern

In the hot humid climates, the wet or dry season has an effect on the daily weather pattern. In the dry season this brings clear and fine weather but more often there are tropical thunderstorms at a point later in the day. This gives heavy rain, wind and high humidity. In the wet season there are prolonged periods of rain which can last for weeks. The daily pattern is simply wet and dank with large amounts of surface water and small diurnal temperature ranges of 5 degrees C. This means that temperatures at night are high with higher humidity (70-80 per cent relative humidity).

Hot humid bioclimatic chart and climate modification strategies

The heavy rainfall at periods of the year and high temperatures mean that more moisture can be absorbed into the air thus increasing the relative

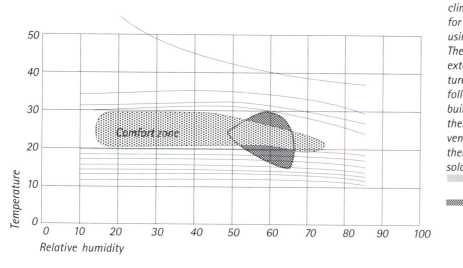

2.8 *The bioclimatic chart and climate modification strategies for the hot humid climate using Cairns as an example. The comfort zone can be extended with in the temperatures ranges by using the following strategies in the building:*
thermal mass (25-28° C) and/or ventilation (28-30° C)
thermal mass and/or passive solar (5-20° C)
Comfort zone

Modification to the Comfort zone by the climate responsive building strategies

humidity. The effect of this for Cairns is that there is excess humidity 100 per cent of the time. Over-heating occurs for 54 per cent of the year. Thus, the climate is outside the comfort zone for a large proportion of the year. Strategies for heating are not required but there is a need for cooling.

The high humidity precludes the effectiveness of evaporative cooling, therefore mass and airflow are the preferred strategies. The use of mass also moderates the internal temperatures particularly for the under-heating period, but does little for the over-heating period. Methods of improving the effectiveness of mass cooling by mechanical night time ventilation is possible (see Chapter 8).

Therefore strategies that reduce humidity and maximize airflow are desirable, with wind speeds up to 2 ms⁻¹. Yet at this wind speed the air velocity created can cause the inconvenience of flying papers and other disturbance. Therefore, any increase above the level of 1.5 m s⁻¹ is not practicable for internal conditions.

2.7 The hot dry climate

These climates occur in latitudes from 15 to 30 degrees north and south of the Equator. The climates are dominated by lack of humidity and seasonal changes in temperature both of which can be attributed to land mass effects. Unlike the preceding climates, the effect on the land is to cool during the winter whilst in summer it heats up creating excessive temperatures of 40 degrees C and above. The lack of water and high temperatures makes this climate the most severe.

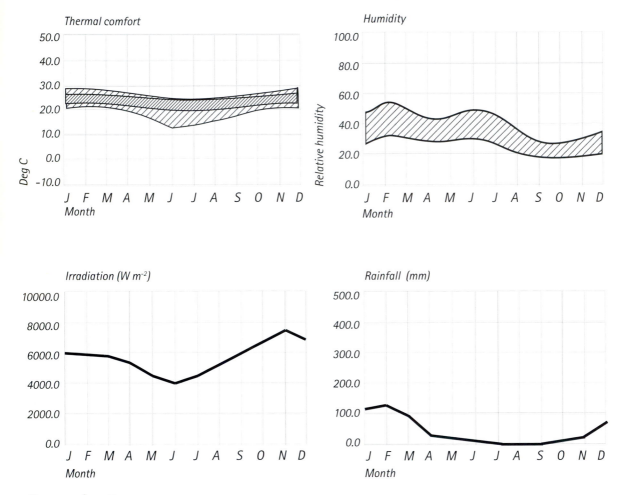

Seasonal pattern

An example of this type of climate is found in Cloncurry, Australia. The relative humidity rarely exceeds 60 per cent. There is a clear cool season in July, with a summer season from November to March. Temperatures in winter are 10 degrees C during the night and 30 degrees C during the day. In summer the night temperatures are 25 degrees C, with daytime temperatures around 40 degrees C. There is very a small transitional period in autumn or spring, where the summer intense heat gives way to winter cool, and as a consequence March through to September is under the Comfort zone whilst the rest of the year is above.

Rainfall is low, with most falling in December to March. The maximum monthly rainfall is just over 100 mm. Irradiation is high with 4000 W m^{-2} for winter and up to 8000 W m^2 for clear sky conditions. Wind speed is low with occasional dust storms.

2.9 Seasonal pattern for the hot dry climate using Cloncurry as an example

 Comfort zone

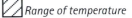 Range of temperature

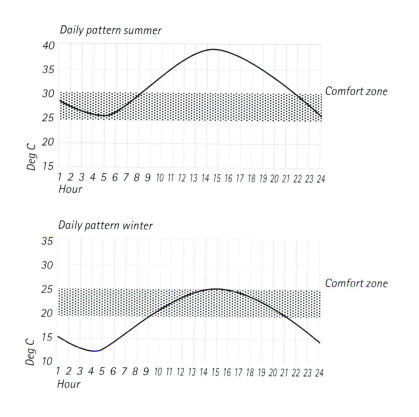

Daily pattern summer

Comfort zone

Daily pattern winter

Comfort zone

2.10 *Daily temperature pattern for Cloncurry in relation to the comfort zone. Note in winter the rise in temperatures in the morning due to solar gain. In summer, the Comfort zone is exceeded during the day but is achieved during the night. The high diurnal range of temperatures should be noted which is characteristic for inland desert climates*

Daily pattern

The daily pattern is similar most of the year. The lack of clouds, clear skies and lack of humidity means the sun is the main source of discomfort. The main feature is the diurnal range in temperature, which can be as much as 12-15 degrees C. This is brought about by the clear sky conditions. The clouds act as a moderator in a more humid climate, shielding the land from solar radiation during the day and retaining heat during the night. The absence of clouds creates more extreme conditions, with heat gain during the day being released at night.

Bioclimatic chart and climate modification strategies

The strategies available for cooling in summer include mass, air, and evaporative cooling. First, the use of air for cooling seems to be the least effective during the day due to the, high external air temperature. Yet some advantage can be taken of the low night-time air temperature.

Second, the strategy of using night-time air with mass can be effective. The process draws air into the building at night cooling the

2.11 *The bioclimatic chart and climate modification strategies for hot dry climates using Cloncurry as an example. The Comfort zone can be extended within building for the following strategies and temperature ranges:*
mass effect and/or direct evaporative cooling (28-30° C);
mass effect with night ventilation and/or indirect evaporative cooling (28-40°C)
mass and/or passive solar (18°C) with 300 W m^{-2}
passive solar (5-10° C with 800 W m^2)

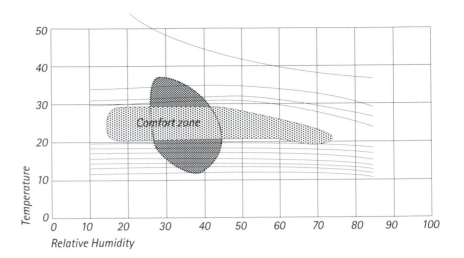

	Comfort zone
	Modification to the Comfort zone by the climate responsive building strategies

2.12 *Buderim house by Lynsey Clare: 1994. The building is located on a creek and sits over the creek bed. Cool breezes travel from the sea and are funnelled under and through the house. High levels of porosity in the building skin harness this breeze and direct it to the interior for cooling*

mass. The coolth stored in the mass can reduce the internal air during the day.

Third, the other effective strategy is to use evaporative cooling. The use of water as a cooling medium is well known; as it evaporates it absorbs heat, thus lowering temperatures. The direct form of evaporative cooling is by sweat from the body. This is effective in these climates up to 35 degrees C with very low humidity. Above this temperature some form of indirect evaporative cooling is required. This can have a localized effect on modifying temperatures through the use of landscaping. Also some form of mechanical system can be utilized producing an indirect form of cooling. This involves bringing air into the building by a powerful fan, passing the air over water which evaporates and thus cooling the air. This system is effective up to 40 degrees C with a humidity level 12 g kg^{-1}.

Finally, for winter a similar pattern to moderate climates can be used. The under-heated period can be moderated by the use of passive solar heating and through mass storage.

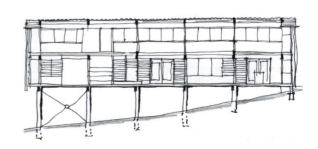

Table 2.2 Climate matching strategies for building form and fabric applicable to domestic scale buildings

Moderate	Hot humid	Hot dry
Materials		
Mass or lightweight materials	Material non-determinant due to little variation in temperature, lightweight preferred for quick response	Mass that is well shaded, light in colour and ground coupled
Plan shape		
Thin plan to maximize cross- ventilation	Thin plan to maximize cross ventilation	Compact but with thin plan depth to facilitate night ventilation to cool mass during summer
Thin plan gives high levels of natural light, avoids dark areas as this encourages mould growth	Thin plan gives high levels of natural light, avoids dark areas as this encourages mould growth	Long axis east-west, with flexibility to shift axis 20 off true west or east without loss of performance
Section		
Open section to maximize	Open section to maximize stack ventilation	Open section to maximize stack ventilation

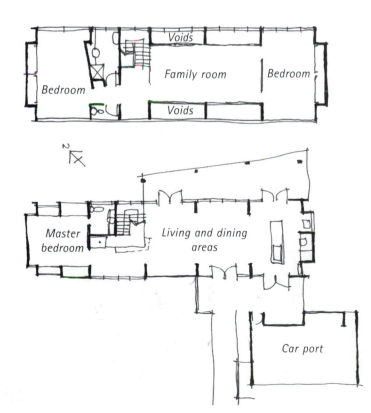

Voids

Bedroom

Family room

Bedroom

Voids

N

Master bedroom

Living and dining areas

Car port

2.13 *Buderim house by Lynsey Clare: 1994. The building has an open section and plan. It is orientated to catch the prevailing wind by placing its longest axis east and west. Voids in the first floor promote stack cooling in low-wind-speed conditions. The use of a veranda to the north provides a buffer space for summer reducing heat loads. In addition, corrugated iron is used to the north and south walls reflecting solar radiation*

Table 2.3 Climate matching strategies for building form and fabric applicable to domestic scale buildings

Moderate	Hot humid	Hot dry
Plan orientation		
Windows facing equator for solar access in winter, facing prevailing breezes in summer for ventilation	Windows facing prevailing breezes in summer for ventilation	Long axis east-west, with flexibility to shift axis 20° off true west or east without loss of performance
Smallest building aspect to east and west to reduce solar gain	Smallest building aspect to east and west to reduce solar gain	
Landscape		
Use of tree canopy in summer to shade building but allow breeze.	Use of tree canopy in summer to shade building but allow breeze.	Water features for evaporative cooling
Heat and glare dissipating planting. Planting to allow solar access in winter	Heat and glare dissipating planting	
Verandas		
Rain and sun protection to walls, external space for extreme heat	Rain and sun protection to walls, external space for extreme heat	Dust and sun protection to walls, external space for extreme heat
Provide diffused light	Provide diffused light	Provide diffused light
Courtyards		
Light and ventilation to deep plan buildings	Light and ventilation to deep plan buildings	Light and ventilation to deep plan buildings
Diffused light and glare reduction	Diffused light and glare reduction	Diffused light and glare reduction
		Contains cooled air from evaporative cooling

2.14 *Buderim house by Lyndsey Clare: 1994. Elevations, left: west, right: east*

2.8 Building form and climate matching

In the preceding section a clear response to climate was developed from an examination of the climatic parameters and strategies suggested. The application of these strategies sounds simple but in reality is more complex due to the range of architectural parameters that come to bear on the building design. The main point of departure for the architectural investigation is the site and building context. Exploration of the potential of the site, both in terms of its macro- and microclimate, is an important stage in development; in particular this involves the use of climate matching to establish the appropriate building response for the climate. In vernacular architecture there is a strong relationship between site, climate and the elements of building in the generation of the building form.

'Although from time to time, these forms have been distorted by architectural metaphors and spiritual requirements, the basic need for the physical performance of the building to respond to the climatic region in which it is placed remains a valid form determinant.'[11]

The term 'form' means the building elements and materials used in the building and associated landscaping of the site. The inclusion of landscaping in the form determinant features is important as this can act as an additional climate modifier to the building. Ideally, the building response should have an integrated landscape and building response. For particular climates a set of generic matching strategies can be developed: these have been adapted from Greenland's taxonomy.[12] These strategies can be split into two levels, the first relates to general building and environmental control characteristics such as materials, plan shape and section (see Table 2.2). The second relates to specific aspects of building form such as the plan orientation, landscaping, verandas, courtyards (see Table 2.3). In addition the main building elements are also related to climate types (see Table 2.4). These are discussed further in subsequent chapters.

2.14 continued, *Buderim house by Lyndsey Clare: 1994. Elevations, left: north, right: south*

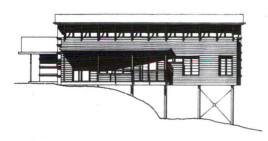

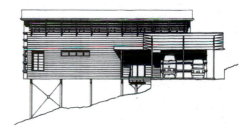

Table 2.4 Climate matching strategies for building elements that are applicable to domestic scale buildings

Moderate	Hot humid	Hot dry
Roof		
Light coloured to reflect solar radiation	Light coloured to reflect solar radiation	Solid and light coloured to reflect solar radiation
Parasol type to maximize ventilation	Parasol type to maximize ventilation	Minimize area of roof lights
Insulation to ceiling for improved thermal performance	Reflecting foil laminate under roof to reflect radiation	
Minimize area of roof lights	Minimize area of roof lights	
Reflecting foil laminate under roof to reflect radiation	Light coloured to reflect solar radiation	
Walls		
Light coloured to reflect solar radiation	Avoid windows to the east and west	Heavy weight with small well-shaded windows in summer
Avoid windows to the east and west	Reflecting foil laminate in walls to reflect radiation	Windows to admit night time ventilation
Light weight or mass, use of reverse brick veneer for mass effect		
Reflecting foil laminate in walls to reflect radiation		
Floor		
Light coloured to reflect solar radiation	Light coloured to reflect solar radiation	Solid, massive and ground connection
Lightweight elevated	Lightweight elevated	

2.15 Buderim house by Lynsey Clare: 1994. View of the house showing the pole frame and support structure

2.9   Building context and microclimate

A similar process can be carried out with regard to the site conditions and building context. The need for careful analysis of the site is required to determine the modification to the macroclimatic conditions. The factors affected mostly by the site are as follows:

- *temperatures:* air temperatures can be modified by local conditions on the site through effects of topography and vegetation. Undulating topographies can cause local katabatic cooling in winter. In still conditions cold air sinks to the hollows, creating cool pools and lower temperatures than on the crests of the hillside. Large features such as rivers act as cooling zones; often sea breezes will follow the river and penetrate inland. In addition areas with large areas of heat absorbing materials as found in cities increase local temperatures and create further climate control problems.

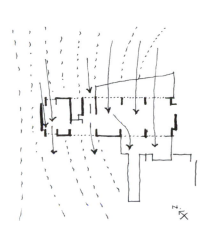

- *solar radiation:* solar access is a constant factor provided by the macro-climate. Shading from vegetation and other buildings affect the light and solar access to the building. This is a particular problem in the urban context. Reflectance from adjacent buildings and ground conditions is a secondary problem. The absence of solar radiation can also be utilized on the site. Access to sky cooling at night can be an advantage in unshaded sites. At night in clear sky conditions the land loses heat to the sky by radiation. The advantage of this phenomenon, dependent on climate and location, is that it can be used in extreme weather conditions for night-time sleeping and is common in many hot dry climates.
- *airflow:* this is modified significantly by ground conditions, and velocity increases with height. The site should be assessed as to the level of exposure provided, indeed sites are selected to maximize exposure to breeze and summer cooling. Thus the elevation and orientation of the site are crucial factors in site selection and planning. The use of major landscape features such as trees which create wind shadows and buffers to buildings can modify and reduce this level of exposure. Winds can become channelled though elements of topography and relative wind speeds are increased and decreased accordingly.
- *evaporative cooling:* the topography and vegetation conditions on the site can often provi tive humidity is low reduces localized air temperatures. This is particularly useful where the air can be contained in a courtyard or natural feature such as a gully. An example of this is found in the Rainforest Gully at the Botanical Gardens in Canberra. An area of rainforest has been created in this gully and the rainfall increase from 600 mm per annum to 1200 mm per annum. This has been achieved by using misting devices and irrigation and reduces temperatures from 30 to 25 degrees C. In this way the use of local misting systems in conjunction with buildings can reduce microclimate temperatures, provided the air is contained.

2.16 *Buderim house by Lynsey Clare: 1994. The diagram shows the cross-ventilation effect at the ground floor. Microclimate control, that is the open space to windward allows the prevailing breezes to easily access the building. This condition is crucial to the success of the ventilation strategy in the building. Left, view of the site showing the hills to the south of the building, which protect the house from cool westerly winds in winter*

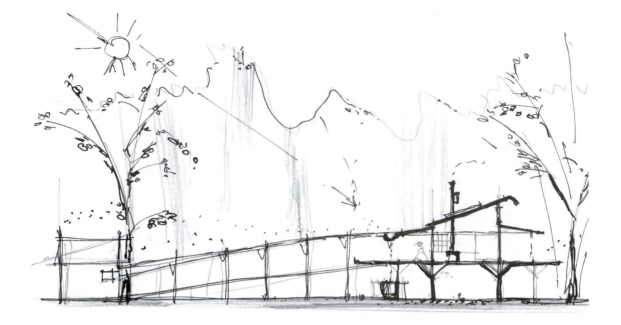

2.17 *The Mapleton house by architect Richard Leplastrier. The section shows the use of a rainforest buffer to shield the building from winds and lower solar gain to the house. The extent of the clearing also reduces humidity normal found in the forest through penetration of sunlight*

The effect of these general site modification effects should be examined in relation to the three main site contexts: the rural, suburban and urban.

The rural context

In the rural context the dominance of natural features as compared to man-made is the key aspect of the building context. The respect of this context is

2.18 *The Mapleton house by architect Richard Leplastrier. The partly roofed deck provides a microclimate between inside and out. In winter it is a warming space whilst in summer it sunlight reduces the humidity found in these forest settings*

crucial as the opportunities and design flexibility provided by the availability of land provide least constraint on the designer.

Two cases illustrate the way the site context can be utilized to maximize climate modification in the building. Both are located in southeast Queensland and are in rural and semi-rural locations.

The first case is a house at Buderim by Lynsey Clare. This is a detached hillside house which takes advantage of the topography and the proximity to the ocean to moderate climate. The site has a large hill to the southeast and the site slopes to the northeast, with a gully running north-south. In winter the hill proves a wind shadow to the site, preventing the main force of cool westerly and southwesterly winds. In summer the northerly aspect provides access for cooling ocean breezes, which are funnelled up the gully and provide an opportunity for increased wind speed. The position of the house on the site takes advantage of the breeze to maximize cross-ventilation in summer. The building has a thin plan and is orientated with its long axis east and west, thus presenting the maximum area to the breeze. In addition, it straddles the gully in order to utilize the increased wind effects from the topography.

The second house, the Mapleton house, is located in a rural rainforest area. In this case a clearing is created in the rainforest make a space for the house. The dominant features of this location is the sheltering and humidity affects of the rainforest. The tall trees shelter the building from exposure to high wind loads but also to breezes. High humidity is a problem, and this has been dealt with by increasing the area of the clearing to allow sun penetration. This sun penetration reduces the local humidity and provides solar heating in winter. In this case the advantages of the forest setting provide a remote location and the need for structure but also generate other problems of lack of breeze and humidity.

2.19 *The Mapleton house by architect Richard Leplastrier. The house is formed from a number of linked pavilions located on the edge of a clearing*

2.20 *House retrofit, Brisbane, Australia. Reduction of interior walls and modification of topography assists with improved ventilation through linking positive pressure at the front of the house with negative pressure at the rear. Architect: Richard Hyde, 1994–98*

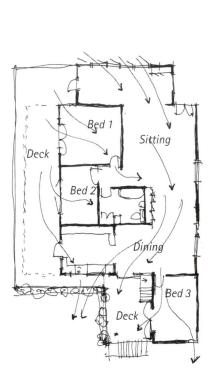

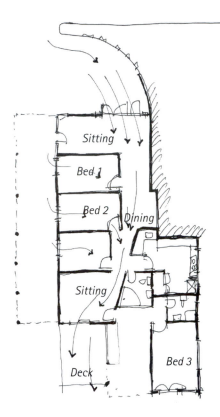

2.21 *House retrofit, Brisbane, Australia. The front courtyard collects the breeze and assists with directing the airflow through the interior. Architect, Richard Hyde, 1994-98*

2.22 *House retrofit, Brisbane, Australia. The external rooms at the rear of the house provide a buffer space to the westerly sun. Architect: Richard Hyde, 1994-98*

The suburban context

In the suburban context one of the main issues is the provision of airflow for ventilation. The higher density of building, the smaller block sizes and increased building height reduces wind speeds at ground level and access of buildings to wind flow. In addition the orientation of plots provides problems where buildings face the street but not necessarily at the optimum orientation. Adjacent buildings and trees can also block solar access. Reflection from adjacent buildings also redirects light and heat to adjacent properties.[13]

One case is examined which attempts to address the site in the urban context through retrofit of an existing building.

The house, located in Brisbane, Australia, was designed as an Austerity model timber framed building in 1945. The original building was a single storey house elevated on columns to accommodate the sloping terrain. The building was located at the front of a 600 m² block with its long axis east and west. This gives optimum orientation to the north for solar gain and breeze in summer. Unfortunately the building did not respect the orientation and faced the street, due east and did not take advantage of its elevated position and northeast orientation. Also, the interior layout consisted of a number of small rooms with little cross-ventilation. A sun space to the east, bedrooms, a kitchen and a deck were added further reducing the climatic response. The house was cold in winter due to the circulation of air under the building and hot in summer because of the lack of ventilation and roof insulation.

The main feature of the retrofit design was to take advantage of the natural features of the microclimate of the site. The first improvement was to improve the airflow for summer cooling through the passage of air from the prevailing northeast breeze. The internal walls were removed and large openings placed in leeward walls. Thus, the prevailing summer breeze was easily admitted to the northeast and exited to the west. In addition the open planning of the interior enabled the connection of a sun space to the east with the rest of the house thus providing better passive heating in winter.

The second improvement was to follow the same principle but on the ground floor. More massive construction was used to provide some mass effect which could be cooled by night ventilation. A courtyard and French doors were placed at the windward and leeward sides to collect the breeze and direct it through the interior to the exterior.

Finally decks were added to take advantage of air movement between the buildings and to provide favourable conditions for the use of external space at different times of the year. The attempts to achieve optimum orientation in suburban blocks is frustrated further by the need for setbacks to the block for fire protection and privacy. Invariably the rotation of the building on the block causes a reduction in efficiency and therefore increases in the height of the building. This then incurs further increases in the dimensions of the setback.

The front setback to the street can be as much as 6 m, whilst the setback to the other boundaries are normally 1.5 m for a single-storey building. Furthermore, for a two-storey building there is a setback requirement of 2 m. The consequence is to reduce further the usable area of the site and thus provide further constraints to the designer. The problem can be solved by using the appropriate spatial concept. In this case a spatial zoning is used

2.23 In the urban context large buildings modify the climate creating the heat island effect with higher temperatures than the rural context. Microscale conditions can be created by natural elements of the urban landscape which improve the microclimate conditions reducing overheating:
left: water acts as lungs to the city providing cooling breezes.
right: use of shade and shade trees are critical elements to offset the heat gain from the many hard surfaces

whereby the primary spaces are formed to within the setback requirements; additional bays can then be added to form additional secondary spaces. In this way the available space can be utilized within the residual space between primary space and setback.

In these two cases, constraints on building design in the suburban site require careful site planning to establish the optimum relationship between building brief, site, setback and orientation.

The urban context

In the urban context the density of building increases substantially. Also the function of buildings shifts from domestic scale buildings to non-domestic scale, multi-use buildings with a greater demand for air-conditioning. The vertical scale of the man-made environment and the extent of the horizontal area of the city often creates its own microclimate significantly deviating from the macroclimate. Thus, it is justifiably common practice to call the urban context, 'the urban climate.'[14] A number of features effect this urban climate.

1. At the macroscale, the fabric and spatial extent of urban context affects temperatures, humidity, wind and solar radiation[15]
2. At the microscale the design features of the urban context such as density, land coverage, height of buildings, orientation and width of streets, subdivision of blocks, the locations of parks and open spaces in particular water features[16]

Macroscale effects

The effect of the density and level of activity in the urban context leads to the 'heat island' phenomena, that is, the nocturnal elevation in temperature as compared to rural temperatures. The maximum difference in temperatures is called the 'heat island intensity'.[17] The spatial extent of the heat island

2.24 *Site investigation of the urban context identifies opportunities for localized cooling due to the venturi effect between large buildings and also problems of shading and reflections from adjacent glass façades*

extends both vertically and horizontally, related to the density of building and the effects of local regional climatic conditions. Still conditions during the day will extend this spatial envelope whilst wind conditions will reduce it. Similarly days of high solar radiation and high air temperature will influence the extent of the differences.

The height of the heat island envelope is related to the height of buildings and the interface with the boundary layer above the city and the air below that modified by the buildings, called the 'urban canopy'.[18] The urban canopy is the area of transition between the microclimate features affected primarily by buildings and that primarily affected by the boundary layer of the macroclimate. The extent of the canopy is normally at a point three to five times the average height of the buildings in the urban area.[19]

The concerning feature of the urban temperature is the high elevations found in the heat island. Furthermore, the waste heat and hard surfaces increase local air temperatures by as much as 8–11 degrees C compared to the countryside. Relative humidity is lower due to water run off and lack of vegetation.[20] The effects of this on discomfort have been documented together with concerns about the use of external spaces and heat stress in internal conditions. The higher temperatures also signal higher heat loads for air-conditioning and other energy systems.

The effects of urban fabric create problem for ventilation. The building height reduces the availability of breeze at the ground plane by up to half of that found in the open ocean. The wind also funnels through and down large buildings. Down-drafts from large buildings bring local increases in wind speeds from a the boundary layer level. This strong turbulence from down-drafts can cause discomfort to users of the external spaces but on the other hand external spaces which are affected by breeze can provide an opportunity to relax outdoors in comfort. Still air allows a build up of carbon dioxide concentration.[21]

The distribution of solar radiation also varies with the density of buildings. Whilst the availability of solar radiation is similar to the countryside, the distribution is different. The higher density means that more radiation is reflected and absorbed by surfaces of buildings unlike the countryside where it is mostly reflected. In warm climates, an advantage is that solar shading is created by large buildings. These buildings form 'urban canyons' where up to

2.25 *Site data collection and analysis are prerequisites for the process of climate responsive design. Sketching in plan and section the environmental conditions of the site help identify the key parameters to be addressed:*
right: two tower blocks on the site block breeze from the southeast, cool pockets can be identified
left: southeasterly sun reflects off the mirror glass façades causing disabling glare and discomfort in the open space

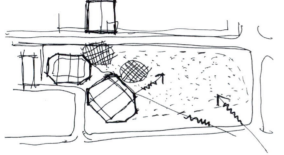
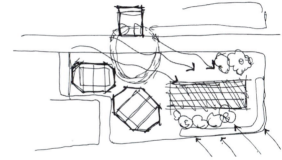

2.26 *In the site data collection and analysis process, the indentification of relationships between existing buildings and open space is important. The urban design of these external space's with respect of the climate should aim to make the external conditions no worse than existing ones. In addition where possible improve should be made to the external environment:*
left: the cathedral site appropriates an adjacent open space but surrounding tall buildings reduce access from cool breezes to the site thus reducing the amenity of the space

60 per cent of midday solar radiation can be transferred into sensible heat. Thirty per cent is absorbed by the building fabric and about 10 per cent from evaporation.[22]

Microscale effects

Yet there are benefits in warm climates from windflow in cities. The creation of shade in urban open spaces provides the ideal environment for outside living especially where large buildings draw air down from the cooler conditions above the canopy. Also large, natural topographical features such as rivers and hills provide higher exposure to prevailing breezes which make for cool spots in the heat island. These natural features provide the lungs of the city, distributing cool air to the heart of the heat island.

In addition, the issues related to the environmental impact of large build-

2.25 continued. *Large buildings such as the two towers shown below should be examined in terms of the shading foot print that is created:*
left: shading can be useful for summer cooling but areas can be exposed to hot low-angle sun and can be problematic
right: solar shading in winter can give under-heated external spaces

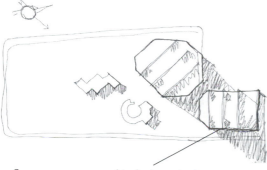

Open space exposed to hot westerly sun in summer

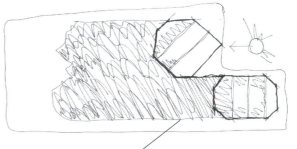

Open space shade by tall buildings from the warm winter sun

*2.27 Sections which analyse
windflow around large
buildings assist with the
understanding of their effects
on open spaces*

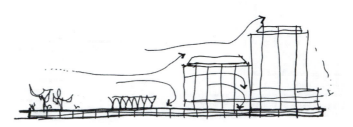

ings is a concern. The shade and shadow from large buildings can create
problems for open space in the city. Winter shading of open space by tall
buildings reduces their use, whilst summer shade brings relief. The location
and planning of large buildings with regard to open space is another important consideration. The shadow from large buildings reduces the available of
light and reflects heat as well as light to other buildings. Large buildings and
urban traffic cause acoustic and air pollution, this is a significant issue where
other buildings use external air for ventilation. The noise generated by local
conditions can have access to the interior through open windows.

Site data and analysis

Site strategies for the city and urban climate require careful consideration of
orientation, airflow and environmental factors. In order to take advantage of
microclimate conditions careful site investigation is required. This involves
a two-stage process. The first stage involves the collection of data on the
microclimate conditions of the site concerning the following:

- windflow and localized building effects for summer cooling and winter
  discomfort
- sun path, sun angles, site shading and shadows
- lighting effects such as reflection and absorption
- acoustic levels and air pollution
- pedestrian and vehicular circulation
- topography
- vegetation
- rain exposure and water run off
- air temperature, location of hot spots and cool spots
- surrounding building density
- soil and water table
- access to views, breeze and the potential for building out this access
- location of natural features and landscape

The second stage uses this data for an environmental analysis of the key

environmental issues on the site. The brief can be examined as to the feasibility of the gross floor area required and the consequences of this in terms of the building volume created and impact on the desirable open space. The application of different development models can be explored.[23] The models vary dependent on the amount of site coverage. Two basic models can be defined. The first is the 'tight fit' developments which have a large building footprint and maximum site coverage, the second is 'loose fit' such as high-rise developments with small footprint and minimum site coverage. The advantages and disadvantages of these approaches can be seen in Table 2.5.

An example of this kind of approach is seen in the site investigation for a proposed mixed-use development in Brisbane. The brief required the creation of an urban space which would reinforce the existing cathedral adjacent to the site. Mixed-use development could be developed for the reminder of the site.

The site investigation revealed that the existing large high-rise buildings dominate part of the site and caused winter shading and blocked summer breeze to the site. The result was hot (4 degrees C higher than other areas of the site) and cold spots in the area most suitable for public open space adjacent to the cathedral. Noise and pollution from adjacent roads further reduced the workability of the open space strategy requiring traffic calming

2.28 *Site data collection and analysis needs both qualitative and quantitative data. Recording the nature of the surfaces of buildings and assessment as to consequences on design is important. Glass façades reflect heat and glare to adjacent buildings (top right), noise can be recorded and the decay in sound plotted (top left)*

Table 2.5 The advantages and disadvantages of different development models with respect to climate and site

'Tight fit' development	'Loose fit' development
Large building footprint	Small building footprint,
Less flexibility to place building at optimum orientation	Flexibility to place building at optimum orientation
Internal open space or atrium	Open space on ground plane
Small scale	Large scale unless podium used
Lack of air penetration at ground plane	Air penetration at ground plane
Lack of setback	Building setbacks can be achieved
Sun penetration to open space	Building shading to open space

strategies. In addition, spectral reflections from adjacent mirror glass in building the façades are problematic requiring careful low level screening.[24]

This form of microclimate study is a prerequisite for climate responsive design particularly where large complex buildings are concerned. The approach allows for consideration of the climate and environmental problems of the external urban space which is crucial to the architecture of spatially adjacent buildings.

References

1. M. Fry, and J. Drew, *Tropical architecture*, Batsford, 1956, p. 24.
2. G. Lippsmeier, *Building in the Tropics*, Munchen: Callway, 1969, p. 28.
3. S.V. Szokolay, *Climate, Comfort and Energy, Design of Houses for Queensland Climates*, Architectural Science Unit, The University of Queensland, 1991, p. 6.
4. Ibid.
5. I. Koenesberger, et al., *Manual of Tropical Housing and Building*, Longman, 1973, p. 13.
6. Lippsmeier, op. cit., 1969, p. 57.
7. Olgay, V., Design with Climate
8. J. Hall et al., *DA Sketch Pad*, Computer Program, Department of Architecture, The University of Tasmania.
   S.V. Szokolay, *ARCIPAK*, Computer Program Department of Architecture, The Univerity of Queensland. The use of the biolclimatic information for this section has been sourced from the above program.
9. Olgay, op. cit.
10. Hall and Szokolay, op. cit.
11. Szokolay, 1991, op. cit., p. 13.
12. J. Greenland, *Foundations of Architectural Science*, University of Technology, Sydney, pp. 7/11.
13. Greenland, op. cit., pp. 7/17-21.
14. Koenesberger et al., op. cit., p. 27.
15. B. Givoni, *Climate Considerations in Building and Urban Design*, Van Nostrand Reinhold, 1998, p. 241.
16. Givoni, op. cit., p. 275.
17. Givoni, op. cit., p. 241.
18. Givoni, op. cit., p. 242.
19. Givoni, op. cit., p. 244.
20. Koenesberger et al., op. cit., p. 27.
21. Givoni, op. cit., p. 278.
22. Givoni, op. cit., p. 247.
23. J.R. Goulding, ed. et al., *Energy in Architecture. The European Passive Solar Handbook*, Commission of European Communities, 1993, pp. 117-118.
24. Koenesberger, op. cit., p. 37.

Climate responsive design

CHAPTER 3

'This is the first and oldest craft of sedentary civilization. It is the knowledge of how to go about using houses and mansions for cover and shelter. This is because man has the natural disposition to reflect on the outcomes of things. Thus it is unavoidable that he must reflect on how to avert harm arising from heat and cold', Ibn Khalddum.[1]

3.1 Introduction

In 1377, the Arab historian, Ibn Khalddum, in his discussion of architecture, emphasized the underlying rationale of building design as needing to respond to climate, in the same way that the fabric should respond to the laws of statics. As was seen in the last chapter, the types of climate lead to broad strategies concerning the response to climate and recognition of the importance of assessing the site and microclimate of the building context. In this chapter the concern is for the implications of these strategies in terms of climate responsive design.

Climate responsive design has a foundation first in the wider context of environmental sustainable design and second in the practice of architecture through effective design management. This involves selection and evaluation of strategies applicable to a particular design problem.

3.1 *Kingfisher Bay Resort, Guymer Bailey Architects 1991. This ecotourist resort uses sustainable design practices and climate responsive design to minimize environmental impacts to a fragile coastal region. The design creates thermal refuges which creates a microclimate that provides an escape from summer heat and winter cool, fostering the intangible measures of climate responsive architecture*

The first part of the chapter, therefore, examines the nature of environmentally sustainable design and the significant part played by climatic responsive design in this field of architecture. The second part examines issues related to the integration in the design process, in particular, how strategies are examined and evaluated.

3.2 Sustainability and climate responsive design

Sustainable design

Climate responsive design is part of an environmental approach to building development called ecological sustainable design (ESD):
'The concept of ecological sustainable development, as it relates to building construction, may be illustrated by reference to built projects. These buildings can be analyzed in a way that broadens the criteria by which buildings are assessed and at the same time illustrates the multi-faceted nature of ESD.'[2]

The significance of this approach comes from the rising concern amongst the design professions for the environment when making design decisions concerning the selection of materials and building systems.[3] This concern has led to the development of methods for assessing these materials and systems in terms of energy use. Energy use has become an important issue as much of the energy used to power industry comes from non-renewable sources and thus is not thought to be sustainable. A number of concepts have been developed to assess energy used in buildings. First, 'embodied energy' has been developed as a way of assessing the energy used to produce building materi-

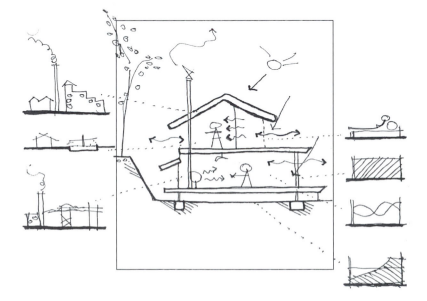

3.2 *Climate responsive design is seen as a subset of environmental design which examines the holistic relationship between the building and environment. The architect's boundary of responsibility can usefully be drawn around the building and site. The main factors represented are as follows left: waste reduction and recycling, use of energy benign sources, efficient use of materials and embodied energy right: minimize site impact, human health and well-being, thermal comfort*

als.[4] This is part of a broader system of environmental analysis and includes 'operational energy', that is the energy used to operate a building.[5]

These factors are also complemented by a range of other environmental factors such as the effect of the building on human health and wider environmental impacts. This broader framework of analysis can be examined not only in terms of the physical dimension but also the temporal dimension. The issues are how the environmental factors interact over time. This framework can be modelled in terms of 'life cycle assessment' (LCA).[6]

It is apparent that the complexity of interactions and breadth of the factors in an LCA framework provide a dilemma for most designers. At the philosophical level most architects would subscribe to this holistic view, yet at the pragmatic level how can the breadth of environmental issues be integrated in design?

A method of resolving this problem is to use an environmental framework.

Environmental framework

An environmental framework comes from the principles of life cycle assessment, which analyse the nature of environmental interventions. These are formed of many interrelated parts and are enormously complex. The essence of the process of assessment starts by identifying the constituent parts of the intervention and defining boundaries of responsibility around the aspects. Thus if a building is examined as an intervention what aspects are architects responsible for in the life cycle of the building?

Clearly it is beyond their responsibility to be concerned with the power generation system and the impact of this in terms of carbon dioxide emissions. Yet to what extent is the architect responsible for the waste and energy use in

3.3 *Kemsey Museum by architect Glen Murcutt, 1990. The building is designed to integrate with the site. Many of its design ideas are generated from biodiversity of natural flora and fauna on the site. The climate response strategies that form part of this ESD approach mean that it reduces energy use by making best use of available daylight, passive solar heating and passive cooling through ventilation*

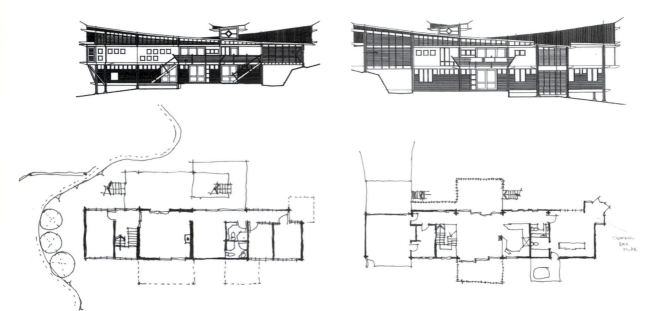

3.4 *Habitat House: Richard Hyde and Mark French, 1997. The design of a prototype environmental house uses an environmental brief to develop the design. The use of climate modification strategies harvests the natural energy of the microclimate resulting in zero operational energy for heat and cooling*

Table 3.1 Design features of the Habitat prototype environmental home

- Spatial organization that provide thermal delight, environmental connectivity whilst meeting user needs and lifestyle choices
- Small building footprint to minimize the area of the site used by the building, thus maximizing the retention of existing vegetation
- Northeast orientation provides shading and maximizes breeze in summer, also provides solar access in winter and solar exclusion in summer
- Lightweight northeast orientated building skin to provide rapid heat gain in winter
- Ground connected mass construction to lower story to provide 'cool pools' for daytime living in summer and 'warm pools' for evenings in winter
- Thin plan form with open section to provide cross ventilation for summer cooling
- The use of an atrium to promote connective cooling in summer calm conditions and to provide light to deep plan spaces
- Utilization of a skeletal frame system that has low embodied energy, is factory made and is prefabricated to a high quality, uses moment joints to resist racking loads and gives internal planning flexibility and maximizes openings for ventilation
- Utilization of composite timber, steel and plywood roof diaphragm that uses monocoche construction to resist wind and thermal loads
- Utilization of materials that have minimum of off-gassing and effects on human health
- Provide storage from hydraulic systems such as rainwater and waste water for recycling and site irrigation thus minimizing mains water usage.
- Installation of grid connected PV (photovoltaic) system to export power to the grid during the day and import power at night
- Selection of energy efficient appliances that minimize power utilization
- Automated building monitoring system to audit performance and security
- Use of gas fuel for heating to reduce carbon production

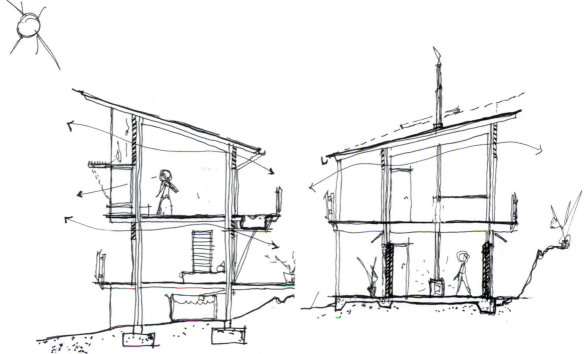

the manufacture and use of building materials and components in the construction process? Furthermore, given the breadth of environmental impacts, a framework is required that begins to define boundary areas within the building process and the responsibilities for these areas. Sound design management requires a clear understanding of the levels of responsibilities and boundaries in which the designer is working. It is suggested that this can be achieved through the use of a design framework and a process that is likely to reduce negative environmental impacts.

Returning to the previous quotation, it is argued that buildings should be assessed and designed by a broader set of criteria, this forms the following framework:

1. The geography of the site and the extent to which the landscape has been modified to accommodate the buildings
2. The degree to which the building fabric has embodied energy over and above that which may have been required using alternative forms of construction, including recycled materials
3. The climate at the site and operational energy demands
4. The potential for reuse and/or recycling of materials and/or assemblies[7]

As can be seen from this framework, the climate is related either directly or indirectly to these principles. The topography of the site is a key issue as this affects microclimate and the energy used to modify the site. Thus it is common practice to bench the site, that is machinery is used to level the site

3.5 *Habitat House: Richard Hyde and Mark French, 1997. The left section through the building showing the lightweight single skin façade which has little thermal insulation. Shading is provided to the façade to allow winter heating during the day but exclude solar heat gain through the wall during summer. The suspended timber floor allows access to a sub-floor water storage tank. The right section shows the 'cool' pool on the ground floor. This is made of masonry with a concrete floor, the thermal mass in these element 's helps lower temperatures in summer. The masonry is shielded from heat gain by cladding materials and insulation to prevent heat gain from outside*

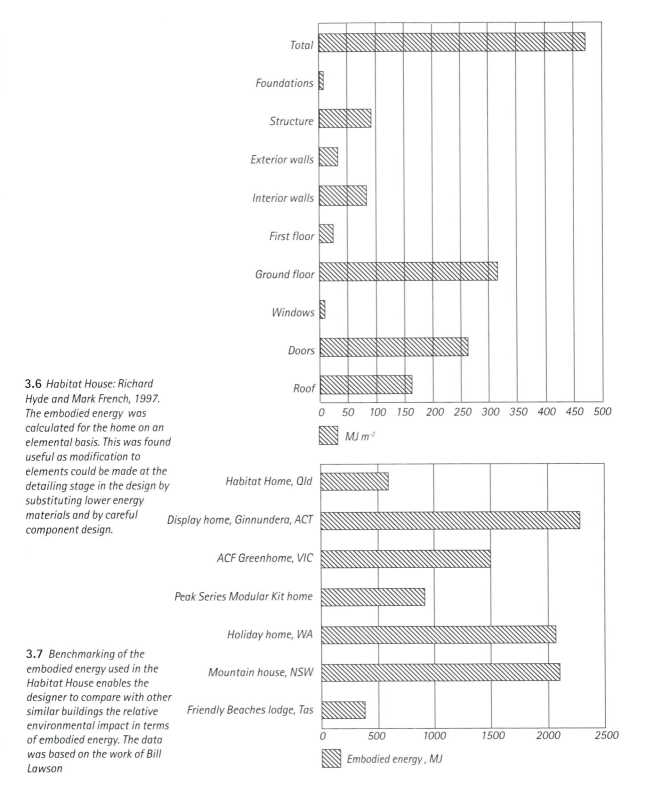

3.6 *Habitat House: Richard Hyde and Mark French, 1997. The embodied energy was calculated for the home on an elemental basis. This was found useful as modification to elements could be made at the detailing stage in the design by substituting lower energy materials and by careful component design.*

3.7 *Benchmarking of the embodied energy used in the Habitat House enables the designer to compare with other similar buildings the relative environmental impact in terms of embodied energy. The data was based on the work of Bill Lawson*

to make a flat platform. This has a number of environmental consequences:

1. The destruction of the natural vegetation and alteration to microclimate
2. The use of non-renewable energy to modify the site, and associated car-
    bon dioxide emissions
3. The use of expensive technology such as retaining walls to provide struc-
    tural support to the retained earth
4. The effects on subground drainage and water runoff increasing hydraulic
    infrastructure

Thus the importance of this aspect is that massive site works may make the building process easier but it has serious destructive effects on the landscape and indeed can create more problems than it solves, both in terms of energy use and site impact on vegetation and wildlife.

The next area of concern is related to materials. In the selection of materials there are two areas of interest, the energy used to produce materials and the impact of the materials on the health of occupants. The use of materials has similar problems to that of site works. The manufacturing process uses primary energy and thus attracts problems with carbon dioxide emissions if non-renewable energy is used. The use of materials that have low processing energy and are from renewable sources is ideal, thus timber provides a useful environmental material from this perspective.[8]

In addition, recycled materials are thought more benign. Most of their embodied energy has been used in their first life and thus can be thought less harmful in their second recycled life. Therefore, recycled materials can offer a useful alternative; it is usually argued that these materials have little embodied energy other than that used in the recycling process. In addition the waste from the building process is reduced, thus quantitatively, the contribution of these materials to the energy budget for the building is small. The concern for the air quality in buildings has grown. Off-gassing of materials and the air quality of air-conditioned buildings are two important issues that affect human health and well-being.[9]

Finally the use of the site and climate with regard to energy efficiency has further potential for reducing energy consumption, that is the operational energy of the building. The energy efficient strategies should be put into context by considering the national energy budget for developing countries. Building energy use constitutes up to 50 per cent of the national energy consumption, and housing contributes up to 60 per cent of that building energy.[10] This environmental framework was applied and taken a stage further with the development of a prototype environmental home.

Habitat home: prototype environmental building

The Habitat home, designed by Richard Hyde and Mark French, is the result of close collaboration with a property developer to design an ESD demonstration building for the suburbs. The Habitat development is a subdivision in the Bridgemond Downs area of Brisbane. The developer has taken specific steps to produce an environmentally sensitive approach to the design of the subdivision with a minimum of site disturbance including the use of landscape buffers and minimizing cut and fill.

One of the prevailing issues in Brisbane is that available flat-land sites are rapidly diminishing and development on steeply sloping sites is becoming more common. The Habitat site is a similar, steeply rolling, afforested hillside. Unfortunately most development of these sites appears to follow flat land practice with extensive use of cut and fill and slab on-ground building systems. The developer is particularly concerned about this practice and is keen to use a development approach that minimizes this strategy.

The design of the Habitat home required an extensive briefing phase to develop both the architectural brief and an environmental brief. With this type of house it was necessary to decide what environmental issues could feasibly and practically be addressed in the project. A notional 'ideal' environmental brief was established, this was then tailored to the particular requirements of the client and site.

The environmental framework was generated with respect for both the requirements of the client and the wide range of environmental issues.

First, with regard to the issues of site utilization and environmental impact, an attempt was made to the retain the topographical and vegetation to minimize the environmental impact of the building. This was difficult with large-scale construction. An elevated house was designed with pad footings to minimize cut and fill and site disturbance. This provided a platform above the site supported on columns on which to construct the house. Further problems were found with the utilization of site resources and the recycling of waste. The aim was to make the site as independent of the council infrastructure as possible for water conservation purposes. In addition some double functioning of elements was used economic benefit as well as environmental purposes. Rainwater and grey-water tanks were designed to integrate as retaining walls in areas where cut was required. The earth was treated as a swail to direct water rather than as a dam to contain surface water run-off, thus attempting to limit impact on the natural water flow on the site. Top soil was retained and reused to maintain the gene pool and natural flora on the site to foster the existing biodiversity.

Second, the embodied energy assessment of materials and impact on human health was a major issue. In the environmental brief the quantitative data on embodied energy and off-gassing was reduced to a set of strategies for ease of application. This is a much simpler approach and avoids lengthy calculations in the design stage. A detailed quantification of the embodied energy used in the major components and the impact of materials on human health was assessed on conclusion of the design. This was used as a benchmark against other similar buildings to assess the relative merits of the design.

Third, energy efficiency was addressed through the use of climate responsive design strategies. The climate parameters of Brisbane indicate that it is possible to design a house without heating or cooling, thus the issue of operational energy use was avoided reducing this environmental impact. The quantification of the benefit was calculated to demonstrate the benefits of the approach.

Finally, the detailing of components to meet life cycle criteria and environmental performance became a major concern. This led to a demonstration of how the components were installed, the tolerances, the crafting of the building elements and possible demountability. The durability and life cycle issues concerned with the detailing were paramount, in particular detailing for environmental performance. An example of this is found in the glazing. Large areas of laminated glass in the building drew considerable penalties with regard to higher embodied energy and cost of replacement if broken. Therefore, small panes with standard float glass were used reducing the life cycle cost and embodied energy. Thus, the detailing philosophy required the designer to work back to environmental and climatic principles to generate an optimum solution.

In summary, within the area of environmental design, climate is a benign way of providing for the well-being of occupants, through thermal comfort and air quality with a minimum of environmental impacts. Another negative impact from buildings is through carbon dioxide emissions, this becomes a further concern and measure of environmental performance. In addition, secondary problems occur through emissions during the production process of buildings. It is an important environmental principle to efficiently construct and operate buildings. This can reduce both embodied energy and operational energy; this minimizes the effects of the use of non-renewable energy sources and thus reduces greenhouse gas emissions such as carbon dioxide and associated climatic effects.

3.3 Climate responsive design strategies

Climate responsive design strategies are a subset of environmental design. The question raised is how this should best be carried out. The approach argued here is one of a strategic design approach where the design process is seen as making a number of decisions to optimize the relationship of people and climate through the medium of site, building fabric, plant and equipment.

Strategies are design directions to solve particular problems posed by the design brief and have both tangible and intangible benefits. The tangible are measurable in physical terms the intangible, from the prosaic and poetic standpoint. The complexity of the design process places emphasis on the need to select, integrating and evaluating alternative strategies that are often competing and contradicting. There are a number of ways this can be achieved, by ordering and prioritizing strategies, grouping strategies into particular models and selecting strategies that are appropriate for particular models and climate types.

3.8 *Prosser house, the Gold Coast, Queensland, Australia, 1999. Architects Richard Hyde and Upendra Rapashka. This environmental home is constructed with a large open section to maximize airflow and uses materials that have low off-gassing qualities. This responds to the client's requirements for a 'health home' to minimize building related health problems. Where possible climatic responsive design can address these other environmental issues emphasizing the holistic nature of ESD.*

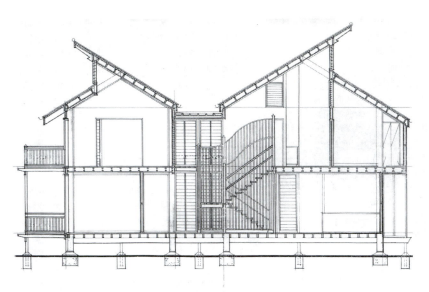

Ordering and prioritizing design strategies

Ordering of climate design strategies suggests that some have a greater impact on climate response than others and this has a bearing on the focus of the design decision-making process. This idea came form research that examined the building as a climate filter where the filtering mechanism be related to three sets of factors.[11]

- microclimate, macroclimate and topography
- building form and fabric
- plant and equipment

The outcome was to suggest that these various factors played differing roles. It was proposed that the climate, building form and fabric provide a 'coarse' form of control in the filtering process, 'finer control' is by the last, plant and equipment. Two examples were cited. First, the case of the hilltop building which is highly exposed. This environmental problem can be rectified by building fabric alone by providing a highly defensive skin. Also, modification to the climate to create a microclimate that moderates exposure can also be achieved. The combined efforts of these strategies is to place emphasis on the need for plant and equipment. Second, the case of the glass box building– the strategy of using only plant and equipment to provide a comfortable environment and still maintain a level of energy efficiency is problematic. In this last case the finer control strategy is used for coarse control. Therefore, it is necessary that the way the strategies are applied is considered if climate response is to be optimized.[12]

3.9 *Prosser house, the Gold Coast, Queensland, Australia, 1999. Architects Richard Hyde and Upendra Rapashka. The site is surrounded by buildings and uses height to gain access to the breeze for cooling. The pop-up roof areas provide ventilation in hot calm periods when wind driven ventilation is not available. Timber louvres are used to prevent glare and heat gain into the roof space when closed.*

An extension of this argument is to suggest that there is a level of hierarchy in the decision making. The first-order decisions are those concerning environmental design strategies that are related to the modification of the macroclimate environment to produce a favourable microclimate environment for the building. The decisions include the positioning of the building with regard to the microclimate and the planning of major elements for climate advantage. Second-order decisions concern the form and manipulation of the building fabric. Third-order decisions concern selection and positioning of service plant and equipment.

This design approach is explained by Hassan Fathy. 'An architect who makes a solar furnace of his building and compensates for this by installing a huge cooling machine is approaching the problem inappropriately and we can measure the inappropriateness of his attempted solution by the excess number of kilocalories he uselessly introduces into the building.'[13]

Active and passive models of climate modification

It may be useful, as a further way of articulating this ordering approach, to group the building aspects of climate modification in terms of active and passive models. A passive model makes use of the 'natural energy'[14] in the environment which is available to the building through the use of first- and second-order decisions, that is, the microclimate as well as building form and fabric are used to modify climate. In the active model primarily third-order decisions and man-made energy is used to achieve climate modification. The framing of strategies in this way enables an intellectual approach to the design problem. Finally, a third model can be proposed which uses a combination of these two models.

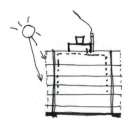

Active building model

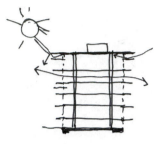

Passive building model

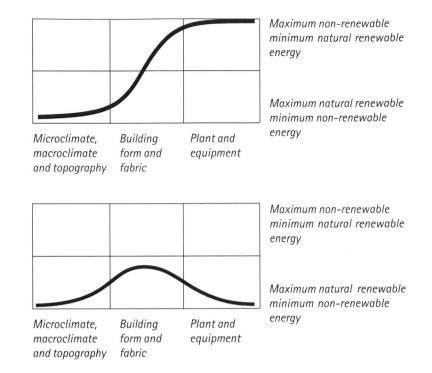

Maximum non-renewable
minimum natural renewable
energy

Maximum natural renewable
minimum non-renewable
energy

Microclimate,   Building   Plant and
macroclimate   form and   equipment
and topography   fabric

Maximum non-renewable
minimum natural renewable
energy

Maximum natural renewable
minimum non-renewable
energy

Microclimate,   Building   Plant and
macroclimate   form and   equipment
and topography   fabric

3.10 *The passive and active building models showing the effects on energy consumption for the three types of climate responses strategies available
- site and climate related
- building form and fabric
- mechanical plant and services
Two main sources are considered, non-renewable and renewable energy. The model is a conceptual tool for explaining energy trade-offs. The building passive model buildings may need a sophisticate approach to building form and fabric consuming large embodied energy but little operational energy. The active model may trade-off embodied energy for operational energy. The use of this approach helps benchmark climate responsive design strategies*

1. *The passive building model*: This uses no plant or equipment to modify climate. This building is called free running as its internal temperature follows that of the climate. The best that can be achieved with this building is that the thermal performance will be kept at the external shade temperature. Problems with this type of building occur when there are high casual gains that add to the environmental loads. The characteristics of performance are variable and the designer needs to assess the number of days in the year when internal conditions exceed comfort criteria and whether this is acceptable to the client and building users. Thus in school buildings it may be acceptable to use all passive systems because throughout the majority of the year the conditions may be within the comfort zone, and only a few days are problematic in terms of exceeding it. In the days when the comfort level is exceeded, behaviour modification can be used to minimize thermal discomfort.

2. *The active building model*: This uses mainly plant and equipment to modify climate. These buildings are called 'conditioned buildings' and guarantee a level of thermal comfort through the active systems. The performance issue in these buildings in not global thermal comfort – this is provided in theory by the plant and equipment – but local comfort conditions and energy efficiency. In many cases designers ignore first- and second-order decisions, relying mostly on the plant and equipment. The consequence here is poor efficiency. Also the use of plant and equipment in this system

Table 3.2 Climate types, climate modification strategies and building tactics for warm climates

Climate type	Adverse climatic elements	Climate method	Response strategies
Moderate	Rain Snow Cold winter winds Summer heat and high humidity	Minimize heat loss in winter Allow solar access in winter Minimize insolation in summer Utilize ventilation in summer	Good insulation Large windows facing the winter sun with solar access Overhangs/eaves for excluding summer sun Roof insulation or ventilated roof Large openings with cross-ventilation
Hot dry	Insolation Large diurnal temperature variation Wind-blown sand and dust Dryness	Minimize heat loss in winter and heat gain in summer Utilize diurnal temperature variation for summer cooling, winter heating Provide dust barriers at openings Utilize small amount of rain and low humidity	Overhangs/eaves for excluding summer sun. Shaded windows Heavy walls with large time-lag Screening Water feature to enhance evaporative cooling to incoming air
Hot humid	Rain Heat high humidity Insolation Small diurnal variation	Minimize heat gain Maximize ventilation Maximize shading	Thin plan with axis east-west Cross-ventilation, high ceilings Ventilated roof Window shading all year Shaded veranda

can lead to often over-sizing and redundancy in the deployment of this equipment to accommodate the environmental loads. Localized problems of thermal comfort occur with poorly balanced plant and localized heat gain from environmental loads.

3. *The hybrid building model*: The model has both active and passive building strategies to modify climate. This invariably requires the use of plant and equipment to modify climate in extreme conditions, generated either through excessive casual gains from occupants or from environmental loads. In addition, the use of microclimate and fabric to provide passive control reduces energy. The term 'passive low energy architecture' mainly applies to this approach. In theory this system sounds ideal, but the complexities of diurnal and seasonal climate change make it a complex problem of building management. The use of building monitoring systems can

3.11 *Prosser house showing the climate design strategies in the planning of the house. The building is orientated on the site to achieve optimum orientation and is broken into two pavilions to improve ventilation from the prevailing breezes. A breeze way is used to allow cross-ventilation to the external deck. A number of other strategies are used to avoid heat gain from the west. Bathrooms and non habitable spaces are zone on the westerly side of the house, bays are used to allow windows to face north-south thus reducing solar penetration and reflective materials as well as radiant barriers are used to prevent heat gain through the fabric of the building*

assist with this problem. These are computer systems, which monitor the building performance in use and can automatically regulate the building control features in an effort to optimize this process and achieve a level of building efficiency.

In addition, different thermal zones can be found within buildings; the passive zones can be found adjacent to the skin of the building, which can provide ventilation and daylighting for the occupants in this area. Normally, the size of the passive zone is measured as a dimension from the façade to the interior. This dimension is taken as a distance equal to twice the ceiling height of the space (see Chapter 7 for further details). Zones that have no contribution from the exterior environment are called active zones and re-quire air-conditioning, mechanical ventilation and artificial lighting.[15] This thermal zoning concept is useful for planning as designers can aim to make the passive zones in the buildings as large as possible and reduce active zones as a strategy to conserve energy.

Climate responsive design strategies and tactics

The next step is to examine these models and strategies in terms of the cli-mates in which they are located. In the previous chapter a number of broad strategies were given for the way the climate could be modified and the

Table 3.3 Climate responsive design compared to bioclimatic design

Climate Responsive Design	Bioclimatic Design
Stage 1: Building examples	Step 1: Climate data
Stage 2: Site study	Step 2: Evaluation
Stage 3: Sketch proposal	Step 3: Calculation methods
Stage 4: Design reflection and	Step 4: Findings
testing	Step 5: Architectural examples
	Step 6: Synthetic application

Note: the conjecturing, analysis and testing activities can be used to assist at the conceptual design of the building to help integrate climate orientated strategies

limits that could be achieved using passive means. It is therefore possible to relate the types of strategy to the climate type as shown in Table 3.2. The basic adverse aspects of climate are identified. This is then related to the strategies for modifying climate and the appropriate tactical design decisions concerning form and fabric of the building. In this way the designer can begin to think of the linkages in the arguments for the selection of appropriate strategies in the building design.

Thus, in a hot humid climate the adverse elements are high humidity, insolation and high temperatures with a small diurnal range in temperature. The consequences of this is to result in a number of tactical aspects such as thin plan forms to maximize ventilation and shading to reduce insolation. This kind of structuring of design information is important for integration in the design approach. The next section examines the integration of strategic thinking in the design process.

3.4 Design approach

In the preceding sections it has been argued that climate responsive design results from selecting strategies appropriate for various climate types. There are a number of first-order decisions that have to be taken with regard to the modification of climate to microclimate, then secondary decisions concerning building fabric, and finally plant and equipment. In an ideal world there is a level of 'fit' between climate and building response that is optimum and that this is primarily the goal of climate responsive design. Two particular difficulties occur with this approach.

First, the process of design is idiosyncratic and particular to the designer, and therefore the approach may conflict with individual design philosophies and goals. Also, many design approaches involving climatic design have been highly deterministic and analytical with a basis on the scientific method. The emphasis on quantitative design issues has caused concerns for the emphasis placed on the mathematical models underlying the climatic analysis when an understanding of broad strategies and design implications is required. For example with the bioclimate approach the designer uses a stepped process to interpret climatic data. The process starts from climatic data which is evaluated, represented through calculation methods and applied to practical and synthetic applications, see Table 3.3. This approach is thorough and exhaustive. It has been carried out by many architects since it was first developed with an emphasis on the descriptive and analytical aspects of the climatic and biological factors. It is proposed here to place more emphasis on the synthesis part of the process in particular on how the designer accommodates conceptually the climate design strategies and the attendant practical implications.

Second, in addition to the synthesis issues, it is becoming increasingly necessary to demonstrate the benefits of climate responsive design. Moreover, there are also difficulties in testing whether the strategies deployed will meet performance requirements. Clients and users need quantitative evidence that the strategies deployed will deliver the level of climate modification anticipated. An approach to climate design that starts with a qualitative view of climate and then moves through strategic thinking, to the provision of quantitative evidence is a desired direction.

Conjecture, analyse and testing

3.12 Large buildings require the work of multidisciplinary teams and analysis to test strategies adopted
left: Student analysis of a proposed tall building shows the effects of airflow around the building. Analysis such as this is useful to assess the implications of massing decisions. The effects of airflow at the ground plane can cause discomfort to pedestrians; with this kind of analysis modifications to the form of the building or through the fabric such as the addition of awnings can be made to avoid problems of this nature
right: Raffles City, Singapore, architect I.M. Pei. The use of a podium of smaller scale than the tall buildings helps reduce the visual mass at the street level but can be a useful strategy to reduce problems from strong down drafts from the taller buildings

The first difficulties of the design approach can be resolved in part by using design procedures that reflect the complexity of climate design. A number of

procedural models are available that have varied emphasis; some focus on analysis, some reflect a conjecturing process, others focus more on testing of building design solutions. The advocacy in this area is clearly difficult to put into operation because the methods of design are particular to the designer and therefore difficult to prescribe. It is simpler to suggest that there are design activities that have benefits in assisting with solving design problem related to the use of climate responsive design strategies. The building design can be viewed as a proposition that is critiqued as a method of resolving the problem; the design follows a number of iterative cycles resolving issues and reworking the proposition.

- *conjecturing*: developing a building proposition, based on a specific set on design issues and the climate design of the building that utilize a number of climate modification strategies
- *analysing*: identification and examination of the climatic factors pertinent to the proposition
- *testing*: evaluating the proposition in terms of the effectiveness of strategies selected to respond to climate factors and provision of qualitative and or quantitative evidence of the effectiveness response

Equally important as the need to consider the substance of the climate design strategies, is the application of these strategies in other stages of design such as design resolution and practice. A number of issues are emerging that are related to the effectiveness of the integration of climate responsive strategies. First, the stage at which these are considered, whether at the conceptual stage or later in the design resolution stage. Second, the nature of the design team and the interdisciplinary organization to what extent this delivers a level of optimization with regard to performance. Third, the method of evaluation and testing the outcome of these design decisions. The initiatives by governments to introduce energy codes to reduce fossil fuel consumption and thus limit greenhouse gas emissions, means that increasingly a prediction of performance of buildings is required before construction. This has led to a perplexing range of tools to assist the designer provide evidence of the performance of the building in use.

Conceptual thinking and design resolution

These later two shifts in practice reinforce the argument for more strategic thinking about climate at the early stage when the major design decisions are made. Too often the issues of climate design are ignored or left until after the conceptual design of the building is complete. In this case the design either uses active systems with attendant energy inefficiency, or a hybrid of passive and active systems.

A case is found with the design of large complex buildings and has led to a number of issues:

1. Lack of concern for the building impact on the site and poor microclimate

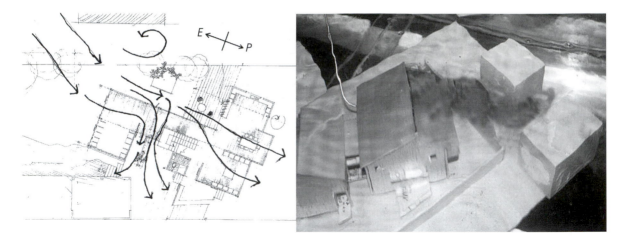

3.13 *Prosser House, architects Richard Hyde and Upendra Rapashka. This house is located in an urban area at Broad Beach on the Gold Coast, Australia*
left: the building and surrounding buildings were modelled using a waterflume to test the microclimate effects on ventilation strategies. Dye is introduced into the building to show the air direction.
right: Graphic analysis is used to record the effects of the modelling. This approach enables a testing of the climate design strategies as well as fine finer grained design decisions about door and window sizes and positions to improve cooling

conditions around the building causing lack of comfort in the external spaces

2. Lack of concern for the building impact on the urban context and the urban context on the building
3. Planning strategies that do not assess the effect of the gross floor area in terms of site coverage and building footprint
4. Planning strategies that do not respect orientation for passive heating, cooling or energy efficiency
5. Planning strategies that increase plan depth whilst also reducing ceiling height and do not maximize the passive zones in the building
6. Use of extensive and complex strategies for climate modification through the skin, for example, the use of shading devices and solar glass, which are high cost and have performance problems ensuing from the technical complexity of the building
7. Skin design that does not meet performance requirements for solar exposure, air tightness, moisture control, heat transfer and vision
8. Plant and equipment that have high levels of redundancy to meet the building and user needs and give rise to service integration problems
9. Lack of amenity in the building to facilitate appreciation of the climate, provide health and safety as well as accommodate differing user lifestyles
10. Lack of user control of the local comfort conditions within and outside the building[16]

Interdisciplinary design teams

The complexity of climate design has led to recognition of the need for an interdisciplinary approach to building design. This involves teams of professionals working in an multidisciplinary group. What is of interest is the growing recognition of the environmental benefits of this approach and the shift in the focus of the interdisciplinary problem.

The benefits of the interdisciplinary approach lies in the holistic resolution that this can achieve. To be successful environmental design requires professionals from many different areas of expertise to solve the problems to balance the needs of the environment with the needs of the economic constraints of the project. Often these competing needs working differing directions. Energy efficiency is a good example, it has been found that reductions in the use of energy and the shift to cleaner more benign forms of energy supply can reduce energy use and greenhouse gas emissions, significant emission reductions can be achieved through better design. That is even without the new technical fixes that are available, the design team and the management team of the building can reduce both the demand for and supply more efficiently the energy used in the building. This is viewed as a major potential yet to be exploited in the design of many large buildings.

This realization has led to a shift in what is perceived as the focus of the interdisciplinary design problem. Historically, the urban atmosphere with its pollution and noise led to the sealed box building with for advanced mechanical and electrical systems to filter the air and provide artificial light. The initial design problem was one of integration, to accommodate the plant and equipment in a rational and structured way. Yet the consequences of this approach was higher and higher energy use and a move to 'low energy design.' Ironically this led to further environmental problems, filtering of the outside effects of climate through high insulation, small windows, venctian blinds and the provision of very little amenity.[17]

The new challenge and focus is to begin to balance the negative and positive factors of climate to achieve both amenity and efficient use of resources. Some see this a design task that draws on models from the past such as vernacular architecture, others on a software approach. This approach focuses less on the hardware such as the specification of plant and equipment in a building and more one the phenomena of climate such as daylighting, thermal reponses and natural ventilation. Thus the understanding the dynamics of building response a multidisciplinary task is seen as a significant new challenge. There have arisen new design professionals to take on this challenge, the 'climate engineer' is a description of a professional now versed in the skills of modelling and designing with climate and developing new ways of using natural energy strategies as well as those that use man-made energy.[18]

Design assessment and building modelling

This shift of focus in the interdisciplinary problem area has led to the need for greater prediction of the performance of the building during design. Design techniques that involve design assessment and computer modelling are now becoming commonly accepted as necessary servised that the team will provide to validate design concepts.

The main performance measures that can be used to assess a building response to climate are lighting, thermal and ventilation factors

Designers can assess the effects of climate design strategies by comparative analysis either through field measurements of buildings or by computer simulation. The former gives broad data on the performance of a building to given a set of climate conditions. It is also useful to measure the solar radiation, humidity, and external shade temperature and wind speed to assist with making comparison between days. The use of this data is only valid for the particular case examined and it is difficult to make wider generalization. On more use is the latter method that of computer simulation. This involves the input of data about the design. A mathematical model is then used to calculate the performance given climatic conditions.

A papametric computer simulation study by Coldicutt and Williamson of a basic house form shows the effects of changes in design strategies on internal temperatures. This gives the designer an indication of the likely effects of design decisions. It should be borne in mind that generalizations based on this information should be examined in relation to how the proposed application of the strategies varies with the example given. Also the study uses computer simulation and therefore the temperatures are indicative of likely performance.[19]

There is wide concern about usefulness of these computer simulation tools as one of the techniques used by architects for design assessment. Many tools claim to assist the architect but it is not common for designers to use computer simulation studies of buildings. This is particularly the case for the early conceptual stages of the design process. The complexity of input into the tool and extent of this kind of evaluation requires a high level of design resolution to obtain practical results. Work has been carried out to clarify the interdisciplinary protocol for integrating climate strategies in buildings and to match types of tool to the protocol.

Three main types of tool can be found:

1. *Rating tool*: these have simplified input and use standard criteria to assess building designs. Normally this is given in the form of stars in a similar way to energy ratings for refrigerators. These are particularly useful for baseline studies with clients to give general information about building performance. Problems exist with the assumptions made in simulation engine and the criteria, hence a rating scheme for warm climates is not likely to be applicable to cool climates.

2. *Conceptual design assessment tools*: the tools are similar to rating tools but do not lock in criteria, rather they give performance data on key indicators such as energy-use, carbon dioxide emissions or thermal comfort. Models of the building can be constructed using a computer aided design interface which can be assessed by the tools engine. Output from this enables an approximate assessment of the climate strategies used sufficient to place the building in the 'right ball park' for optimum design.

3. *Design development evaluation tools*: these are used to assist with the specific sizing of plant and equipment and to give detailed evaluation of the main energy and building fabric decisions. These tools can involve sophisticated computer simulation tools, for example the use of computer fluid dynamics studies to test airflow in atria and the use of lighting tools to optimize

Table 3.4: Thermal performance measures used to compare effects of changes in building design variables on internal temperatures

	Optimum orientation	Adverse orientation	Square plan	Rectangular plan
Peak external temperature	40	40	40	40
Peak internal temperature	37.5	37	37.5	37.5
Temperature difference	2.5	3	2.5	2.5

Drawn from the work of Williamson and Coldicutt

daylight and electrical lighting.[20]

The value of using these tools based on three arguments.

First, the tools provide the designer and the client with quantitative data of performance in an area which can be a largely subjective and largely unequivocal area decision making.

Second, traditional design activities such as using principles in design can only take the designera small way along the design path. Significant improvement in design can be achieved by the interrelation of the main design factors. For example the need to optimize daylighting and electrical lighting which involves balancing design factors such as shading, glazing area and room depth. Simple manual calculation methods to achieve this are slow but with design tools an optimization approach can be used which is far more effective.

Third, tools give the implication of using a range of strategies concerning the skin and form of the buildings. The benefit of this approach is that it can begin to demonstrate the holistic resolution of technology to address environmental problems. In this way designers learn not only the basic concepts concerning environmental technology but also how to develop technical strategies to address environmental problems.

The wider application of the conjecture, analysis and testing procedure requires careful focus on the question of analysis and testing. At the foundation of this are a number of performance and evaluation measures that can be used to highlight the efficacy of the building proposition. The next section examines some measures that can be used as evidence to support benefits of integration of climate design strategies in the design problem.

A number of tangible measures can be used that indicate the likely climate performance of the building. These are described briefly below, and are used in the subsequent discussion on the strategies described in the chapters that follow. Other professionals adequately cover an extensive description of these measures, and therefore only the main issues are presented. The evaluation measures can be applied at a number of levels:

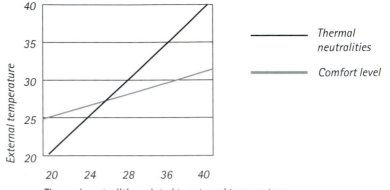

3.14 *A comparison of thermal neutrality temperatures for thermal comfort to external temperatures to show the effects of acclimatization*

1. *The global level:* the measures that give information specific to the spaces within the building and outside the building
2. *The local level:* specific to individual areas, zones and components of the building form and associated elements
3. *The personal level:* the experience of individuals and groups in a space and associated behavioural response

3.5 Design performance measures

The performance measures used during the design stage vary with the strategies used. If the building is free running using primarily passive systems then it is appropriate to use thermal comfort as the main indicator of performance. Where it uses active systems then the mechanical systems provide thermal comfort, in this case the main indicator is energy use.

Thermal comfort

Comfort can be defined as the complete physical and mental well-being.[21] Thermal comfort is a subset of the broad definition of comfort and relates to human and environmental factors. It is a complex area of study in fundamental terms, but for the designer the key issues relate to the building and environmental factors that affect comfort since these are amenable to manipulation in the design of the building. The main environmental factors affecting thermal comfort are as follows:

- air temperature
- radiation
- air velocity and air movement
- humidity

Research has pointed out that basic physiological response to thermal comfort is moderated by acclimatization to respective climate conditions, thus people living in temperate climates may have a different sensation of climate to that of people living in tropical climates. The person-specific nature of comfort means that defining precise levels of comfort for buildings is fraught with difficulty. Despite these difficulties, research has generated some methods whereby designers can measure performance of buildings in terms of thermal comfort

The global effects are defined as the level of comfort provided by the environment in which the building is located. Thus for a given air temperature and humidity a zone of comfort can be found (see Chapter 2). Methods for assessing comfort based on mean monthly external temperatures are also available. A number of researchers, using empirical research, have developed formulae for converting this temperature into an internal temperature, at which people are comfortable. This gives an internal thermal neutrality temperature, the temperature at which a person should be neither too hot nor too cold. From the neutrality temperature a comfort zone can be defined as 2 degrees C above and below the neutrality temperature. The neutrality temperatures for warm climates can be based on the analytical work of Bromberek.[22]

Given the global temperatures at the ambient air temperature. Clearly, though, where the external air temperature exceeds the comfort level then efforts to modify that climate to reduce internal temperatures below ambient are required. The passive strategies using first-order decisions concerning microclimate modification and the second-order decisions using the building fabric to achieve this are desirable but predictably difficult to achieve. The building therefore should move from a free running state to a conditioned state.

Local effects on thermal comfort are found at specific parts of the building and should be thought of as both negative and positive. For example the radiant effects from solar glass is a common problem in high rise buildings that cannot be overcome by reducing air temperatures and requires careful design of the building fabric.[23]

Energy performance

With the increased concern for energy use, arguments have been developed to assist with the savings of energy use through life-cycle costing. In principle this involves the computation of both the capital cost of the building and the cost of operating the building over its projected life. The energy costs often exceed the capital costs of the building over time, this condition has focused design efforts to reduce the need for and use of active systems. Often the cost of plant and equipment is around 40 per cent of the capital cost of a complex building and therefore strategies that can reduce the demand for this type of equipment will reduce capital costs. In addition the need to save operational energy in the running of active systems has focused attention on the design decisions that contribute to energy saving.

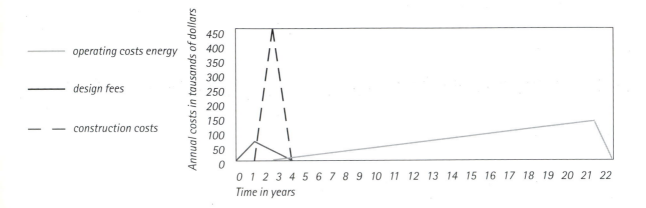

operating costs energy

design fees

construction costs

3.15 Life cycle costing of a building showing a comparison of operating cost to capital cost; note the operating costs exceed the capital cost and the relatively small cost of design fees. Arguments for more resources for design to reduce operating costs come from this kind of analysis (R. Flanagan and G. Norman, Life Cycle Costing for Construction, RICS, London, 1983)

Energy use can be divided into two sets of factors for efficiency purposes, demand side and supply side efficiency. Supply side efficiency comes from the elements of the building that drive the need for power in the building whilst the demand side efficiency is related to elements that use power.

The first important way to save energy is to use less of it, so the first goal is to cut demand, and second goal is to supply power in a manner that is benign (use of renewable energy sources) and efficient as possible. The assessment of the demand side of energy use in buildings is therefore best served at the conceptual stage in the design process. It is at this stage that the brief can be questioned with regard to power requirements. The form and shape of the building through the application of passive low energy architectural strategies can provide the optimum design to reduce energy use. Following the application of these strategies the second important way of delivering efficiency is through the selection of plant and equipment to deliver service needs efficiently. Ways of assessing the effects of demand side efficiency that result from fabric and form decisions are available to the

3.16 Diagrammatic plans of deep and narrow floors of an office building used to compare energy efficiency

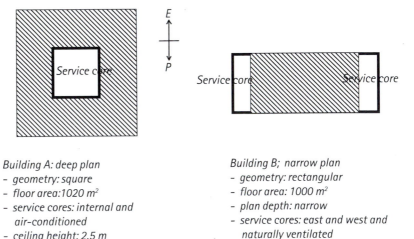

Building A: deep plan
- *geometry: square*
- *floor area:1020 m²*
- *service cores: internal and air-conditioned*
- *ceiling height: 2.5 m*

Building B; narrow plan
- *geometry: rectangular*
- *floor area: 1000 m²*
- *plan depth: narrow*
- *service cores: east and west and naturally ventilated*
- *ceiling height: 3.5 m*

Table 3.4 Efficiency measures that can be used
in the demand for and supply of energy in buildings

Demand side	Supply side
- Building Planning	-On site generation
Optimize orientation	-Integrated PV Systems
- Naturally ventilated core	-Alternative generation
Solar blocking by the core	-Gas fuel cells
- Thin building Plan Depth	-Thermal energy storage
- Maximize passive zone	-Ice storage
- Increase ceiling height	-User control
- Skin design	
Passive cooling	
- Natural cooling	
- Thermal performance	
- Glazing control	
- Shading	
- Light diffusers/maximize aperture/	
solar glass	

designer. These can provide quantitative data on building energy efficiency. This can be achieved by computer simulation, but this process is complex and time consuming. Simplified tools are available for use at the conceptual stage which are more appropriate for designers.[24] The approach is typified by a simple experiment: two building propositions were examined. The first was a square, deep plan office building; the second was a narrow plan office. The former had a central core; the latter had cores to the east and west.

By using the narrow plan building and orienting the building with cores east and west, the passive zone is increased and active zone reduced. Furthermore, by naturally ventilating and lighting the cores a further area of

3.17 *Comparative energy use for different plan types and climates. Note that the narrow plan geometry is optimized for climate response and to achieve energy efficiency. The consequence it uses approximately 30 per cent less energy. The energy saving is from lighting energy*
1. *Deep plan, cool climate*
2. *Narrow plan, cool climate*
3. *Deep plan, Mediterranean climate*
4. *Narrow plan, Mediterranean climate*
This analysis used the energy design tool called LT Method

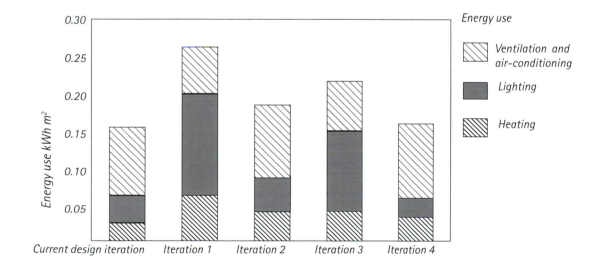

Energy use

Ventilation and air-conditioning

Lighting

Heating

Current design iteration   Iteration 1   Iteration 2   Iteration 3   Iteration 4

conditioned space can be reduced. These two buildings were used to compare energy needs to establish the overall influence of shape and orientation. Other variables were kept similar. The climates selected were used to compare both situations of heat deficit and heat surplus.

The results from the experiment show that an approximate 30 per cent saving can be achieved by using the narrow plan strategy with high ceilings, naturally ventilated cores east and west, as opposed to the square, deep plan building with low ceiling and central core. This does not mean that the narrow plan is the optimum solution in all cases; it indicates that the use of simplified energy tools can give meaningful advice to designers on the energy efficiency of buildings at the conceptual stage. In addition they are an iterative and comparative tools. As climate modification strategies are applied further design iterations are made and energy consequences compared. It should be recognized that these simplified tools are model reduction exercises and thus only give indicative performance but are useful at the conceptual stage when broad strategies are evaluated.[25]

Visual comfort

Lighting is required for functional purposes in the building to enable the completion of visual tasks and for human safety. The principles for satisfying these requirements are climate independent.

The climate dependent issues come from the quality and quantity of daylighting in found in the different climates. This in turn is related to the sky conditions and the levels of solar radiation, which vary in the differing types of warm climate. Hot humid climates are fairly cloudy during the year, with 60-90 per cent cover. Illuminance from the clear sky is high but is reduced with overcast conditions to approximately 12 per cent of the clear sky conditions. Solar radiation is less than that for the hot dry and moderate climates. The high humidity causes a reduction in the transparency of the atmosphere, leading to lower solar radiation. The clear sky conditions in both the moderate and hot dry climates give high light levels and solar radiation.[26]

It is clear from Table 3 that there is ample daylight for interior lighting, but the large amounts of solar radiation admitted into the building is the

Table 3.5 Typical lighting levels and solar radiation for warm climates

	Hot humid	Hot dry	Moderate
Typical sky luminance, lumins			
Clear skies	7500	10800	100000
Overcast, obscured	9000	9000	20000
Typical solar radiation, W m^2			
Clear skies	750	1080	1000
Overcast	90	90	200

3.18 *Kingfisher Bay Resort, Guymer Bailey Architects 1991. Optimization of lighting is achieved to provide a level of visual comfort. Control of the external environment through landscaping and verandas reduced reflected light and heat. Large glazing areas can be used giving a transparency between inside and out. The clear storey windows bring daylight to the centre of the buildings and are shaded to reduce sky glare. Electric lighting is used to complement daylighting and avoids contrasting external conditions.*

main concern. Particularly in the moderate climates where there are long periods of clear sky conditions this is a difficult problem. For example a 1m² square skylight will admit up to 1000 W of heat, equivalent to the sensible and latent heat load of six to seven office workers. In moderate climates there is an abundance of natural light; the challenge for the designer is to utilize this natural light to avoid electric lighting without heat gain.[27]

The quality of light in these climates also varies considerably. In the moderate climate brightness of light, due to the high intensity, gives high contrast between sunlight and shaded areas. This contrast can cause high levels of reflected glare from highly reflective surfaces. The main problems occur with interior spaces where low light levels are used. Glare can be found from contrasts between the exterior light levels, sky glare and the wall surfaces around the window.

Lighting can be separated into both electrical and daylight. A further distinction should also be given with regard to sunlight and diffuse light. Daylighting can contain both sunlight and diffuse light. Diffuse light is the indirect light that is light reflected from external surfaces, whereas sunlight is the direct light from a clear sky. The main concern with daylighting in warm climates is that the access of sunlight into the building brings heat and ultraviolet light. The use of glass traps the heat by virtue of the greenhouse effect and thus contributes to the heat load. Diffuse light, on the other hand, is more benign; it has a much lower component of heat. Hence the need to shade openings to reduce the direct solar access and increase the amount of diffuse light. Yet this simple strategy represents a high degree of complexity, which centres on the performance requirements and design strategies for windows.

Indeed there is increasing concern for the design of windows for warm climate arising from conflicting performance requirements. Aynsley points out that:

'Sadly, in many recent buildings in the rapidly developing urban, warm humid tropical regions, there is little apparent design effort associated with window design. In housing particular window openings are often formed in unshaded walls and fitted with the least cost aluminium sliding sashes. This leads to rapid indoor overheating, extreme indoor glare and reduced airflow as the effective area of sliding windows is only 50 per cent.'[28]

The concerns raised by Aynsley are founded on the need to unpack the various conflicting constraints involved in window design. There is the need to provide for the ingress of light but also the reduction of glare. The high level of daylights found in warm climates come from clear sky conditions. This generates the need for shading to reduce thermal loads through the glass but the shading systems also reduces the amount of daylight. This is in turn compensated for by the use of electrical light. The optimization of shading, daylight and electrical lighting design is a main design concern if energy efficiency is to be achieved. The window may also be expected to provide ventilation, airflow, view as well as acoustic and visual privacy. It is clear that given the complexity of these requirements it is hardly of surprise that the design of these elements is found wanting. A better strategy is to accommodate each as a separate environmental control system by separate elements and not attempt to integrate all into one element. Thus some 'windows' may be for ventilation only whilst others are for daylighting, and others as vision panel for view. This may not simplify the problem but it does focus the designer on the role and issues associated with the design of the skin of the building. The climate responsive design issues concerned with daylighting are:

1. *Diffuse light*: the use diffuse light where possible, rather than direct sunlight, to avoid heat gain and ultraviolet degradation of interior materials and furnishings

3.19 Types of mechanical ventilation systems used in buildings. Left: desk or pedestal fans, used to bring external air into the building if placed adjacent to the window right: ceiling fans used to re-circulate air, the balance of these fans is important to avoid noise and reduced efficiency. Also the number and pitch of the blades causes noise, for noise-sensitive areas consider 4 bladed types. Reversible motors are available for winter use to avoid staticifaction of hot air at the ceiling. For summer use ceiling fans can be linked to a thermostatic control in a similar way to air-conditioning systems. This is advisable fo night time comfort when early morning temperatures drop to below the comfort zone

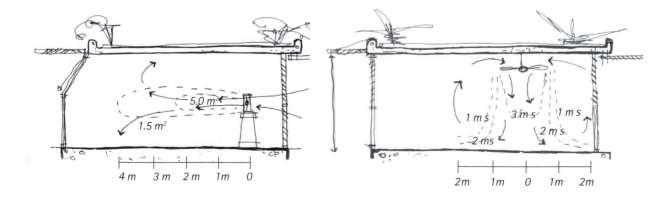

2. *Heat gain from glazing*: the provision of external shading to reduce direct solar gain but allow sufficient lighting for natural lighting; optimize the glazing ratio to provide appropriate natural lighting conditions, and provide ventilation to remove the heat gain associated with glazed areas

3. *Glare*: use materials and colours to avoid high contrast in the external and internal lighting conditions; elements such as landscaping, tinted glass and screens are of use as buffers to moderate internal and external conditions

4. *Light transitions and thresholds*: in situations where contrasts occur, avoid sharp contrast in light levels to avoid disabling glare; set electrical lighting threshold for smooth transitions from natural light[29]

3.6 Ventilation strategies

Ventilation can be defined as the effects of air movement in the building. There are three main functions of ventilation. The first is the provision of a sufficient quality and quantity of air for people's life processes and activities. This is therefore the provision of healthy ventilation, air that is free from pollutants or other harmful substances. Also, in the case of urban sites, where buildings are built next to areas of high levels of acoustic and atmospheric pollution such as around motorways, the location of fresh-air input to buildings has to be carefully sited to minimize these effects.

The second main function of ventilation is to provide occupants with personal cooling; sometimes this is called thermal comfort ventilation created by the passage of air across their bodies. This is related to the availability and velocity of cooling air from outside the building. The velocity of air to achieve thermal comfort increases with temperature until the skin surface temperature is reached at approximately 35 degrees C. In the hot dry climates this is a problem. The summer air temperatures can peak at 42 degrees C, in this case the air is dry and dusty, as well as above the comfort zone, and to

3.20 *Types of mechanical ventilation systems*
left: use of roof mounted axial fans to service spaces; the roof space is used as a plenum to bring in cool air from gable vents, the roof skin should be highly insulated with radiant barriers to reduce heat gain to the plenum, the rooms can be pressurized in this way which keeps out insects
right: a ducted system using remote axial fans, this reduces fan noise and provides a low energy form of air-conditioning without the refrigerant cooling

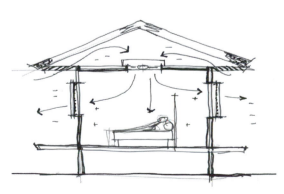
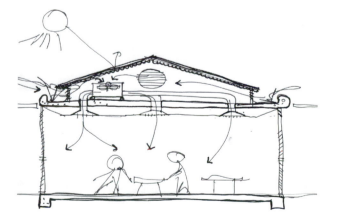

3.21 *In these units on the Sunshine Coast in Queensland, the air-conditioning has replaced climate design features for this western orientation unit, this transfers the heat load to the air-conditioning system and created higher energy use*

bring this air into the building is problematic for personal cooling. Other forms of cooling are required such as evaporative or mass cooling.

Ventilation's third main function is to cool the fabric of the building, commonly called structural cooling. The amount of cooling provided by the air will depend on the relative temperatures of the materials and the air. Air entering the building that is cooler will absorb heat from the materials and vice versa.[30]

The consequences of the functions of ventilation suggests that ventilation is highly context specific; general levels of airflow from mean wind speeds are modified by the site and through the building skin through the disposition of elements. In addition occupants compete for personal cooling with the need for structural cooling of the building. Thus, the amount of mass, the volume of airflow through the building as well as temperature difference are crucial parameters for the effectiveness of ventilation. Thus in designing for ventilation the main issues are the exposure provided by the site, the amount of opacity in the skin and the function of the ventilation, i.e. to cool the people or the building or both. There are two main types of ventilation: natural and mechanical ventilation.

Natural ventilation is generated by pressure differences in and around the building. These pressure differences come from air movement generated by air temperature and by wind. Temperature-driven ventilation is usually the lesser pressure of the two, and thus where both are expected to occur at the same time the wind pressure will prevail. Temperature driven ventilation is called 'stack effect' because it uses the natural buoyancy of the hotter air to rise and displace cooler air. Stratification will occur in a space with hotter air at the top and cooler at the bottom. Advantage is taken in buildings where the external temperature is lower than the internal temperature. The internal

3.22 *In these units on the Sunshine Coast in Queensland a generic unit design is replicated for a number orientation. High glazing ratios in the skin of the building reduces the thermal efficiency of the building to accommodate low angle sun found with east and west orientation. This can give high internal air temperature swings requiring air-conditioning to achieve comfort. Air-conditioning plant and equipment installed on the exterior of the building can lead to problems of service integration (external ducting and trunking), maintenance and visual pollution*

air will rise up and exhaust from the building, bringing in fresh air. In warm climates the effectiveness of stack is questionable, the temperature differences between inside and out are small. Since stack is driven by temperature difference, the pressures are small. Wind-driven ventilation therefore is commonly used in warm climates. The design factors affecting ventilation are as follows:

1. Reduction of plan depth and increase openness of section to facilitate cross-flow and vertical flow of air
2. Optimum orientation of rooms to the prevailing breeze and the linkage between leeward and windward side to utilize pressure differences
3. Maximize the skin opacity through the number and size of opening, single-, double-or three-sided openings to rooms, horizontal versus vertical stacking of openings
4. Reduction of internal obstructions
5. Site selection and building situation to increase exposure to airflow effects[31]

In principle it is best to conceive of rooms and spaces as large ducts that can moderate and direct airflow. Any obstruction will direct or block the airflow and provide friction, reducing its energy. Ideally, wind flows from the windward side to the leeward side by pressure difference through the linking of internal spaces. The deeper the building and the more cellular its internal form, the more friction and therefore less airflow.

In situations where for functional reasons, such as where there are high casual gains from occupants and the need for cellular spaces, natural ventilation may not be feasibly provided. In addition when the forces of nature

Table 3.5: Rating of air-conditioning systems based on performance and technical integration. Energy use is not considered as this is dependent on plant type and the building context

System	Least capital cost	Ease of retrofit	Low sound generation	Efficient reduction of humidity	Provision of fresh air	Efficient disposal of condensate	Total
Continuous velocity	1	1	5	5	5	5	22
Chilled water fan coil	3	3	3	1	4	1	15
Split coil/fan	4	5	5	4	0	1	19
Window conditioner	5	3	0	3	3	1	15

fail then mechanical assistance for natural ventilation is required. This can be provided in a number of forms:

1. Floor- or desk-mounted fans can be used to bring in external air if placed next to the window, this is useful for providing individual cooling due to local air movement
2. Ceiling-mounted fans, which recycle the air in the space and give air movement. These cannot lower the air temperature in the space but give cooling due to the movement of air across the skin. Subjectively the internal air temperature is reduced by up to 3 degrees C.
3. Exhaust-fans, which extract air from the space and draw in external air to provide cooling
4. Ducted air using input fans to bring external air into the space. The efficiency of this system is improved if air can be brought in from a cool location. This type of system is useful for moderating peak loads from environmental or high casual gains. A computer simulation study of school classrooms in Queensland, Australia, illustrates the application of this system. On days where there was little breeze, peak internal temperature were found to exceed the comfort zone by 5-10 degrees C. The use of the ducted air system was found to reduce peak temperatures to that of 1-2 degrees above ambient temperature.[32] The use of ducted external air is also a more energy efficient form of conditioning than full air-conditioning. This is because with full air-conditioning, energy is required for air movement and for temperature reduction. In ducted external air, only energy is required for air movement. At best the use of these systems can only bring the external temperature to the ambient air temperature yet it does provide this temperature consistently. Thus in design conditions where behaviour modification cannot take place, i.e. classrooms, this consistency of temperature is a crucial factor. In this way natural ventilation can be supplemented by mechanical ventilation with a lower energy component than full air-conditioning.

3.7 Mechanical ventilation and air-conditioning

Natural ventilation relies on the quality of the external environment of the building to provide clean, fresh air to service the air quality and cooling needs of the building and its occupants. In the late nineteenth century, the industrial revolution and high population density led to the deterioration in the quality of the external environment. Noise and air pollution, particularly in cities, reduced the environments capacity to provide a source of energy to service the building.[33]

A consequence of this was the provision of mechanical ventilation, which became available in the late nineteenth century and was adopted in landmark climate responsive solutions like the Larkin Building by Frank Lloyd Wright. Mechanical ventilation allowed the sealing of the building to reduce the penetration of externally generated noise, and the use of filters to remove pollutants.

The facility to provide temperature-stable, dry, indoor air has been available since the 1930s. With this development came the capability to not only filter external air but cool and dehumidify it. High internal heat loads from people and equipment, called casual gains, could thus be removed to create a stable environment. The comfort and commercial benefits of this technical development led to its speedy penetration into the building industry. The benefits of air-conditioning in warm climates is similar to the provision of heating is to buildings in temperate climates. The energy solution is increasingly seen as a prerequisite for climate modification.

A further consequence in the twentieth century is the expansion of the highly mechanically serviced building . To service this type of building, a sophisticated technical support programme for its design and management was required. Moreover, the complexity of interdisciplinary work called for teams of architects, engineers and builders to enable the successful synthesis of design and technical issues. The development of integrated heating, ventilation and air-conditioning systems (HVAC) came from a number of factors, chiefly and innovation in the design of various types of mechanical plant and systems as well as the availability of cheap energy to run these systems. Furthermore, the social status attached to this type of building increased and it became potent symbol of industrial development and progress.

The prevailing opinion is that air-conditioning in buildings is relatively new and expensive, providing year-round comfort. Unlike heating, which is seen as a basic need in cool climates, air-conditioning is seen as a privilege and therefore requires justification.[34] Five main reasons are used by designers for justifying the installation of air-conditioning:

- *design flexibility*: the use of air-conditioning removes planning strategies associated with providing access to the external environment for passive cooling, that is, application of thin floor plans, large window sizes, use of solar shading, application of optimum orientation
- *site utilization*: allows dense site coverage, 'tight fit' site utilization strategies can be used as ducts, air wells and courtyards are not required for

light and ventilation
- *constant air quality through temperature and humidity control*: thermal comfort can be regulated, by using refrigeration in the mechanical system, to provide air to within one degree below or above the desired comfort zone, and to within 5 per cent of the desired humidity. In the commercial office this is thought to reduce absenteeism and in the retail sector it is marketed as a commodity and as a thermal refuge. It can also be used to protect specialized and climatically sensitive plant and equipment
- *thermal comfort in high population density*: in conditions where there is a high density of people using a space, for example in conditions of under $1m^2$ per person, then the high casual gains and deterioration in air quality, necessitate the use of air-conditioning.[35]

The issues facing the designer when installing and integrating air-conditioning range from the technical complexity of accommodating the plant and equipment in the building to the issues of air quality and energy use. In addition, the use of air-conditioning has received attention from those that promote its use and those concerned with environmental impacts. The plant and equipment manufacturers are readily promoting the comfort benefits in the press and on television. A small room air-conditioner comes with a remote control like the television and the VCR. One can dial up the optimum comfort level from your armchair whilst watching a favourite movie. Air-conditioning comes standard in your car along with the air bag and the anti-locking brakes. The privilege of owning and using air is no more; it has been deemed a necessity.

The initial impact that started in commercial buildings is rapidly spreading to domestic ones where passive systems have previously been used. This is a concern in an energy conscious world, where the cheap energy to drive these systems comes from non-renewable sources and contributes to greenhouse gas emissions. It is from this energy efficiency perspective that many of the criticisms of air-conditioning are mounted. Additional concern has come from the point of view of human well-being; the constantly filtered 'clean' air seems not to be as benign as once thought and the technology has difficulty delivering the quality expected for a reasonable capital cost. The main criticisms are:

- high market penetration of sophisticated HVAC systems has progressed rapidly at the expense of less energy active systems
- to avoid high energy consumption, less fresh air is drawn into the system and more recycled air is used thus raising concern about air quality
- central control of temperatures has been used to cut demand by preventing users from altering thermostats and other parts of the building for microclimate control. In particular, windows are sealed to prevent tampering
- air-conditioning has been assumed to replace the need for climate design features in buildings creating poor thermal design and high energy use.

The capital cost reduction of this approach is transferred to higher life-cycle energy costs and negative environmental impacts
- the quality of air due to excessive recycling and poor maintenance of plant has led to 'sick building syndrome' where the indoor air quality has led to problems of users' health
- concern for the long-term well-being of an increasing indoors, sedentary population, that has become acclimatized to the constancy of air-conditioning. It is postulated that this will reduce occupants' physiological thermo-regulatory mechanisms, increasing the risk of climatic stain when returning to the warmer external conditions[36]

It is evident that whilst these concerns are about the design issues associated with air-conditioning there is also strong criticism placed on the management of these systems. This stems from the practice, akin to 'climate determinism', of using constant prescribed temperatures and humidity day in, day out and throughout the year.[37] The result is the building is disengaged from the place in which it is located and from the natural cycle, promoting in humans a range of behaviour similar to that of sensory deprivation. This is indicated in feedback from one user survey of air-conditioned buildings. The problems are as follows:

1. Beliefs held by the occupants are that air-conditioning is related to health problems, yet there is little clinical connection between environmental cause and health effect.
2. Health issues are possibly related more to the psychogenic hypothesis of sensory deprivation.
3. Lack of control of microclimate control the environment, building managers are likened to 'zoo keepers' as they tend to be viewed as regulating the environment on behalf of the occupants and curtailing freedom.
4. Large temperature differences between inside and outside can cause thermal stress and lack of comfort[38]

The survey also shows that there is little preference for an air-conditioned building over a non-air-conditioned; occupants in passive buildings like passive buildings, and similarly in air-conditioned buildings. The one important finding is that preference is based on climatic experience, and this has an important role in determining the preference of users. For example, only 18 per cent of Darwin residents (the hot humid tropics), have a preference for air-conditioning in the cool season whilst in Brisbane (the moderate climate), 68 per cent prefer air-conditioning in the warm season. The warm season in Brisbane is similar in temperature to Darwin's cool season. This would suggest residents benchmark their thermal comfort against seasonal extremes and not against absolute comfort criteria.[39]

There also appears also to be some coincidence between the adoption of energy efficient measures in the management of air-conditioned buildings and the effects on human health. From the author's experience, this is a combination of lack of user control and the use of energy efficient measures. For example, measurements of temperature and humidity taken in one hotel bedroom in a hot humid tropical climate showed particular problems. The internal air temperature in the room was found to be 19 degrees C and relative humidity at 60 per cent. The air speed from the incoming air speed was about 1.5 m s[-1]. The thermostatic control did not function. Even with the author wearing extra layers of clothing, the room became uncomfortable and it was vacated. In addition, condensation appeared on the outside of the windows and obscured the view. In this case, clearly the air temperature was lowered to reduce humidity from the incoming air but for energy saving reasons this air was not reheated to a comfortable level.[40] The thermal stress and the frustration with this form of management of an air-conditioning systems is clearly problematic. This warrants further research into the relationship between the thermal comfort in air-conditioning and energy efficiency measures related to the climatic experience of the occupants. There is the technology and knowledge to create internal environments to suite differing needs for comfort. It seems the 'zoo keepers' need to realize there are a variety of different animals in the zoo and that conditions should reflect their needs. The evidence from the foregoing leads to some recommendations:

- a primary goal of air-conditioning is to provide thermal comfort. It therefore seems self-defeating to achieve energy savings through management practices that compromise comfort and human well-being; a similar statement could be said of passive systems.
- energy savings should be achieved by applying design strategies that control energy use through effective design of the building form and fabric, plant and delivery system
- air-conditioning *per se* is a technical solution to the cooling problem in warm climates and is benign if designed and used effectively. The global use of non-renewable energy sources to provide electrical energy to power these systems is not benign, and it is probably not feasible to power these systems from clean sources such as on-site photo voltaic systems due to the high power consumption. Therefore, in the absence of building control measures, the designer has an ethical responsibility to reduce the demand side of power consumption through appropriate building design and management
- the cost of energy to run these systems is low compared with the cost of using passive systems to achieve the same ends, hence there is little incentive to investigate or apply innovative passive systems or indeed passive design of buildings[41]
- ethical changes in society and the design professions in favour of more benign practices is leading to the development of alternative approaches, including more efficient air-conditioning systems and less wasteful management to address human comfort issues and health complaints from sealed buildings
- the development of design models and tools for architects which can

facilitate and integrate the energy efficient strategies currently available. The tools should be appropriate to the conceptual stage and demonstrate the benefits of any efficiency to clients and users. This integrated approach in conceptual design is currently lacking, leading to problems of retrofitting energy efficiency measures during the design resolution if at all.

Application of air-conditioning in domestic-scale buildings

The application of air-conditioning is examined in relation to small-scale buildings as the principles and concepts found in these types focus on range of prevailing practice options. The common practice is not to air-condition private homes, apartments, schools and institutional buildings except in extreme climate conditions.[42] This practice seems to be changing with the improvements in the efficiency of air-conditioning plant, the reduction in cost and changing lifestyles. The traditional 'window rattler' room conditioning systems which has a single packaged unit of plant located in the window apertures, is being complemented by the availability of split fan and condensor systems where the air-handling plant (the fan and coil) is placed internally and separated from the refrigeration plant (the condensor). The costs are relatively similar. A window air conditioner retails for about A$1500 installed and draws about 15 amps; a 20 amp split system which can cool about 20 m², retails for about A$2500, fully installed. Portable room conditioners that can be attached to room power sockets are available for conditioning rooms and are at a similar cost to room conditioners.

The strategy with these systems is to use them not necessarily for full air-conditioning, but for part air-conditioning of selected rooms in the building. There are also different management strategies for these systems. Interestingly, this approach seems to be one of providing intermittent use, similar to providing a cool refuge in the building, as an alternative to traditional methods. The traditional refuges such as the veranda and the swimming pool may be replaced with an air-conditioned room. Not only is there a practical advantage, there is also a cost advantage. The construction of a swimming pool and a veranda can cost a minimum of A$4000. The running costs and maintenance of the veranda are the least; the pool has more maintenance than the air-conditioning systems.

The application of air-conditioning systems to domestic-scale buildings is a similar process to large complex buildings except that the thermal loading is different. With some exceptions the predominant problem is the environmental loads from air temperature, humidity and solar radiation. The designer should resolve a number of issues. These can be grouped into those related to plant and equipment such as the selection of the air-conditioning system and requirements for maintenance, those related to the building form and planning and envelope design and specification. In addition there are other issues concerning the management of the building and plant to meet lifestyle choices.

Table 3.6 Design priorities for the planning, building form and fabric of a small-scale, air conditioned building

Design priorities for warm climates characteristics and building strategies

Priority 1: the energy costs of air-conditioning the building can be reduced by cutting demand through partial air-conditioning
Strategies: zone the building into conditioned and free running rooms and areas. Use seasonal variations in temperature to shape the zoning, for example some parts of the day or year the building can be conditioned whilst others are free running

Priority 2: hot air has a natural buoyancy whilst cold air is dense and sinks.
Strategies: use of natural density and buoyancy to contain cold air in pools for functions requiring cooling. Avoid cold sinks where cold air drains from the building due to lack of containment. This is an energy drain and can be avoided with draft lobbies

Priority 3: external air temperatures differences to the comfort zone are small, 5-15 degrees. The lack of large thermal gradients between inside and out reduces the amount of energy needed to cool the building. There is therefore little advantage to super insulating the building, as the cost of energy savings is not likely to pay back the cost of the extra insulation
Strategies: provide nominal levels of bulk insulation to walls and ceilings. Avoid cold bridges between inside and out where condensation can form, that is where elements of the building are cooled by the internal air and protrude from the interior to exterior

Priority 4: high levels of solar radiation, at both low and high angles of incidence, mean that there is significant heat load from solar gain
Strategies: use passive means to achieve optimum orientation and shade to reduce solar heat load on the building, reflective surfaces with reflective foil insulation are important particularly to the roof

Priority 5: in humid, warm climates there is a vapour pressure difference between inside and out. Moisture will move towards the inside if some form of preventive barrier is not provided
Strategies: use vapour barriers on the warm side of the insulation. Provide air seals to the building, including draft lobbies, rials on the outside of buildings cause condensation and mould growth

Priority 6: localized cooling of air can be provided particularly in hot dry climates, by humidifying the air. In moderate or hot humid climates this can be achieved through refrigerant air curtains
Strategies: where localized cooling of one person or a small group of people is required then small units of plant can be used.

Selection of system

The options with regard to selection of an air-conditioning systems depend largely on the cost versus performance of the systems, but also there are other issues concerning the ease with which the system can be integrated into the building fabric. The designer has choices from large centralized conditioning units to smaller independent decentralized units, for small-scale buildings some form of packaged system is used. The options are as follows:

1. *Constant volume systems:* these use refrigerant cooling through direct expansion and provide a constant velocity of air, which is distributed indirectly through ducts to ceiling registers from usually from a central plant room.
2. *Fan coil systems*: these use chilled water from a central chiller plant which is distributed to the fan-coil unit in the space to be cooled
3. *Split fan and condensor systems*: these are similar to the fan coil but use refrigerant instead of chilled water; air is distributed directly from fan coil unit located on an internal wall, the compressor and condenser are separated from the fan coil and joined by refrigerant pipes; the compressor and condenser, which are noisy elements, can be placed in a cool, remote location to avoid annoyance and improve efficiency
4. *The window air-conditioner:* this uses refrigerant cooling and has the compressor and condenser integrated with the fan and coil in one unit; it is usually located in the external wall or window so that air can be drawn into the unit from the exterior, the conditioned air is distributed directly to the room[43]

In the selection of a system the designer should consider a range of factors as shown in Table 2.1. These have been given a rating from one to five with five being the most advantageous. From this analysis, the centralized constant velocity system performs best in terms of providing a high level of technical performance but suffers with respect to higher capital cost. A centralized plant area or room is usually provided. Decentralized units can also be provide as an alternatively located on the roof-top, in the false ceiling or as a floor-based packaged unit. The centralized system has advantages of economies of scale over many decentralized single units. The disadvantages come from the problems of integrating the duct distribution through domestic-scale buildings. These can be routed through ceiling voids and on the outside of the building but there is often difficulty where the construction depth of the floor is thin. Chilled water or refrigerant is a more convenient distribution system, as the pipes are relatively small compared with ducts and can be easily integrated in the floor depth.

The split system has a cost advantage over the centralized system. Its main disadvantage is that it gives no provision of fresh air and requires the removal of condensate. The air-handling unit has a fan coil element that is usually housed on internal walls and simply recycles internal air. There is a

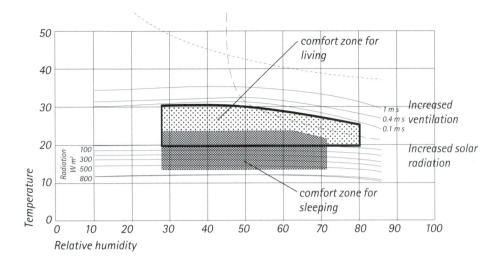

3.23 *Thermal comfort for domestic activities based on environmental temperatures[45]*

reliance on infiltration to provide fresh air and this can be problematic if the building is thermally sealed with no facility for trickle ventilation (small permanent ventilation through a wall or window vent). A reduction in air quality will result from this system if ventilation is not provided. One alternative method to trickle ventilation is to periodically purge the internal air. This is achieved by opening the building when the system is not in use.

Another problem is with the water waste from the air-handling unit. As the internal air is cooled by the coil, condensation occurs. This is collected and reticulated in a small diameter (25 mm) gravity waste pipe to the storm drain. The installation of this type of plumbing is visually problematic and without adequate disposal leads to the growth of mould, bacteria and insects.

The split system has some benefits for humid environments and where a small number of rooms require cooling as the refrigerant cooling can effectively accommodate the latent heat load from dehumidification. The main problem with the fan coil system using chilled water is the effectiveness to deal with the latent heat load arising from humidity in tropical conditions, particularly where a large volume of air requires conditioning. Also the chilled water is required, commonly serviced from a centralized chiller plant. This type of system is ideal where there is a centralized cooling plant for chilled water and a number of small domestic scaled buildings requiring cooling.

Finally, the window conditioner has long been used as an expedient low cost solution to decentralized cooling needs. The problems of visual intrusion and noise are evident both within and outside the building. Where a number are working at once on a wall there is considerable noise pollution. The disposal of condensate is equally, if not more, problematic than with split systems, since the window locations mean that pipes need to travel across the façade of the building creating a lack of integration. Moreover, these window conditioners can easily become overloaded and use excessive amounts of energy in humid conditions where they are working to reduce

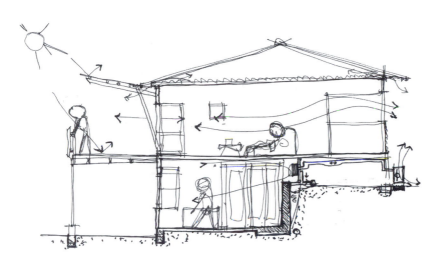

both humidity and temperature over a continuous period of time. The economy cycle in these systems is designed to bring in external air when the temperature is low. In high humidity environments this results in the needless ingress of humid air causing damp conditions. The economy cycle is more appropriate in drier low humidity conditions where external air can be brought into the building without an impact on comfort.[44]

Maintenance

Lack of maintenance reduces the efficiency and minimum power consumption of the system and increases running costs. A number of basic maintenance rules are:
- keep filters clean to minimize the resistance of the filter and permit the maximum flow of air
- keep coils clean to allow efficient heat transfer
- maintain sufficient levels of refrigerant in the system to maximize heat transfer
- use the manufacturers guidance for use and maintenance schedule[46]

Comfort levels, building form and planning

The planning strategies for a building in a cool climate is primarily defensive to conserve heat and address problems of low air temperatures and high thermal gradients between inside and out. This gives rise to the need to create a compact building which minimizes external walls. There is an advantage in providing high levels of insulation in the envelope, reducing window size and infiltration to avoid heat loss. Often the form and planning of air-conditioned buildings in warm climates is thought to be similar to these strategies. Yet there are marked differences in the climatic parameters. The major climatic factor for warm climates may not necessarily come from the external air temperature but can be from other sources such as high solar radiation or high humidity. Also the behaviour of cold air is different to hot air and this leads to different priorities in the form and planning.

The application of these priorities depends on a number of issues concerning the lifestyle, level of activity and state of health of individuals to be accommodated within the air conditioned building. The first priority is to rationalize the need for air-conditioning based on the needs of occupants. The comfort zone varies dependent on these of needs, as, for instance, for the elderly people or the sick; there may be a need to use lower thermal comfort levels than normal and this may necessitate the need for air-conditioning. A number of cases have been found where there has been careful synthesis between the building form, planning and selection of air-conditioning systems to meet these needs.

The first case is based on research carried out to determine the acceptable levels of comfort for domestic activities.[45] The upper limit of comfort zone for sleeping is the between 22-24 degrees C (environmental temperature) depending on humidity. With higher relative humidity, 70 per cent or over, the comfort zone is reduced to 22 degrees C. In many hot humid climates the night-time temperatures may only be 25 degrees C but the relative humidity is in the range of 80-90 per cent. In these conditions occupants find considerable difficulty sleeping even with level of ventilation. This is exacerbated in urban areas where there is a high building density, high levels of external noise and little breeze for ventilation. The environmental conditions in this situation usually dictate the need for a window air-conditioner. The drone

3.25 *In this case, for a hot humid climate, the building is zoned to provide selected air-conditioned rooms. In this case window air-conditioner is placed in the wall to cool a bedroom for a shift worker who needs to sleep during the day. The single skin construction offers lower thermal resistance and possible condensation problems in the high humidity conditions although the hardwood timber offers some insulation*

of the fan provides a white noise for masking external sound whilst the conditioning mainly reduces humidity. In this way acoustic and thermal comfort can be provided. Thus, whilst the remains of the house or apartment is naturally ventilated, the crucial sleeping areas are conditioned.

The second case involves the use of air-conditioning in living spaces and offices in homes. The changes in lifestyle means that the home is becoming a multi-functional building needing to accommodate work, domestic and leisure activities and requiring the connection to the wider electronic communication system. For example, one client building a new home wished to be able to switch on his air-conditioner whilst away on business overseas so that when he arrived home it would be comfortable. These activities and modes of management rely on a range of electrical appliances and require differing thermal comfort conditions in the building. Issues that arise from this come from the need to protect this valuable and often sophisticated equipment. Thus there is a need to provide longevity for a range of household items such as books and equipment such as computers. This is a major concern, particularly in the hot humid climates. With free-running buildings, the high levels of humidity can create mould in areas where there is little light, destroy books and reduce the life of sensitive equipment. This can be achieved with passive means by using dehumidifying storage systems but often air-conditioning is seen as an easier alternative. The strategy is to collect sensitive material and equipment in one area which can be sealed and continuously air-conditioned.

Where the reasons for the use of air-conditioning come from the need to provide thermal comfort, the necessity for its use and the cost effectiveness of the installation should be examined. This can be seen by examining the comfort zone for living areas in domestic buildings. In this case the upper

3.26 A *light weight timber building in Cairns uses a raised timber platform. The rainforest setting creates high levels of humidity. Materials used in construction are not hygroscopic therefore do not encourage moisture up take, reduce mould and respond quickly to temperature changes. Airflow can move under the house to create additional cooling. Selected air-conditioning in this building primarily reduces humidity and rather than reduction of temperatures. The lightweight single skin construction is inefficient for reducung heatflows if low internal temperatures are required*

limit of comfort is 27 degrees C (environmental temperature) with a maximum humidity of 70 per cent. The availability of breeze can extend this to 29 degrees C. Where the building site or location cannot provide the passive cooling the air-conditioning is justified (the provision of this kind of ventilation in buildings is difficult in the tropics especially where calm periods are prevalent). The cost versus performance issue can be gauged from the number of days when these comfort conditions will be exceeded and whether the expense of installing plant outweighs the benefits. A stronger justification comes from situations where occupants have no other options to seek thermal refuge, where people are required by health or functional needs to remain in their location.

One particularly useful planning strategy is where the living area is used as a thermal refuge. It is often useful to integrate the benefits of air-conditioning with the passive effects of ground cooling. In this situation the under-storey of a house can be air-conditioned whilst the remainder is left free running.[46] A way to achieve this is to use a split system as the air-handling unit can be placed on the internal wall and the condenser, fan and compressor placed in the cool shaded area behind the house. The earth integration reduces the heat loads to the internal air, thus improving energy efficiency. Location of the air-handling unit so that the vanes direct the cool air to the occupants also enables a reduction in set points. Care should be taken in selecting systems with low capacity and high fan speeds to avoid noise and drafts.

In some situations it is desirable from an architectural and functional standpoint, not to fully contain the conditioned air in a space. Normally the cool air is contained within a space by a defensive skin, which is used to moderate energy loss from heat transfer and infiltration. It is increasingly being argued that this seal box approach with steady state conditions is unacceptable from the human health and user control perspective. In addition greater flexibility can be afforded if a mixed use approach is used, that is natural ventilation and air-conditioning are mixed. Priority 2 suggests the use of the natural buoyancy hot air and density of cool air.

One way to do this, without excessive energy use, is to create a cool pool in the building.[47] In this arrangement the natural density of cool air is used to

3.27 *A section through a cool pool design strategy integrated within a building. This relies on stack effect for the hot air to rise through the building and escape at higher levels. Cooling can be delivered to the pool by displacement air-conditioning. This system is ideal where intermittant cooling is required as the building can operate as passively when internal heat loads are small*

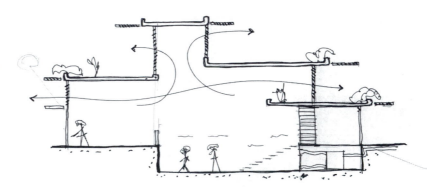

create a shallow insulated enclosure which is conditioned. As warm air is created by the occupants in the pool, the air rises and is removed by ventilation. The advantages are:

1. In hot humid climates where there is intermittent use of air-conditioning, this creates unpleasant odours, dampness, condensation and low levels of ventilation.
2. The energy cost is reduced due to a reduced volume of air
3. Reduction of the cooling load to sensible heat load only, thus avoiding condensation
4. Provision of natural ventilation, available when the pool is conditioned and when free running[48]

The main issues concerning the design are that heat gain to the pool occurs from the two sources, through the walls of the pool and from the free-running air above the pool surface, which mixes with the cool pool air through turbulence. Design guidelines for this type of approach is as follows:

- keep airflow to a maximum of 1.5 m/s^{-2} to reduce heating from turbulence
- the proportion of the depth to length 0.1 to 0.25 to minimize eddies and turbulence between the ventilating air and the air in the cool pool
- use louvres to control and direct entry of windflow
- use a shaded roof to control heat gain
- the reduction of air temperatures cannot be reduced below the dew point; otherwise local condensation can occur

A further issue is with the occurrence of condensation. In moderate climates and hot dry climates, the relative humidity is in the range of 60-70 per cent. Thus at an external dry bulb temperature of 33 degrees C cooling can reduce the air temperature in the pool by 5 degrees C without problems of condensation. In more humid conditions where the relative humidity is higher the margins are less, 2.5 degrees C.[49] Thus the use of cool pools can provide a way of providing local cooling for activities without the need for full air-conditioning. They provide for the benefits of reducing energy consumption and use natural ventilation to improve air quality. The problems lie in high

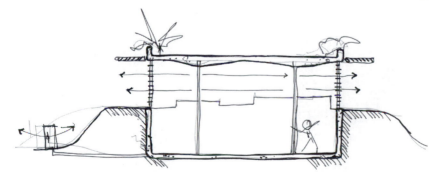

3.28 *A section through a cool pool design strategy. Burming can be used to provide mass and help insulate the pool. The pool requires containment of the air on three sides, doors into the pool should have draft lobbies to avoid the loss of air by gravity seepage. Cooling can be delivered to the pool though by chilling the floor and walls. Problems of condensation occur on these surfaces if the temperature reduces below the dew point. The system is most effective; a laminar flow in air across the pool is maintained avoiding disturbance and mixing of the cooler pool air and the ventilating air*

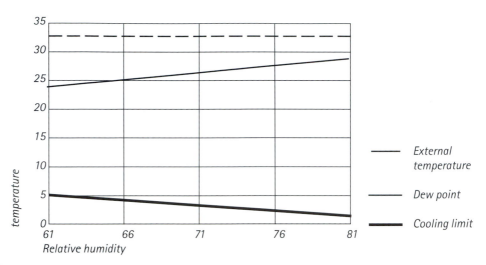

3.29 'Cool pool' cooling limits varies with the external temperature and humidity. The internal temperature cannot be reduced below the dew point to avoid condensation. In this graph for an external temperature of 33 degrees C the effect of differing humidity is given. Thus for 60 per cent humidity a 5 degrees reduction in temperature is achievable, for 80 per cent only 2.5 degrees is possible

humidity areas where local condensation may occur if the cooling limits are not maintained.

Building envelope

The fourth and fifth priority concerns the building envelope. High levels of solar radiation, at both low and high angles of incidence mean that there is significant heat load from solar gain. The use of passive means through optimum orientation and shade can reduce solar heat load on the building, reflective surfaces with reflective foil insulation are important particularly to the roof. Thus an important strategy is to make the building element defensive to heat gain.

Furthermore, in humid warm climates there is a vapour pressure difference between inside and out. Moisture will move towards the inside if some form of preventive barrier is not provided. Strategies for air sealing and the use of vapour barriers on the warm side of the insulation is important. In addition the provision of air seals to the building including draft lobbies to avoid infiltration is necessary. A significant problem is that of using, porous 'cold' materials on the outside of buildings which can lead to condensation and mould growth on the outside surfaces.

Localized cooling

The use of localized cooling of air can be provided and in particular an island in the building to provide comfort for small groups or individuals. The use of ceiling fans is described as a way of providing this kind of cooling and is a common form of low energy system used to provide cooling through air movement. Other options are available using stand alone small-scale pieces of conditioning plant. For example in hot dry climates cooling can be

3.30 *Roof-mounted axial fans can be used to provide local cooling to areas in the building. In this case an evaporative cooling unit is attached to the fans. This is effective in hot dry climates and provides an area of cool in a larger open space. This is ideal for retail operations where there is a single control point and cooling is required around that area. Vanes below the unit can direct air horizontally as well as vertically if required.*
Below: a misting fan used to provide localized outdoor cooling in Singapore is accommodated in an external shelter

produced by humidifying the air. Thus an evaporative cooling air-conditioning unit can be used to direct air down to create a cool island in a larger open space. The coolth will soon dissipate due to the mixing with drier air but this does provide a minimum cost system. The use of this approach is not particularly energy efficient but in situations such as retailing activities it is necessary. The provision of barriers to heat gain to air-conditioned spaces can be achieved by using a draft lobby. But the set of double doors used in these lobbies creates a separation between inside and out, reducing the marketing potential. Often an open façade is needed to facilitate human circulation is a necessity. In moderate or hot humid climates energy efficiency can be achieved by refrigerant air curtains. Cool air is blown down in front of the opening from a small fan coil unit.

The above set of priorities are not necessarily priorities for a building design, all strategies are equally important, the priorities are important in the timing and sequence of design consideration. Thus priorities 1 and 2 are primarily briefing and planning issues that are considered at the conceptual stage, whilst others such as envelope design have more emphasis in the design devolvement stage. Thus gaining some sense of the relative importance of factors in relation to the sequence of design gives further order to the design management process.

System management and comfort

Once the decision to air-condition the building has been taken to solve one particular problem, that is to provide comfort and/or protection for belongings, care should be taken not to create others. This is often the outcome of poor design synthesis and/or lack of concern for appropriate management of the systems in place.

In the latter condition, problems are found with the intermittent way the air-conditioning system is used and how the humidity in the air is accommodation. In these conditions where the air-conditioning system is used intermittently either through thermostatic control and/or user selection, the building environment has to change from free-running to air-conditioned conditions. For example where there is a sharp reduction of internal air temperatures and increases in water vapour, this can give rise to the air often feeling damp and

chilly. This is exacerbated by acclimatization to the tropical conditions. The small diurnal and seasonal range in temperatures tends to make the body far more sensitive to temperature and humidity change. A solution to this is careful regulation of the set points (thermostat settings) to meet local comfort conditions. Similarly when the air-conditioning system is turned off, the building fabric internal furnishings are relatively cool as compared to the outside air and therefore condensation can occur as moist warm air enters the building.[50] The conclusion from this discussion of practice is that management of the building is as important as the design synthesis of the form and planning of the building if an integrated solution to the problem of comfort in air-conditioned buildings is to be achieved.

3.7 References

1.   P. O'Sullivan, 'The Building as a Climatic Filter', *Built Environment*, July 1972, pp. 267–269.

2.   B. Lawson, 'Embodied Energy of Building Materials', *Environment Design Guide*, Pro.2, RIAI, 1995, pp.1–6.

3.   V. Papanek, *The Green Imperative: Ecology and Ethics in Design and Architecture*, Thames and Hudson, London,1994.
     S. Curwell, 'Greenprint for the Future: Environmental Design', *Architects' Journal*, Vol.192, No. 24, 1990, pp. 45–48.

4.   G. Treloar, 'Assessing the Embodied Energy Savings from Recycling Alternate Materials in Buildings', *Solar 95, Renewable Energy: The Future is Now, 33rd Annual Meeting*, Tasmania, 29 Nov.–1 Dec. 1995, pp. 213–218.

5.   Treloar, op. cit., p. 214.

6.   P.A. Mitchell, 'Ecological Sustainability and Innovative Potential of Plywood', 1995, *Plywood Association of Australia Annual Convention*, Gold Coast, Qld., Nov. 1995. pp. 24–26.

7.   Lawson, op. cit., p. 68.

8.   S. Baggs and J. Sand, *The Healthy House*, Harper Collins, 1996, p.153.

9.   Baggs and Sand, op. cit., pp. 217–220.

10. Lawson, op. cit., p. 62.

11. Pitts G, *Energy Efficient Housing - A Timber Frame Approach*, Timber Research and Development Association, 1987, p. 8.

12. O'Sullivan, op. cit., p. 267.

13. H. Fathy, *Natural Energy and Venacular Architecture, Principles and Examples in Hot Arid Climates*, University of Chicago Press, 1986, p. 9

14. Ibid.

15. N.V. Baker and K. Steemers, 'LT Method 3.0 – a Strategic Energy Design Tool for Southern Europe', *Energy and Buildings,* Vol. 23, 1996, pp. 251–256.

16. R.A. Hyde, 'Lighting, thermal and ventilation (LTV) design tool for non-domestic buildings in tropical and subtropical regions: prelimi-

nary assessment of design integration', *Proceedings of the ANZAScA Conference,* The University of Queensland, 1998, pp. 41–48.

17.   Michael Hopkins and Partners, 'Research into Sustainable Architecture', *Architectural Design,* 1997, pp. 27–38.

18.   M. Hiller and M. Schuler, 'Energy concepts for low energy buildings-an interdisciplinary process', in P*roceedings of Solar 99,* Geelong, Australia, 1999.

19.   S. Coldicutt S. and T.J. Williamson, *Design Guide for Energy Efficient Housing Adelaide,* Department of Architecture, The University of Adelaide, 1986.

20.   R.A. Hyde and A. Pedrini, 'An architectural design tool (LTV) for non-domestic buildings in tropical and subtropical regions: critique of the solar design strategies for energy efficiency,' *proceedings of the Solar 99 Conference,* Geelong, Australia, 1999, p. 52.

21.   S. Szokolay, *Climate Comfort and Energy, Architectural Science Unit,* The Department of Architecture, The University of Queensland, 1991, p. 16.

22.   Z. Bromberek, 'Passive climate control for tourist facilities in the coastal tropics', unpublished PhD thesis, The Department of Architecture, The University of Queensland, 1995, p. 237.

23.   E. Harkness, *Precast Concrete Energy – Cost-Effective Building Façades,* The Precast Concrete Manufacturers Association of New South Wales, 1987.

24.   Baker and Steemers, op. cit., p. 273

25.   R.A. Hyde, 'An architectural energy conservation tool (LTV) for non-domestic buildings in subtropical and tropical climates,' presentation at the *Australian Building Energy Council seminar on Energy Tools,* Dec. 1999.

26.   O.H. Keonigsberger et al, *Manual of Tropical Housing and Building,* 1973, Longman, p. 23.

27.   I. Edmunds, 'Advanced glazing systems for subtropical and tropical climates', unpublished paper, School of Physics, Queensland University of Technology, 1997.

28.   R. Aynsley, 'Tropical daylighting strategies', Australian Institute of Tropical Architecture, James Cook University, unpublished paper, 1997, p. 1.
Aynsley, op. cit., pp.1-3

29.   N.V. Baker, *Energy and Environment in Non-domestic Buildings,* Cambridge Architectural Research, 1994.

30.   B. Givoni, *Man, Climate and Architecture,* Van Nostram Reinhold, 1969, p. 259.

31.   Givoni, op. cit., Chapter 15.

32.   R.A. Hyde and M. Docherty, *Computer Simulation Study of Queensland Schools,* Education Portfolio, Queensland State Government, 1998.

33.   R. Thomas, ed. *Environmental Design,* E&FN Spon, 1996, p. 119.

34.   R.P. Parlour, *Building Services: Engineering for Architects,* 1994, Integral Publishing, p 1.

35.   Parlour, op. cit., pp. 2–4.

36.   R. de Dear and A. Auliciems, 'Air-conditioning in Australia II – User Attitudes,' *Architectural Science Review*, Vol. 31, 1998, pp. 19–27,.

37.   de Dear, 'Criteria for the management of indoor climates', unpublished paper, the National University of Singapore.

38.   De Dear and Auliciems, op. cit., pp.19–27

39.   Ibid.

40.   Discussion with Professor Peter Woods on air-conditioning practice in hot humid climates.

41.   R. Thomas, ed. op. cit., p. 120.

42.   Parlour, op. cit., p. 4.

43.   Ibid.

44.   J.B. Jones et al, *Energy Conscious Residential Design for a Tropical Isle,* Guam Energy Office, 1989, p. 59.

45.   T.J. Williamson and A.B. Coldicutt, 'Comparisons of Performance of Conventional and Solar Houses – Computer Simulation Study', in *Proceedings of the Institution of Mechanical Engineering Symposium on Solar Energy Utilisation in Dwellings*, Melbourne, 1974.

46.   Jones et al, op. cit., p. 76.

47.   R. Aynsley, 'Cool Pools for Buildings in Warm Climates', in *Designing the Well Tempered Environment, ANZAScA Conference,* Perth, 1992, pp. 121–125.

48.   Aynsley, op. cit., p. 124.

49.   Ibid

50.   Jones et al, op. cit., p. 77.

Strategies

PART 2

Building structure

CHAPTER 4

'Ideally the hot-wet tropical house is a thing of point supports, a light framework allowing of the maximum of openings for adjustable louvres, windows, mosquito screening and whatever devices can be invented to induce ventilation, and keep out sun, rain and insects...'
Maxwell Fry and Jane Drew.[1]

4.1 Introduction

Structure is an intrinsic part of the building form; it responds to the conditions of climate through the effects of environmental factors. The wind, thermal and snow loads are important determinants of structural form to avoid deformation and collapse. The first part of this chapter examines the climate induced loads that are specific to warm climates. In addition, as Maxwell Fry and Jane Drew suggest, there is also a concern that there is an essential duality in the notion of structure. The successful architectural solution is not simply a matter resolving the structural integrity of the building to withstand loading conditions, but of relating structure to a range of other issues concerning 'visual appearance, function, weight, texture, light, shade and shadow.'[2] This wider definition of structure has enabled a closer examination of structural systems used in warm climate buildings and the extent to which the structural systems are used assist with the climate response. The following strategies are examined:

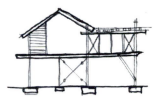

- the timber frame and diaphragm
- light steel frames
- skeletal frames
- the cantilevered column
- shade structures

The use of these systems and the effects on the climate response is discussed through examination of a number of building examples.

4.1 *Strategies to resist wind loads:*
- *the braced light frame and diaphragm*
- *light steel frames and skeletal frames*
- *the cantilevered column*
- *shade structures*

4.2 Wind forces

An examination of the nature of many tropical trees reveals quite clearly the way these types of plant have developed structures which respond to the forces of wind. Indeed, over time the wind forces as well as other climatic factors have

led to the evolution of the unique shaped of the trees.

The Ansarna tree is a good example. It is found in many tropical rainforest locations. The root structure and base act as an exaggerated and enlarged foundation. It is only a surface-rooting tree and the base acts as a buttress to the trunk. The trunk can be a metre in diameter at the base and acts as the support structure where the structural forces are largest. The trunk tapers to the top and keeps the canopy at high level above other trees; the canopy acts as the kinetic element responding to wind flow. So while the base and trunk are steady, the canopy bends and deflects to the racking force of the wind. As the wind increases so the movement increases bending the canopy. And shaping it to provide the least line of resistance to the wind so as to prevent uprooting. This dynamic response of the tree to the force of the wind is found in buildings in the tropics particularly in storm conditions. The palm tree is known to resist even the most severe storm by streaming its leaves to leeward, and often many leaves are shed to drag.

The organic form of the tree can be used as a metaphor in design. Gabriel Poole has designed buildings which resemble the structure of a tree. Coastal buildings on the Sunshine coast in southeast Queensland have predominantly a sandy soil. The response to these site conditions is to either use a pile system or pad and raft. The pile is analogous to the tap-rooting forms of tree whilst the pad and raft is similar to surface-rooting trees. The branching forms at the base of some plants such as the Pandanas palm can act as a

4.2 *Gabriel Poole, The Hastings, Noosa Heads, 1984 and the Towers-Walker house, Sunshine Beach. Coastal building in Australia shows design integration of structure, construction, site and climate above: steel view of the Hastings showing the Pandanas palm below left: use of K and X bracing to give transparency and racking resistance at the ground plane of the Hastings right: Quadrapod structural systems used in the Towers-Walker house.*

bracing structure and buttress the plant. This principle is found in buildings where transparence is required at the ground plane. A light steel framework of square hollow sections and 'C' sections can be used to form a skeletal system. This is braced at the ground plane by 'K' and 'X' braces in a similar way to the Pandanas palm. The frame at the first and second floor is braced by plywood diaphragms. In Poole's quadrapod design a space frame system is used to support the platform of the house at a high level but with a small building foot print.[3] The likeness of living in the canopy of a tree is clearly evident.

In this case, the effect of the wind on buildings in warm climates has two main characteristics dependent on the speed of air flowing across the building. At low and medium wind speed it can be harnessed for ventilation and cooling. The building responds through aerodynamic features that direct and filter the wind for ventilation. At high velocities such as associated with storms and cyclones the wind speed is high and destructive. The building responds to these extremes in velocity through the design of the skin and the structure.

The challenge is to develop a design that uses the forces of the wind to advantage rather than to disadvantage. How can the aerodynamics of the building be such than it makes the building stronger as the wind strength increases rather than structurally weaken as the structure reaches its the ultimate limit stated by the design? This question is perhaps best resolved by closer examination of the nature of wind.

4.3 The Hastings, Noosa, architect Gabriel Poole:
left: a section through the building showing the four levels of structure and the methods of bracing to resist environmental loads. Note the use of lattice for gable ventilation and the truss structure
right: exterior elevation showing the prefabricated wall system providing cladding and bracing to upper levels

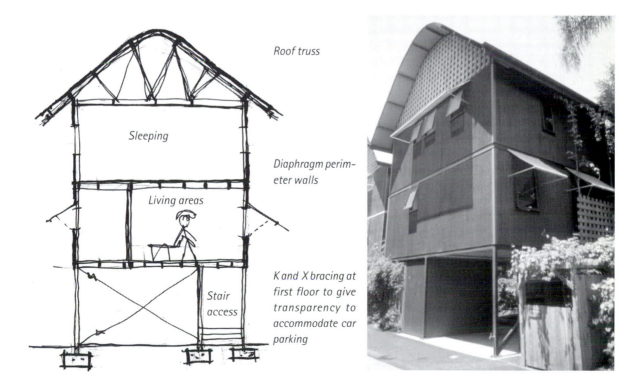

Roof truss

Sleeping

Living areas

Diaphragm perimeter walls

Stair access

K and X bracing at first floor to give transparency to accommodate car parking

Table 4.1 Wind pressure histories showing the variation over time

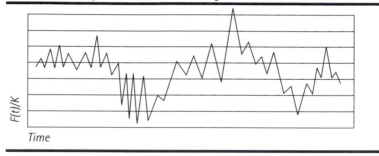

Wind characteristics

The main self-evident characteristic of air is that it is experienced mostly when it moves. Air that is still is lifeless and in the tropics brings little relief from the heat. Yet once air has movement it is transformed into a different entity. Air movement across the surface of the earth has a spectacular and dynamic effect on the landscape, shaping and moulding it in every respect. Buildings, in contrast to nature, are far less responsive to changes in wind speed; we seldom see buildings leaning in the breeze like a palm, its foliage excited by the gusts of wind. The sight and sound of the physical interaction of wind with nature is perhaps an area for architectural expression that is yet to be developed. Thus, speed and movement are important aspects of wind that shape the design of buildings. The wind speed can be measured in terms of velocity in metres per second. This is can be translated into a wind pressure which acts on the building (N m^{-2} = velocity/1.6).[4]

Yet wind pressures are not constant, they vary over time with peak pressures in times of storm. Histories of wind pressure show the likely changes in a broad-band random manner. The building responds to these pressures through the friction and elastic stiffness of the structure. A closer examination of this process reveals how the building structure responds. The wind force is rarely static in the typical force history. Rather it can be said to be randomly gusty with peaks and troughs about a mean wind velocity. If the wind speed is on average of 25 knots it will have peaks of 30 knots and troughs 20 knots. This effect is to create a sine wave represented by the major peaks and troughs.

As a gust of wind strikes the building it will cause the building to deform. A thin cantilevered column can be used to demonstrate the behaviour of the building. As the wind speed increases it will bend and deflect. A gust of wind will establish 'free vibrations' in the column. The column will move backwards and forwards even after the wind has stopped, yet the 'free vibration' of the column will not continue indefinitely; the elastic stiffness will dampen the vibration until all the energy is dissipated. The column in this way acts as a damping effect on the wind force.

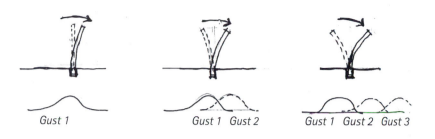

Gust 1   Gust 1   Gust 2   Gust 1   Gust 2   Gust 3

4.4 *Wind effects and building behaviour; the diagram shows the effect of gusts on the behaviour of a flexible column with ground restraint. As the gusts hit the column the pendulum effect occurs; if the sequence of the gusts is the same frequency as the swing of the column then a resonance will occur which will significantly increase the loading on the column*

As further gusts strike the column, the force of the preceding gust is amplified, causing more deformation. This can induce a resonance between the wind pressure and the damping response of the column. The wind has a natural frequency of gusts, and it is this frequency that can be the most destructive rather than the mean wind speed. The mean wind speed will set up a static pressure on the column but when the column is excited by the dynamic amplification of the wind, then the magnitude of the loads increases significantly. If the natural frequency of gusts matches the resonance of the column, then effects can be catastrophic.

The building response to dynamic forces is of concern particularly in high-rise buildings. The cumulative force of this kind of wind pressure can create major oscillations and sway and can lead to displacement of floors. This can cause discomfort to occupants and malfunction of parts of the building such as lifts. Engineers examine the aspect ratio of the building to establish the potential stability of the structure regarding resonance and sway. Additional mass dampers can be added to the top of high-rise buildings to tune the frequency of the structure so that it is not in phase with the natural frequency of the wind. Aspect ratio is the relationship between the breadth and height of the building. As the building becomes taller and narrower this ratio becomes larger but as the breadth becomes wider and the height lower so the ratio is smaller.

Design wind speed and return periods

The design method for establishing the design wind speed for a building is contained in Building Regulations, National Standards and Codes of Practice. Establishing the design wind speed is related to the following steps:

- selection of a return period for high wind frequencies
- determination of a basic standard wind speed corresponding to the selection of a return period
- modification of the standard speed to account for site specific conditions that will affect the structure of the building

Weather data is used to gain detailed information of the histories of wind

4.5 *Map of the regional basic wind speeds and design wind categories for Australia*

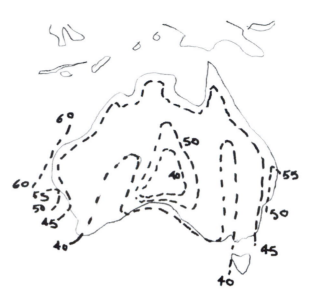

speeds. The mean velocities are measured and also the fluctuation in velocities over time. The occurrences of such phenomena as storm conditions, cyclones and other high wind activity are of particular interest as these are likely to place high loads on the building. In addition the time interval between the occurrence of these high wind speeds in monitored. The greater the interval between the occurrences, the less the risk to the structure, and therefore smaller values for wind speeds can be selected.

This interval between the occurrence of a specific wind speed is called the 'return period'. It can be between 25 and 200 years depending on the projected life of the building. Temporary structures therefore have low return periods whilst the wind speeds for those buildings with a longer life span can be based on return periods of 100-200 years. From this analysis the return period of the wind, the standard or basic design speed for the building can be determined.

The basic and design wind speed

The basic wind speed is determined from the return frequency and it is also related to a number of other factors to give the design wind speed as follows:

- terrain
- topography
- height above ground

The use of these factors modifies the wind speed over a specific return period; 25 or 50 years is used to give location specific data for design. In addition data also available for peak gusts of 2-3 second duration. Engineers calculate the likely wind load on the structure using design wind speeds.

These design wind speeds are set for particular regions. For example in Australia, the regional basic design wind speeds have been classified into four basic regions, ranging from a normal wind speed of 33 m s^{-1} to severe tropical cyclones of 60 m s^{-1}.[5] Therefore, to summarize, the wind speed at a particular site is determined by the following:

1. The selected return period for extreme wind conditions. This will differ for long-life structures as compared to short-life temporary structures
2. The basic standard wind speed corresponding to the return period
3. Adjustment for height, terrain and topography[6]

The use of these design wind speeds has had a considerable effect on building design. The location of the building on the site with regard to elevation and exposure is important. The more exposure the higher the design wind speed and therefore the size and number of elements to resist wind forces. Yet the higher the exposure the better the ventilation and the possibility for cooling. Here lies the conundrum of design, the optimization of structure and climate modification strategies require careful integration to avoid the problems of these competing factors. In particular the natural disasters caused by cyclones such as Cyclone Tracy in Darwin have led to the revisions in design standards.[7] The two particular building-related problems with cyclones:

1. Total collapse of the structure due to wind forces exceeding the design ultimate strength of the structure
2. Local damage to components to the structure. For example roofing tiles and roof sheeting can be ripped off due to localized suction or pressure on the external skin of the buildings

The consequence of this is to set two particular sets of design criteria, the first relating to strength of the structure, the second to serviceability. Strength is concerned with the permissible stress that the structure should take given

4.6 Effects of excessive wind pressure on the building right: total collapse due to insufficient racking resistance left: localized damage due to failure of cladding components

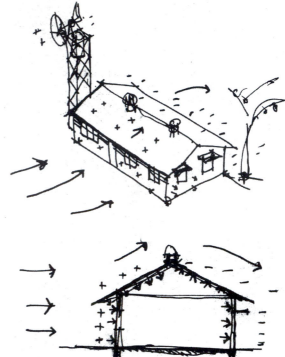

4.7 *Windflow effects on and across a building:*
right: note the positive pressure at the windward side, negative pressure on the leeward side, also the suction effects produces an outward force from inside the building, in cyclones the pressure differ-ence between inside and out becomes large resulting in uplift of roof elements
top: effects of uplift showing the disintegration of the roof structure

the ultimate load created by the extreme design gust speed. Serviceability is concerned with the effects such as deflection caused by the more commonly occurring lower wind speeds. Thus, for strength a wind speed of 55 m s^{-1} may be used, whilst for serviceability a wind speed of 39 m s^{-1} is used. In wind load conditions, the structure will therefore start to show distress in the clad-ding materials at 39 m s^{-1} but will not fail until over 55 m s^{-1}. The main reason for this categorization is to provide some level of efficiency in the design process.

There are other considerations in the general design of the building which have climatic consequences on the internal environment. First, to reduce wind loads it is advisable to reduce the height of the roof; flat roofs produce less drag than high pitched roofs. Also, height of the roof above the ground increases drag, therefore there is an advantage in reducing the overall height of the building. This has the consequence of reducing ceiling heights and therefore the volume of air for cooling.

There is an advantage in reducing window openings and increasing the wall area for bracing. This reduction of the skin transparency is advisable as it reduces the area of glass susceptible to wind damage during extreme wind conditions. Unfortunately all these structural advantages to resist extreme wind conditions are counter productive to the climate response of the build-ing for the normal wind conditions. The increasing use of the cellular nature of plans reduces ventilation and the small windows restrict the access of air to the building. Research has shown a kind of 'bunker mentality' where build-

ings are optimized for extreme wind conditions and not for the normal climate conditions, leading to poor thermal performance.[8] The use of structural systems that are appropriate for the climate to promote the desirable climate modification strategies is preferable. This draws attention to the effects of wind forces on particular elements of the build. The designer can select where the stiff parts of the structure are located to assist with the integration of the climate modification strategies. The next section examines the consequences of these decisions in structural and climatic terms.

4.8 *The effects of high wind speed on buildings:*
left: wind load has affected the racking resistance of these walls causing collapse
right: lack of anchorage of the is building has caused rotation and overturning although the structure appears intact

4.3 Effects of wind forces on structural elements

In a building, certain parts are identified as the primary structural elements. In a masonry structure, the masonry elements are the structural unit; the mortar is simply the interface element that accommodates the tolerance in the bricks. The masonry elements take only a compression load. For structural purposes the plaster lining and cement render are not used to assess the structural integrity of the walls nor the mortar binding the bricks as the tensile capacity is not considered to be of structural importance. In a timber frame structure there is a similar structural rationalization: the studs are the main load-bearing element, the plasterboard and timber weatherboard cladding are assumed to take little load, although in reality they will contribute to the overall structural stability. Therefore, one of the first principles in the structural considerations with regard to wind loads is to decide which parts of the structure are to take the loads, and to assess what forces these loads generate?

There are three main effects of wind loads, which contribute to the failure of the building. These are:[9]

1. Racking
2. Overturning
3. Uplift

The first structural action is racking. One of the effects of wind loads on the building is to cause collapse of the building by the rotation of elements

4.9 *Methods of stabilizing build-*
ings to resist wind loads:
top left: racking forces from the
horizontal component of the
wind load cause sway and col-
lapse
bottom left: this sway and col-
lapse can be resisted by bracing,
either cable bracing in the X form
or through walls which act as
stiff planes or diaphragms, if the
weakest link now is in the foun-
dations or anchorage to the
ground over turning will occur
top right: if the foundations are
sound and the structure is an-
chored then components of the
structure can be affected by the
vertical component of the wind
load, through uplift

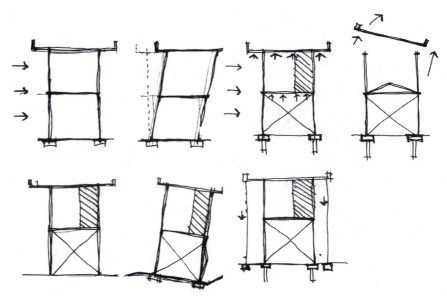

through inadequate support and restraint. For example, a wall frame with simple pin joints will deform from a rectangle to a parallelogram with the rotation of the vertical elements. The addition of triangulation is one method of providing a support that resists this rotation.

Racking is the term given to the rotation of elements in the building due to the effects of the application of horizontal wind loads, which is resisted by using a form of bracing. Two types are found, rigid bracing and flexible bracing.

The characteristics of rigid braced structures are that pin joints are used to connect the elements. The loads are taken axially through the elements of the structure, the elements are not required to resist buckling and as a consequence are usually of smaller cross-sectional area. The disadvantages are that more members are required but the structural size of the members is smaller. The characteristics of flexible braced structures are that rigid joints are used. The loads produce forces perpendicular to the elements, causing buckling. The elements are therefore larger in cross-section area and require complex joints to create rigidity. The advantage of flexible braced structures is that fewer elements are required but they are of larger size than those found in rigid braced structures.

The second action is overturning. As seen above, the objective of bracing is to resist rotation in elements caused by wind forces but there are cases where the structure retains its integrity but whole building rotates. This is usually called overturning. The designer has a number of options with regard to overturning. The most common is to rely on the foundation system to resist the vertical and horizontal forces. The problem is that complexity increases where flexible braced systems are used. This includes the sophisticated design of the joints and connectivity to the ground. The capacity of the ground to resist forces becomes a crucial issue, as will be seen in later examples.

Finally, there is the third action of the local effects of wind on parts of the structure. As the windflow across the building, the windward side receives a positive pressure whilst the leeward side is negative. The interior is also normally negative if all the openings are closed. In particular there are suction effects on the roof and walls, which cause uplift and pull-out forces on the wall elements. The lack of snow loads in warm climate means that the prevailing environmental load is the wind load, which can amount to the main structural force on the building

For structural efficiency reasons the roof is usually a lightweight element, with the aim to reduce dead load where possible. In this case, therefore, the main method of resisting uplift forces is using load transfer. This process requires transferring the uplift force from the roof plane to a stabilizing element within the building, in the foundation or on the site. An example is found in timber frame housing where the load from uplift is transferred from the rafters by metal plates called triple grips to the top plate of the wall frame, and from the top plate to the foundation by cyclone rods.

An alternative to this is to increase the dead weight of the roof structure thus countering the uplift forces. The use of heavyweight cladding such as cement or clay roofing tiles, for example, will substantially increase the roof dead load compared to steel sheeting. Yet in exposed areas where high wind loads are experienced, the forces exerted on the structure are likely to exceed the forces from the dead load offered by traditional heavyweight cladding. Thus, whilst the increased dead load strategy may be effective for small domestic structures in unexposed locations, the lightweight strategy is more efficient in high exposure for long span roofing design problems. The methods of providing stiffness to resist forces is examined next using a number of cases studies.

4.4 Timber stud framing and bracing diaphragm

A diaphragm is a stiff plane of material that can resist vertical and horizontal wind load.[10] For example, a masonry has little transverse stiffness and, lacking any tensile capacity, buckles. For stability, the wall requires lateral

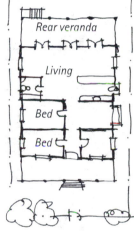

4.10 *Stud framing and diaphragm walls are used in this Queensland workers cottage:*
right: the plan of this building shows that it has been modernized with an open plan living area and back veranda. The traditional cellular form is shown in the front of the house.
top: the back veranda uses the traditional framing systems, post and beams for the veranda sides and the house walls of studs with bracing elements
top left: view of the front veranda showing the post and beam construction with non-structural lattice work for privacy

support through piers or additional buttressing walls. A similar pattern occurs with vertical timber walls; although they have greater inherent resistance to tensile forces, they still require buttressing for stability. These diaphragm walls are ideal to resist racking forces. Thus, by using a combination of walls and floors that interconnect, a cellular form of structure can be created. This usually corresponds to the rooms required in the building.

The evolution of the this type of diaphragm structural system for warm climates is interesting as it is a progressive synthesis of a number of factors concerning not only structural determinants but also cultural, economic and construction factors. There has been a transformation from the single skin timber construction found in the traditional Australian house to the current brick-veneer housing system which uses timber frame walls supporting an exterior skin of brickwork.

In southern and northern Queensland the traditional housing uses a combination of structural systems. The house normally consists of a central building form with verandas that are wrapped around the exterior skin. The veranda is constructed using a post and beam system. The inner and external walls are formed from a light timber frame of 100 x 50 mm or 75 x 35 mm hardwood studs. The studs are mortised into a top and bottom rail a single skin of timber tongue and groove boarding is attached vertically to the studs and rails. The conventional height for the ceilings is 3–4 m. In some cases where these ceiling heights are larger, additional horizontal rails are used with larger studs.

The structural capacity of these walls is sufficient to resist vertical axial loads but not racking loads, and therefore bracing is required and is located between the studs. The amount of bracing depends on the degree of exposure; in some buildings with low exposure to wind forces, little bracing is used, mainly at the corners of the building or in selected structural bays. This not only produces the characteristic aesthetic quality of these single skin structures but also produces a lightweight building skin. Some architects have made modern interpretations of the traditional house and have used these forms of bracing as structural expression in buildings.

The evolution of this form of structure is contentious; some suggest the origins are found in American balloon framing; some in British technology. It seems though that the use of the single skin construction was based on economic and environmental conditions.[11] In the mild climate of southern Queensland and the tropical north, the walling system provided settlers with a low cost and climatically appropriate skin which was amenable to prefabrication and transportation to remote locations.[12]

In recent years though this single skin form of stud wall has received criticism and the climate response of the houses using this type of structural system has been assessed.

First, in hot dry climates a high mass skin with high capacity materials is optimum due to the resistance required to accommodate the high diurnal range in temperature; the mass moderates temperatures during the day and is cooled during the night.[13]

Second, in hot humid climates the lightweight skin is seen as less of a

problem due to the small diurnal range of temperature. This means the skin should offer little resistance to temperature change, and indeed it is advantageous to have a skin that responds quickly to cooling. The main area of contention is the cellular layout of these buildings required by the structural systems. With the high humidity and temperatures found in these hot humid climates, the main issue is to provide airflow. Methods of ventilation such as cross-ventilation and stack effect are required to provide thermal comfort. The cellular house form found in the traditional house offers only small windows and therefore little cross-ventilation, but has high ceilings with ceiling vents connected to the roof to aid stack ventilation. The conclusion reached from this analysis is that user behaviour is required to seek optimum thermal comfort. This means users move to the verandas for sleeping and living when internal conditions are uncomfortable. Hence the characteristic of these traditional houses becomes integrated in lifestyle and cultural factors; the Australian traditional house is designed to be lived in and around to provide a range of spaces which are optimum for differing times of the day and the year.

Third, in moderate climates, such as warm climates that have cool winters and hot humid summers, both the sets of disadvantages are found as in the hot humid and hot dry climates. It is argued, though, that in these climates the transitional conditions between the warm and cool periods are large and therefore the user behaviour through various adaptive strategies enables thermal comfort to be achieved. The use of supplementary radiant heating in winter and appropriate clothing allows thermal comfort to be achieved in these buildings.[14]

Further evolution in recent years of the timber frame structural systems for the Australian house have followed a number of directions. One of these directions is to improve the structural performance of the structural system and second the thermal performance.

First, the structural performance has improved by substituting modern materials for traditional elements. Plywood diaphragms have replaced cross-bracing to resist racking loads and through Code systems the minimum number

4.11 *Timber bracing and diaphragm walls*
right: the traditional single skin construction has been replaced with double skin construction and plywood is used as the main bracing element
left: single skin traditional construction with cross-bracing

of bracing walls for a particular design and location can be calculated. Roof tie-down systems have been improved and extended. High levels of prefabrication through modular factory made panels are used to improve quality and buildability.

Second, to improve durability, masonry has been attached to the exterior of the skin destroying the single skin aesthetic without improving thermal performance. Studies have shown that the masonry is best placed inside of the timber wall to provide some mass to the building to assist with moderating temperatures. The single skin and elevated timber floor have been replaced with masonry and concrete. The consequence of this is to move away from the lightweight aesthetic of timber structures and to establish a hybrid modern form of construction.

The question remains as to whether this evolution has produced a more climatically appropriate form of traditional architecture. It is clear that the traditional house is a blunt instrument for climate response, it is a compromise of cultural, economic and social factors and thus in an attempt to address a wide range of issues, trade-offs are made in terms of climate response. The more interesting question is how designers have addressed the deficiencies in the traditional house, not by adding brick veneer, but by exploring the use of a number of alternative structural systems to support the integration of climate responsive design directions.

4.5 Light steel framing

The use of steel structural elements in early traditional Australian forms of housing were replaced by timber systems due to good availability and problems with importing materials from overseas. In recent, year this trend has been reversed, as many steel elements are now manufactured in Australia. The elements most useful in housing are cold-formed sections, which can form into studs to substitute for timber studs. Hot rolled sections are also used, with the 'I' and 'C' sections used most commonly for beams, whilst square and circular hollow sections are used for columns.

Improvements in the design of the climate responsive house have in-

4.12 The O'Donnell house, architect Charles Ham, shows the use of lightweight steel columns with glue laminated timber beams and cross-bracing to the veranda. Diaphragm walls are used in the interior of the building, the illustrations show the necessary bracing in all three planes of one bay of the house
left: the house is braced in the vertical transverse plane at the end gables with plywood behind the weatherboard exterior cladding, ironically this cladding is not considered a bracing material for structural purposes
centre: the veranda has only one bay braced which is sufficient to give racking in the vertical longitudinal plane
right: the cross-bracing at the ceiling and the floor provide bracing in the horizontal plane

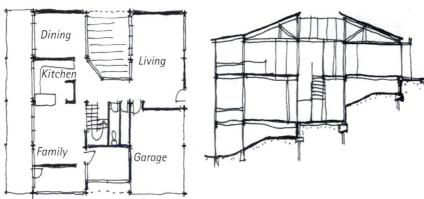

4.13 *Plan of the O'Donnell house showing the light skeletal steel frame. This framing system is ideal for steep sites as found in this case. The frame can easily be located on piles or pads depending on ground conditions, it is craned into position and floos provide a working platform for the constructing the walls*

creasingly utilized steel structural elements. These elements have been used in a number of structural systems to make improvements to the construction and structural engineering of the traditional house.

The first development has been to enhance summer performance for the moderate and hot humid climates through improved ventilation of buildings. This had both planning and building form consequences.

The traditional Australian house, is designed as a compact building with a deep plan building form. A double-loaded corridor is placed down the centre of the building with rooms leading off this circulation space. This gives single sided ventilation which is best facilitated by opening doors at the front and back, allowing air through the centre corridor, and pulling air from the adjacent rooms. Modern improvements have been made by reducing the plan depth and by making buildings a single room depth to allow cross-ventilation.[15]

The crucial issue is to provide openings in the walls and the roof to for airflow. Koenigsberger suggests that 'one of the most difficult problems which a designer must attempt to solve is to provide large openings, but at the same time protect from driving rain, insects, smells and noise without radically reducing air movement.'.[16] This poses a structural problem; as greater transparency is required in the external wall for ventilation, there is less area for structural bracing.

Designers have used two strategies to address this issue:

1. The use of selected lightweight steel post and beam construction with selected use of diaphragm or crossed bracing walls.
2. The use of a knee brace at the joint between column and beam to provide racking resistance

The O'Donnell house, designed by Charles Ham, is an example of the first strategy. Steel hollow sections, 75 mm square, are used as columns and connected to glue laminated timber beams which, in turn, support the floors and trusses at the roof plane. This provides the basic frame of the structure. A

4.14 *Tent house, architect Gabriel Poole, 1991: a steel portal frame structure*
right: the use of the P column creates a knee-braced structure for transverse stiffness to resist racking loads
bottom: longitudinal bracing is created from alternating bays of plywood

combination of horizontal and vertical diaphragm floors and walls is used to brace the structure. At the eastern edge of the building a large degree of transparency is needed to provide views. Cross-bracing is placed in plane with a veranda structure and avoids large diaphragm walls at the line of enclosure of the living spaces. The use of the steel system integrates well with the 'H' plan form, which minimizes plan depth and maximizes ventilation to all rooms. The advantage of the steel column system is as follows:

1. Columns and beams connected into a pin-jointed system with rigid bracing reduce section sizes and simple bolted connections aid buildability
2. Small structural section, 75 mm square or circular hollow section sizes, is designed to take dead loads only. The wind load is taken by bracing walls, and uplift is resisted by a continuous column
3. Pad foundations reduce site impact
4. The connection system can be fabricated so that it is integral with the column facilitating buildability by using plates welded to columns to accept bolted fasteners
5. Small section can be integrated in walling system

The second strategy uses a knee brace in the transverse line of structure spanning across the building. The changes in planning strategy for longer thinner building forms and away from the cellular form of building means there are less bracing walls. Structural advantage is found by using closely spaced transverse frames with increased rigidity. This permits the building to be opened in the longitudinal direction. In addition the reduction of the transverse span to 5 to 6 m means that beams rather than trusses can be used for spanning purposes. A steel system developed by Gabriel Poole in the Tent house uses this approach. In the transverse direction the knee brace is used outside the line of enclosure to create a 'P'-shaped column giving considerable rigidity at the joint providing racking resistance. The rafters are connected to the column and a horizontal compression strut to form the triangular knee brace. This rigid element forms the basis of the frame that supports a fabric outer and inner roof. In the longitudinal direction of the building,

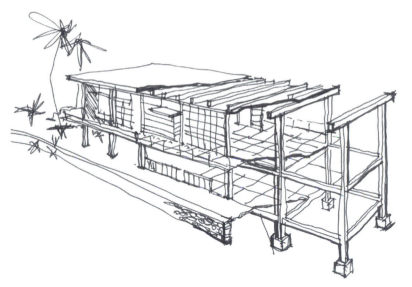

4.15 *Concrete skeletal frame house developed for Guam, by Raymond and Rado, 1952*

alternating bays of single skin plywood diaphragms and lifting walls are used to provide bracing and ventilation.

These two strategies describe the way structure has evolved to facilitate the integration in climate design strategies in smaller domestic buildings.

4.6 Skeletal and portal frames

Traditional shelters in hot humid climates commonly use a post and beam structural system made of timber. These light skeletons are designed to take more of the raking load, with less load on the walls. A structural combination of the column, the beam and the joint, is used to offer resistance to racking. In this case the walls become lightweight and filtering elements that permit the passage of light and air thus ventilating the inner space. The application of this type of system using the materials of timber, steel and concrete has been attempted in more domestic scale buildings. The essential

4.16 *Steel skeletal frame used at the Kempsey Museum, Glen Murcutt, 1980*
left: the tubular steel framework takes dead load from the roof and transmits it to the foundations, racking loads are resisted by buttressed masonry walls
centre: steel gussets provide bracing in the longitudinal direction
right: racking loads are resisted by masonry elements which are gravity loaded to provide reactions

4.17 *Details of the timber skeletal framing systems used in the Habitat home. The joining system makes use of a cruciform timber column. This reduces the visual mass of the column yet still provides racking resistance through the joints in two direction*
top: the skeletal system with a hypar roof geometry to give in-plane horizontal racking resistance
bottom: details of the joints at ground plane, first floor and roof. The columns and beams are fixed by epoxied dowels to give a 'high tech.' system

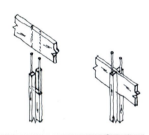

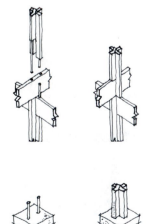

feature of these structural systems is to use flexible bracing in one or more planes of the building.

Early development work by Fry and Drew suggested the development of the rigid frame for tropical buildings.[17] Their suggestion was to use the work of Mies van der Rohr and architects Raymond and Rado house for Guam, as a model. The rigidity of the monolithic concrete frame in the case of the Raymond and Rado house, could be designed to resist wind up to 140 miles per hour. The design flexibility offered by this system enabled Fry and Drew to propose a skin that could be modified to accommodate varying internal functional conditions and exterior environmental conditions.

Hence, the conception of the skin as a mechanism, with infinite permutation, was born from the advances in this type of structural development. This also represented a major development in the notion of climate response in buildings, no longer were occupants required to select the appropriate environment to occupy, as with the traditional Australian house. The filtering wall could be devised with a number of screens and louvres to moderate airflow, rain and sun as required. In addition the design flexibility offered by the rigid frame both in terms of functional planning and environmental performance presented additional advantages in more complex buildings such as offices. It has resulted in new construction systems in Southeast Asia where a single skin brickwork to provide a low cost building skin to in fill between the frames.

The extension of this work has seen the development of both steel and timber skeletal systems which seek to address some of the main problems with the monolithic concrete frame. Whilst this form of construction is cost effective for large span commercial buildings where fire resistance and high dead loads are found, in smaller domestic structures the scale and cost of structural members is questionable. Portal frames can be 350 x 70 mm in section size for a 6 m span. Hence, the use of alternative systems of timber and steel, yet even with these types of systems the complexity of joints and the high cost of the structural elements raise additional design problems.

Two strategies are found to reduce the scale and cost in these rigid frame elements by using load transfer. In essence the main thrust of these strategies is that wind loads in a building will always travel to the stiffest part of the structure for racking resistance. Designers have options as to where this stiff part of the structure is located. Is it to be in the walls, in the joints or in the foundations?

The first utilizes selective load distribution, i.e. dead load and uplift are taken by one part of the structure whilst racking is taken by another part. In a traditional timber frame the dead load and raking loads are taken by the bracing walls whilst the uplift is accommodated by tie downs to the slab.

In a rigid frame structure a similar process can be used; the rigid frame can be used for dead load and uplift whilst the raking load is taken in a different part of the structure. The Kempsey Museum by Glen Murcutt is a useful example. In this case a two-way rigid frame of tubular steel is used to accommodate the dead load and uplift load. Tie down is through the structure. Racking resistance is achieved by connecting the structural frame to a masonry structure. This masonry structure clearly has sufficient mass to resist racking forces and also buckling in the column. In this way the frame can be kept slim and elegant whilst most of the raking load is transferred to the bulk active masonry structure.

The second strategy is to reduce the rigidity in the joint creating a semi-rigid structure. This transfers load to the column and beam forming an elastic structural system. This behaves in a similar way to a reed in the breeze, bending and deflecting but not breaking. Racking forces on the building result in deflection in the structure, but still within the limits of safety. Skeletal systems in timber often display this kind of behaviour. A case study that uses this form of structure is the Habitat house (see Chapter 2). This building uses a two-way semi-rigid frame.[18]

The term two-way semi-rigid means that the structure is rigid in both the transverse and longitudinal directions of the structure and that the joints have limited stiffness. In the longitudinal direction the opportunities for cross-ventilation is increased because the frame gives the potential for maximum opacity in the skin. In addition, in the transverse direction, the structural

4.18 *Cantilevered column used in the Queensland School system*
left: the plan shows the position of perimeter columns which support transverse beams without internal bracing walls. This provides open planning and maximizes cross-ventilation
right: the columns provide flexible bracing for the vertical component of the wind load without internal bracing walls. Diagonal bracing between the roof beams provides horizontal racking

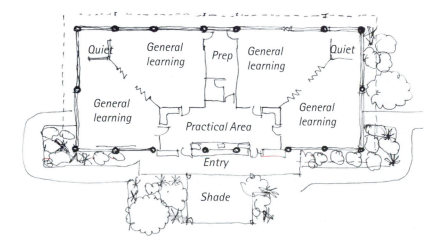

4.19 *Cantilevered column used in the Queensland School system*
left: open planning provides cross-ventilation to internal spaces without interruption of bracing walls
right: lightweight wall panels can be used as in fill to increase the response of the building to climate change and rapidly shed heat

depth of the roof is reduced as compared to the normal truss roof construction for houses. This increases the internal volume for a given height and creates a more open section. This improves stack ventilation and allows for permanent ventilation at the higher levels.

4.7 Cantilevered columns

4.20 *Mapleton house, Richard Leplastrier, shows the use of underfloor bracing system to support the cantilevered columns*

The use of cantilevered columns is a way of providing a bracing system in single- or two-storey buildings, yet still providing spatial transparency in two directions as found in the skeletal frame systems. The structure in this case shifts the major point of stiffness to the ground plane as opposed to the first- or second-floor joint as with the skeletal system. The structural diagram shows either the use of ground restraint or through a stiffening element such as a slab in the ground plane. The consequences of this type of structural system is that the structural capacity of the foundation and column is increased. The effective length of the column is twice that of a column with end restraint and therefore the thickness of the column is increased.

The use of this approach is found in buildings that require functional

4.21 *Collaborative Design Laboratory, the University of Queensland, Donovan Hill architects, shows the use of cantilevered columns and beam grid. The beam grid is connected to a plywood diaphragm, which provides an elegant bracing system to resist the horizontal component of the racking load*

flexibility and an open space section for ventilation. A school system in Queensland uses this approach to provide a variety of building types. The typical classroom space requires a clear span of 6 m to accommodate a class of 30 children. Perimeter cantilevered concrete columns are used which support universal steel beams for the primary roof structure. The column system allows a large part of the wall to be used for louvres to provide efficient ventilation. Using high ceilings and open planning, spans of up to 12 m can be achieved with this economical structural system. None of the internal walls are load bearing and therefore can be of lightweight construction for demountability and flexibility.

A similar approach has been used for a laboratory building. In this case a two-way grid of flitched Laminated Veneer Lumber is used to form a trafficable roof. The beams could be cantilevered from the columns to further increase the roof overhang. The timber system allows flexibility to cut skylights for additional light and ventilation when buildings become deep plan, and the plywood deck provided a timber diaphragm to rest racking in the horizontal plan. The integral structural action of the system provides an environmental, structural and aesthetic solution to a difficult design problem.

There are a number of knee-braced systems which can also be used to assist with the stiffening of the column. In the case of the Mapleton house by Richard Le Plastrier, a large under structure is used below the building to resist racking forces. These diagonal braces are bolted to 200 mm thick hardwood posts. Connections at the floor and roof are pin jointed. In this case the stiff part of the structure is below the building as with the other cases, but the elevation of the floor provides an additional functional area. As with the other systems the ends of the cantilevered column require restraint, and therefore are embedded in the ground.

In all cases, the use of the ground plane as a method of restraint to a stiff column which can resist the horizontal component of the wind load facilitates an openness of section for functional flexibility and ventilation. The interesting aspect of this building is that this system takes advantage of the shelter location. The house is set in a rainforest location which shields the house from extreme wind conditions. This reinforces the notion of engineering and architecture as design activities, which must accommodate the dictates of the location to make a climatic responsive architecture.

4.22 *Bracing systems used for shade structures, surface action from fabric, cable bracing with ground anchors, cable bracing using tie downs to buildings*
top left: a cable grid is used to form the support for landscape elements such as vines to provide shade for the skylight system
top right: a frame support system is used to the cable grid
bottom: the cable supports are connected to ground anchors and turn-buckles used to provide tension in the cables

4.8 Shade structures

The use of shade structure is an increasing popular structural type in warm climates particularly in areas which have many hours of sunshine per day and high levels of ultraviolet radiation. The abundance of sunshine and warm temperatures suggests a benign climate. But there is increasing concern for the health and safety of people particularly the young due to the extreme conditions of ultraviolet radiation. Sun related illness such as skin cancer is becoming increasingly problematic. Personal measures can be made to provide protection through clothes and chemical barriers to the skin but particularly in the work place or in public places such as pools, an overhead physical barrier is needed. This physical barrier is usually a shade structure which not only protects users of these facilities but also prevents the ground (or pool) from becoming a heat sink, thus dissipating the sun's energy more effectively to the air.[15] With these kind of structure there is a key relationship between openness to achieve breeze for cooling, opacity and reflectance of the shading material to protect and reflected light from above. There are also attendant problems of heat and glare from the ground surface.

The question that faces the designer is two-fold. The nature of the fabric to be used for the roof surface and the type of support structure used to tension the fabric. First there are four main types of support structure.

- pole hung
- pole supported
- frame supported
- beam supported

Second, the type of material used in the fabric is important. A common strategy with the design of fabric structures is to use surface action and cable bracing. These structures are lightweight, can span large distances and be retrofitted to existing buildings relatively easily. The disadvantage of this

strategy is that the fabric used may not give sufficient protection, moreover the structures can give a false sense of security to the user. There may be a subjective sense of protection from the sun when in fact the perforations in the fabric still allow the transmission of large amounts of ultraviolet light through the material. These types of perforated fabric are reasonably economical and due to the perforations have negligible uplift forces thus simplifying the structural loading problem. More opaque and solid forms of PVC and Teflon coated fibreglass fabrics have higher shading coefficients, hence better protection and can substantially reduce light and ultraviolet transmission. The performance of these fabrics with regard to ultraviolet degradation and transmission should be verified with manufacturers at the outset of the project.

Strategies for stabilizing these structures normally utilize a cable bracing system. Cables are stretched through the fabric which is cut to make an antisyclastic form. This displacement gives the fabric its stability after stressing. These cables take high tensile loads and require considerable anchorages and tension devices. Use of ground anchors in the form of friction piles, mass counterweights or rock anchors can be used. The connection of cables to existing buildings is also possible but it requires careful consideration of whether the building can resist the additional loading. The other significant problem is reflected glare. Whilst it is advantageous to use light fabrics to reflect light for shade purposes, the reflectance from the structure can be problematic from the outside. This can reflect light and heat to adjacent buildings increasing the mean radiant temperature and cause visual interference.

Overall, these types of structure require careful design of the form of the structure; the characteristic saddleback shape is required to give sufficient stability to the fabric, also careful location of the cable braces to avoid functional problems and circulation of people around the structure is necessary.

4.23 Typical shade structures, careful selection of roofing materials is required to reduce reflected glare and transmission of ultraviolet light
right: exterior view of this pole supported structure, not careful positioning of guys to avoid the interfering with circulation around the structure
left: interior view showing the increase in the fabric density at the ridge where stress concentrations occur, the catenary form at the edges provides stability at these points

4. 9 References

1.   M. Fry and J. Drew, *Tropical Architecture in the Humid Zone*, Batsford, 1956, p. 62.

2.   B.N. Sandaker and P. Eggen, *The Structural Basis of Architecture*, Whitney Library of Design, 1992, 7, pp. 12-13.

3.   A. Ogg, *Architecture in Steel, the Australian Context*, Royal Australian Institute of Architects, 1987, p. 222.

4.   Sandaker and Eggen, op. cit., p.12

5.   Timber Research and Development Advisory Council of Queensland, *Timber Framing Manual,* W50, Queensland, 1990, p. 7.

6.   R. Aynsley et al, *Architectural Aerodynamics*, 1984, p. 116.

7.   Bureau of Meteorology, *Understanding Cyclones*, Commonwealth of Australia, Global Press.

8.   R.A. Hyde and M. Docherty, 'Thermal performance of housing in the hot-humid tropics of Australia,' *Architectural Science Review*, 1997, 40, pp. 105-112.

9.   Timber Research and Development Advisory Council of Queensland, op. cit., p. 18

10.   Sandaker and Eggen, op. cit., pp. 16-17.

11.   P.R. Skinner, 'A Design Investigation of Critical Regionalism Theory: Light Timber Portal Housing for South East Queensland', unpublished PhD thesis, Department of Architecture, The University of Queensland, 1996, p. 99.

12.   Skinner, op. cit., p. 103.

13.   B. Saini and R. Joyce, *The Australian House*, Lansdowne Press, 1988, p. 20

14.   Ibid.

15.   I.O. Koenigsberger et al, *Manual of Tropical Housing and Building*, Longman, 1973, p. 217.

16.   Koenigsberger, op. cit., p. 219.

17.   Fry and Drew, op. cit., p. 60.

18.   R.A. Hyde, 'Application of Composite Steel and Glue Laminated Timber to Skeletal Frame Housing Systems for Warm Climates', *World Conference on Timber Engineering*, Montreux, Switzerland, 1998, pp. 2-516.

19.   Queensland Health, *Shade for Public Pools, Guidelines for Shade Protection Against Ultraviolet Radiation at Outdoor Public Pools*, Bookmark Publishing, 1996, p. 22.

The building process

CHAPTER 5

'People build homes as easily as birds build nests', Hassan Fathy[1]

5.1 Introduction

It is probably self-evident that the method of building should reflect the climate and location of the project. Yet with the development of sophisticated material handling systems and methods of industrialization of construction, along with greater needs for standards of construction and international practice, the role of the region and location seem often to be inconsequential. It is important, therefore, to reaffirm the concept that the method of construction should relate to the location and climate in order to achieve efficiency in the construction process.

This chapter examines the underlying relationship between climate, location and building, which was brought home to me while teaching brick laying construction to students in Singapore. Large amounts of physical effort were required to lay English bond walls in the hot humid climate. As well as problems of keeping the mortar sufficiently hydrated to enable laying, the bricks had to be prewet to facilitate effective laying. Timber construction, by comparison, seemed more appropriate. The elements of construction such as posts and beams can be pre-fabricated into components that connect and interlock thus making the erection process easier, faster and thus allowing less exposure to the climate. Although this seems an advantage in terms of construction sequence, there are limitations with timber that have to be taken into consideration in the design process.

This experience of building in the tropical environment raised the first concern: determining the most appropriate method of building that is specific to climate and location. All climates share common attributes of rain, sun and wind and yet how these act as agents of destruction on the building form and its construction process seems to be the main concern. Furthermore it is apparent that a number of strategies can be drawn form the analysis of the common practice of building in warm climates. These are as follows:

- materials selection for climate
- use of climate orientated traditional ways of building
- modernisation of traditional methods for urban infill
- top down construction sequence

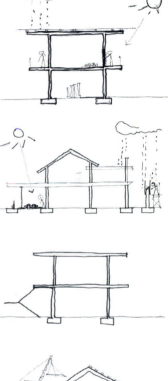

5.1 *Strategies for the building process:*
top: materials selection for the climate
next: use of traditional building methods for climate
next: modernisation of traditional methods
bottom: top down construction

Table 5.1 Categorization of materials and construction systems

MATERIALS

FABRICATION   WEIGHT

WET   DRY   HEAVY   LIGHT

Liquid curing   Mechanical   Small component   Large component

First, though, it is useful to make a preliminary analysis of materials and systems and their relation to climate.

5.2 Material classification

A broad classification of building systems for climate can be developed with regard to the density of materials and method of fabrication. This can be further linked to the extent that these elements are more or less climate sensitive.

In this respect timber and aluminium materials are considered to be lightweight since they have lower mass per cubic metre whilst masonry and concrete are heavyweight, having higher mass per cubic metre. The weight is directly related to the size and lifting restrictions of components and this indirectly relates to the speed of construction. For example in the construction of precast concrete cladding panels, glass-fibre-reinforced concrete is

5.2 *Precast concrete panel systems, glass reinforced materials halve the dead weight as compared to steel reinforced systems improving speed of construction:*
right: glass reinforced panel system, Hong Kong
top left: panel units for circular columns
bottom left: panel units under construction

often preferred to steel reinforced concrete panels because they are half the weight.

As a consequence the panels are more easily handled and can quickly be craned into place. An alternative is to use larger panels, this reduces the number of panels in the façade, and thereby improving speed of construction.

In addition to weight, the method of construction is also particularly weather-sensitive. Where tropical climates have clear, distinct wet and dry seasons, or hot and cool seasons, it is often useful to organize construction so that the most weather-sensitive parts of the fabrication process (such as foundations and frame) are carried out in the dry cooler seasons. The fit-out and finishing can then take place in the weather-protected environment of the partly completed building in the wetter/hotter seasons. The concern for the timing of the construction system in relation to climate underlies many of the traditional forms of construction.

5.3 Traditional ways of building

Traditional ways of building are useful to examine because the method of construction is usually highly place-specific, the materials and construction systems have developed based on the availability of local materials and in response to the local climate. Indeed many of the customs of building are deeply woven into the culture of the peoples of the region. The connection

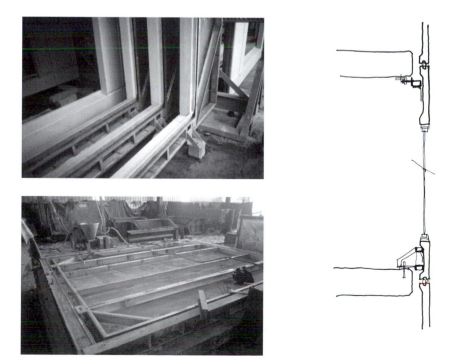

5.3 *Precast concrete panel systems, glass reinforced materials halve the dead weight as compared to steel reinforced systems improving speed of construction: Right: section through a typical construction assembly with steel connections to the structure*
Top left: panel units constructed, note the steel haunches used to connect the panel to the main structure
Bottom left: Panel units under construction. Note steel subframe.

5.4 *Front elevation of the experimental Malay house. This building was built to understand the process of construction. It includes a number of rationalised features to simplify the jointing for non-traditional builders*

between building system, climate and culture should be examined further with some analysis of the rationale for the use of the particular construction system.

The first example that is of interest is the indigenous houses of Southeast Asia. These have been recognized for the appropriate nature of these building systems for the climate and the location.

The Malay house is a useful example. The form of construction is categorized as lightweight and uses mainly dry systems of construction. The structure of many of the buildings uses a post-and-beam system for carrying the major loads.[1]

The building is formed of a primary structure of columns and beams which in turn support a secondary system of beams and rafters. Each of the four columns forms a bay of the structure that can be added repetitively to form the house. The cladding is usually lightweight and made of a single skin of material, such as timber boards, rattan or attap.

Experimental work with this house type revealed the essence of the construction system. A bay of the structure was built by students at the National University of Singapore. The aim was to establish the nature of the construction system and sequence of construction. The findings from this study indicated that the system was easy to reduce into a series of components. These components could be prefabricated in a location separate from the final location of the building. This enabled a number of building teams to be established, each responsible for the manufacture of particular components. It was found that these teams could work independently of each other and thus accelerate the manufacturing time.

The organizational plan suggests that the manufacture of the components could take place in a linear sequence, that is foundation components first, then framing components and so on. In practice this did not occur; it was found that more and more elements of the experimental bay could be prefabricated, resulting in a parallel process where framing components were manufactured at the same time as cladding components. This led to a considerable saving in the completion time of the building.

Therein seemed to be the first major advantage of the lightweight traditional system: it is designed as a kit of parts that is readily amenable to

5.5 *The building of the experimental Malay house required prefabrication of components. Teams of builders were used for each set of components. These were then brought to final building for erection. The traditional building system in warm climates can be built off site in dry sheltered locations beneficial for workers health and safety. Many characteristics of the traditional system are found in modern building practice*

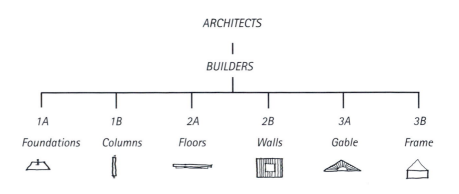

prefabrication. The building construction process is then a simple assembly process. In the experimental bay of the Malay house, the advantage of this process was self-evident. The components could be carried to the site and erected in a short space of time. In this respect the construction system was less exposed to the weather.

The research found that the keys to this form of construction are the frame of the building and the jointing system. In the joints extensive use is made of the mortice and tenon joint with timber dowels and wedges as connectors. These joints at first seem quite simple, but in fact the reverse was found. The joints operate in a number of ways. Visually they are often articulated to emphasize this part of the frame. Structurally, they are used to resist sway in the structure. And finally the construction provides not only the bearing support for the beams but over-sizing in the vertical plane provides opportunities for levelling the beams. This aids buildability and improves field flexibility. The joint between floor beam and column is a good example. The column is routed at the centre point so that the beam can pass through the column. At first glance this would seem to be weakening the column, but in fact the location of the route is in the zone of the neutral axis of the column and therefore it is the part doing the least work, as bending stress is much less than at the extremities of the section.

Furthermore, the route is over-sized in the vertical dimension to allow the beams to be slotted through the column with little difficulty, and the vertical tolerance provided allows for levelling of the beam using shims and wedges. Finally, the joint is locked in place with timber dowels driven horizontally through the column and beam. The friction fit of these joints helps

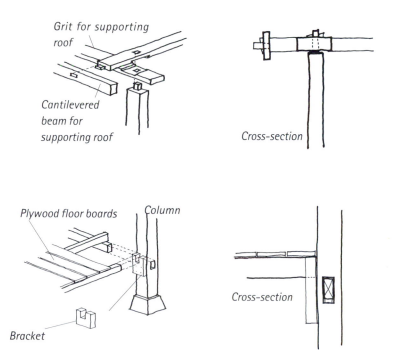

Grit for supporting roof

Cantilevered beam for supporting roof

Cross-section

Plywood floor boards   Column

Bracket

Cross-section

5.6 Joints used in the experimental Malay house:
Top: roof beams are connected with an interlocking mortice and tenon joint to the column. The connection gives rigidity to the frame to resist wind loads
Bottom: for simplicity the floor joits were connected with a bracket to the column

5.7 *A detail of the joint between column and floor beam in the experimental Malay house. Floor beams penetrate through the column and are fixed with horizontal wooden dowels. The floor is levelled by use of a wedge. These joints are multifunctional providing a simple aesthetic expression, giving structural rigidity and useful for ease of construction*

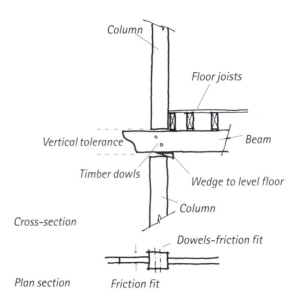

these joint types enables the speed of construction found in the building system. What is also of interest is the absence of metal connectors to achieve restraint and the interlocking nature of the timber elements. Both these characteristics contrast with present theory on timber jointing, which argues that timber should not be reduced at the point of connection since this weakens the timber elements, and that high-strength material such as steel should be used for connections to facilitate load transfer. The joints found in the Malay house seem to confront these principles but also function at both the visual, structural and construction level.

The type of construction system found in the Malay house demonstrates many of the concepts found in modern construction practice: the high levels of prefabrication of components, the use of assembly base methods of construction and the minimization of on-site construction time, which reduces vulnerability to climate.

It is interesting to note the extent to which these principles have been incorporated in modern construction methods in Malaysia and Singapore.

5.4 Modern frame construction in Singapore and Malaysia

The extent to which modern construction practice in Singapore and Malaysia has followed the traditional system as found in the Malay house is debatable. Rather it appears to be a hybrid form of construction that responds to climate location and principles of reinforced concrete construction. Closer examination reveals that the main resemblance to the Malay house lies in its use of a frame – concrete not timber – as the main structural system.

Similar to the Malay house most resistance to wind load is taken through the joints, thus relying on full-moment connections. The consequence of this is a large stiff concrete framing system which bares little resemblance to the elegance of its Malay predecessor.

Initial observations of this system of construction and its relation to climate can be assessed by examining its origins and comparing it to the set of improvisations that have taken place to fit it to climate and context.

The precedence for this type of design is seen in the work of Le Corbusier, in particular the Domino house. The principles for this kind of construction were developed in France in the 1950s. The method of construction was designed to solve post-war housing problems in particular the shortage of materials and labour. Corbusier devised the use of the concrete frame as a substitute to load-bearing masonry wall construction, which was commonly used. It had advantages both from an aesthetic and technical standpoint.

One technical advantage was the availability of large quantities of brick rubble from destroyed buildings. This rubble could be reconstituted to form non-load-bearing cladding elements which could then be utilized in the concrete-frame structural system. Another advantage was with regard to the use of the concrete frame. It could be built with relatively unskilled labour. This had clear advantages over the traditional system of load-bearing masonry, which required skilled bricklayers and good quality bricks for the construction process to be effective.

This system of construction appears to have been transferred to many parts of the world, including Singapore and South-east Asia, where there is a similar shortage of skilled labour and quality of materials. It has also been transformed to accommodate the conditions found in the local climate. It is useful to examine this transformation in detail.

In Singapore it appears to have been adapted to the island location and the climate in specific ways.

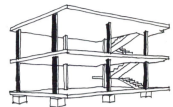

5.8 *The early form of the concrete skeletal frame as found in the Domino house by architect Le Corbusier*

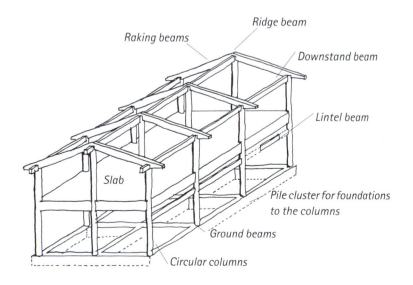

5.9 *The modern form of the concrete skeletal frame as found in many warm climate countries such as Singapore. Raking beams are used for the pitch roof construction. Unlike traditional building much of the construction is not prefabricated but built on site and is exposed to the weather. The frame in concept is similar to the traditional system in other respects such as the rigid structural system and the cladding which is non load bearing*

5.10 *Typical section of a modern concrete frame building in Singapore showing location of cladding elements*

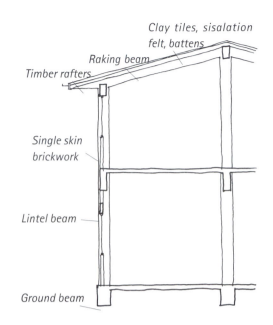

Clay tiles, sisalation felt, battens

Raking beam

Timber rafters

Single skin brickwork

Lintel beam

Ground beam

Many areas of Singapore are part of an emergent coastline which is rising out of the sea. This produces large areas of wet lands which in turn produce soil and ground conditions that reflect this change, with a large amount of sedimentary rocks and soil deposits such as marine clay and sand. These conditions often provide poor or variable soil conditions with little bearing capacity. As a consequence, most buildings require displacement piles to support the frame structure. Treated timber or concrete piles are usually driven as a cluster under each column of the frame. The cluster of piles is connected to the column through a pile cap.

This pile cap has two functions: first, to distribute the load from the column to the pile cluster and to provide continuity of structural action and second, to help stabilize the head of the pile to resist rotation. In very weak soils at the ground plane, large ground beams are used to assist with this function. In some cases the ground beams can be used to support the ground-floor slab. This therefore becomes a suspended slab rather than a ground-

5.11 *The modernization of traditional construction using concrete column and beams:*
Left: a sloping site with column formwork in place
right: concrete frame and floor slab complete and infill non-loadbearing masonary cladding under construction

bearing slab. The principle advantage of this system is that the suspended slab is less likely to suffer cracking and failure due to poor bearing capacity of the soils, or where site conditions during construction are poor due to monsoon rain. Also, if a suspended slab is used, waterproof expansion joints are required between the frame and the slab.

It should be noted here that the poor site conditions in these areas with large amounts of free water from high daily rainfall provide considerable constraints on the nature of the foundation work.

A similar problem is found with the frame. The use of wet systems in the tropical environments has a number of disadvantages. The high temperatures, large amounts of free water from rainfall and high humidity provide constraints on the placement and curing of concrete. Without adequate quality control of the process of placement, there is a potential loss of strength and building failure. The methods that can be used to avoid these problems include night-time pouring of concrete and modifications to the mix, such as increase in the percentage of concrete, to avoid loss of strength.

The frame is normally designed to reduce the number of additional materials used in construction in order to minimize the number of additional trades used on site. At the roof level raking and ridge beams are substituted for trusses or other lightweight systems to keep the structure as homogeneous as possible (see Figure 5.10). Secondary roofing elements such as rafters are fixed to the primary ridge and longitudinal beams.

Finally, cladding elements that are attached to the structure follow the Corbusian model, with single skin brickwork used as a cladding. The brickwork usually has high porosity which will readily absorb water if left exposed. The skin is made water resistant by the addition of two coats of sand and cement render. In addition, a paint system is applied to enhance the water resistance of the cladding.

Where high exposure to sun and rain is found such as in high-rise locations, additional improved specifications of materials and detailing is required. Brick cavity wall construction is often used on east and west walls to prevent solar gain to rooms in these orientations. Careful detailing is required which integrates this type of assembly in a frame construction.

5.12 *Concrete frame construction in Singapore:*
left: elevation showing concrete raking beams for the roof and the installation of timber rafters
right: form work under construction to support the concrete floor slabs

5.5 Modernizing traditional construction for urban infill

A useful example of this is a strata title office building designed by Rex Addison Associates in Brisbane. This low-rise office, called the Hill House, is part of a mixed-use development which includes housing and the office complex. The frame in this building has been designed to achieve economic efficiency as well as appropriate climatic design. A concrete frame is used throughout the building (as with the Singapore example), apart from the roof where timber trusses are used as a lightweight alternative. In addition, rather than down-stand beams as found in the Singapore frame, flat slabs with drop heads are used where possible. This minimizes the floor-to-ceiling height in the carpark to approximately 1.8 m, thus reducing the overall height of the building, and contributes to keeping the building to a domestic scale.

The cladding utilizes double-skin 100 mm concrete masonry unreinforced in plane with the structural frame to provide improved thermal performance and water resistance. Concrete masonry blocks are porous, so an additional layer of masonry paint is used to improve the specification of the wall. The architect uses a mix of paints; a high-build textured paint similar to a render is used on the lower floors whilst exterior masonry paint is used on the upper floors. This is intended to weather with age thus denoting the vertical partition of the building façade in a similar way to rustic buildings in Europe. The more permanent and durable material is at the base with lighter materials towards the roof. The consideration for the way the climate interacts with the fabric has coloured many of the decisions about the design and construction of this building.

There are also a number of construction advantages to this type of system for the climate, one further advantage is the construction sequence facilitated by this type of frame construction.

5.13   Hill House, Rex Addison Associates, Brisbane. Concrete frame construction is used with lightweight roof of timber and steel. This is protected from fire by a lightweight ceiling which has a sixty minute resistance to incipient spread of flame. Water penetration is prevented and increased thermal insulation provided by a cavity concrete masonry system in plane with the concrete frame
right: a steel veranda is created on the front elevation to provide protection to pedestrians. A concrete balcony cuts into this veranda to form a feature on the façade. Careful detailing of the rainwater systems is used to take water from the main roof to the street gutter

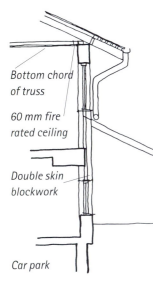

Bottom chord of truss

60 mm fire rated ceiling

Double skin blockwork

Car park

5.14 *Corner views of the Hill House. Note the finishes to the concrete masonry to prevent water penetration*

5.6 Top-down construction sequence

The climate not only affects the materials and their construction but also the sequence of construction. Sequence of construction in this case means the order in which the elements of the building are fabricated and also the location of this fabrication, in situ or prefabricated. In situ means the component is fabricated in its final location in the building whilst prefabrication is fabrication in a place other than in its final location in the building.

In this way we can begin to conceive of the building as a kit of parts, comprising prefabricated components which can then be simply assembled to form the building. The important features of this approach are three-fold. First, the manufacturing process of elements is less dependent on the climate, i.e. components can be made indoors in a factory controlled environment. Second, the assembly sequence can be designed to minimize exposure of the builders and the already completed fabric to the climate. Third, the assembly process itself can be less weather-sensitive as the on-site construction sequence can be reduced.

The beach house on North Stradbroke Island, Queensland, designed by Donovan Hill Architects is a useful example of this approach. The house was designed for a retired couple. The site is on a north-facing ridge and slopes gently from the road and then ascends steeply at a slope of approximately 45 degrees. The house is positioned at the transition from the gentle-sloping and the steeper-sloping section of the site. This offers a potential of a semi-enclosed courtyard to the south and spectacular views to the north.

The main building is built with a primary steel frame prefabricated in the workshop and bolted together on site. The frame grid is 3.6 m², three bays deep and two bays wide. Walls are of timber stud frame and sheeted with plywood, and are kept separate from the frame where possible. The walls only engage with the frame when lateral loads are to be restrained or where the brief requires the enclosing of a bay of structure. The result is that the frame becomes articulated and ornamental. The use of taper flange beams (cut from a standard Universal Beam) is an example of this, with the

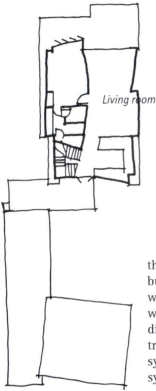

Living room

5.15 *First floor plans of North Stradbroke House, Donovan and Hill Architects:*
right: north facing elevation showing the lightweight steel and timber construction system

thickening of the structure at point of maximum bending. The walls in the building contribute to the design in a number of ways. In some cases the walls become perceptual elements suggesting solidity and permanence as with the masonry walls facing the hill. In some cases walls are used for directing air movement. The curved walls connecting front and back illustrate this well and are articulated and detailed accordingly. The battening system used to fix the fibre-cement sheeting is reminiscent of the fixing system used in the original beach shacks on Stradbroke Island.

The building responds to climate through the construction sequence and the selection and disposition of the fabric of the building.

First, the fabric of the building. Walls facing west are double-skin; plywood cladding is used externally, Sissilation felt and quilted insulation is used in the interstitial space with a plasterboard liner to the internal face. This assembly reduces heat gain from low westerly sun, particularly in summer. Other walls are single-skin to reduce mass to facilitate summer cooling, and the large number of openings to the north and south maximize ventilation.

The roof is disconnected from the walls with a glazing strip directly below the overhanging eaves, which allows diffused light into the building. The roof truss is of interest as it is segmented. The first segment consists of a primary section between columns which is bowed in section to increase stiffness at maximum bending. It is made of circular hollow sections of differing sizes: top chord 65 mm OD (overall diameter), webs 20 mm OD, bottom cord 38 mm OD. The second segments extend from the truss as outriggers, providing overhanging eaves which are connected directly to the roofing iron and sun breakers - partly solid and partly faceted - to reduce solar gain and still provide ventilation.

These elements are cut from 75 mm equal angles and tapered from truss to edge. The use of the roof as primary element and secondary element in this way articulates the structure as well as providing both a weather-proof

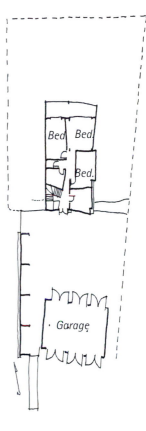

enclosure to interior spaces and a shading device to walls.

Second, the construction strategy facilitates the aesthetic expression but also the integration with climate. This method has been called 'top-down construction'. In recent years, the concern for rapid construction and health and work place safety has resulted in a number of innovations in sequencing construction which facilitate making the building site a safer place to work. In Australia in particular the concern for skin damage from solar radiation and heat stress have prompted builders and architects to consider buildability of projects so that the least damage is done to the building and associated personnel during construction.

Top-down construction is one strategy that is employed which results in early completion of the roof of the building so that the assembly of other elements can take place in a semi-protected environment. This has fortuitously coincided with moves towards increased prefabrication of building components and in particular factory-based manufacturing systems. These two strategies assist with providing a greater degree of control of the building environment, which promotes higher degrees of quality of the finished building and well-being for building personnel.

Many of these principles are found in the Donovan Hill House, North Stradbroke Island, Brisbane. The sequence of construction is as follows procedure.

5.16 *Ground floor plans of North Stradbroke House, Donovan and Hill Architects: right: masonry and lightweight construction is used at the top of the hill. A court is created between the garage and the building*

Prefabrication of the primary steel frame and detailing of frame

The frame consists of prefinished members which are galvanized and coated to resist a coastal environment. Simple bolt connections are used so that the integrity of the coating is maintained. No site welding is used, as this provides a potential for future corrosion problems and reduces the speed of construction. Square hollow and circular sections are used so there is a flush

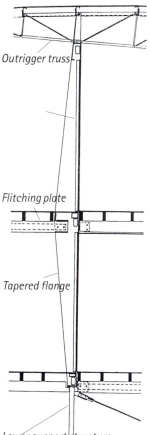

Outrigger truss

Flitching plate

Tapered flange

Lower support structure, 75 x 75 mm steel square hollow sections

smooth surface to facilitate adhesion of the protection system and minimize areas where water may collect; sharp corners or angular elements reduce the thickness of protection systems, and provide the potential for corrosion of steel elements.

Site interface

On the steeply sloping site only pad footings are required due to the low dead weight of the structure. This minimizes site damage and reduces site works. In an area such as Stradbroke Island which is mostly sandy soils, fragile ecology and considerable scenic beauty, the minimal site impact is important. Disturbance to vegetation and water run-off with large-scale site works can have a substantial ecological impact which is not easily regenerated. Careful consideration should be given to the layout and levels of the pads. Site tolerances of 25 mm are often used, which is incompatible with a steel frame designed to 5 mm of tolerance. Adjustment of the frame is not economically feasible on site for the above reasons of maintaining the integrity of the protection system of the elements.

Early completion of frame and roof

After the pads are complete the elements of the frame can be assembled incrementally. In this case the structure was in two parts, a lower frame supporting the ground-floor timber floor, the upper frame providing support to the second-floor platform and the roof. The partitioning of the structure in

5.17 *Donovan and Hill Stradbroke Island House: right: section showing the cross-braced steel support structure used to address the steep slope of the site. Balconies are supported by props from this structure made of cropped steel 'I' beams. top: detail section through the frame. Note the lightweight curved truss with outriggers to support the sunshades*

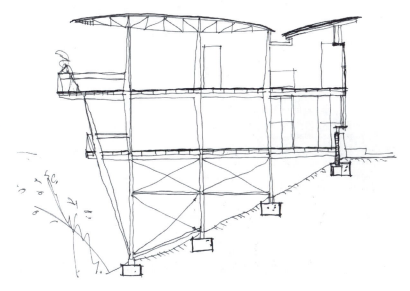

this way on a sloping site is advisable as it provides a safe working area for building personnel. To erect the frame in a single sequence requires specialized riggers to connect and install the elements in space from pre-erected scaffolding systems. The use of the frame as a working platform is an important principle obviating the need to use additional scaffolding and thus saving cost and time.

Completion of cladding and fit-out

On completion of frame and roof, cladding and fit-out can be completed in a semi-enclosed environment. In this case, timber stud framing is used as the structural support to the cladding. Plywood is used as an external skin to provide weather resistance and bracing. This double function of the material makes the use of plywood cost-effective in this kind of location.

To further improve buildability the external cladding is set out on a modular system of dimensional coordination. The module used is based on the standard manufactured sheet size of plywood (2.4 x 1.2 m). This eliminates cutting and reduces wastage. Joints between sheets are made of a preservative-treated timber cover strip.

5.7 Appropriate technology

The conclusions reached from the above case studies suggest that where technology is used then it should be used in an appropriate manner. With the shift to international standards of construction and engineering practice it seems that to determine what is appropriate is a contentious issue. Whilst it

5.18 *Construction sequence of North Stradbroke House, Donovan and Hill Architects.*

5.19 *Details of cladding of North Stradbroke House, Donovan and Hill Architects right: sunshades and balconies left: plywood vertical sunshade to reduce the westerly low sun angle. Translucent sheeting is used at the line of the truss to provide top light to the interior spaces*

is possible to use engineering definitions of the word 'appropriate', that is use of technology such that it has 'fitness for purpose.' In this case appropriate technology is that which serves the needs of addressing the physical laws of nature. It seems that there is also a need to broaden the notion of appropriate technology to not only meet the needs of the physical laws of nature but also the ecological laws.

The case studies discussed here, and in particular, the last discussion of the Donovan and Hill House at Stradbroke Island, suggest that this is possible. Climatic responsive design is not simply how the building responds to climate once built but also how the building construction and structural system can mesh with site and climate to provide well being for building personnel and improve buildability.

References

1. H Fathy, Guest lecture to the School of Architecture, National University of Singapore, 1982.
2. Lim Jee Yuan, *The Malay House*, Institute Masyarakat, 1987, Pulan Penang, p. 104.

The roof

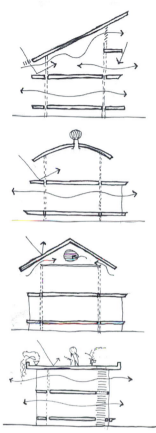

CHAPTER 6

If God is in the details then climate is in the building section', Peter Woods.[1]

6.1 Introduction

The roof design of buildings is a complex problem of attempting to provide a form of enclosure that resists the forces of nature – wind, precipitation and thermal conditions. This can be understood better by comparing the response of a warm climate and cool climate buildings. In cool climates the roof is a potential source of cooling since the building is mostly in a heat deficit. The roof is therefore highly defensive and has a dual function of retaining heat and preventing the ingress of precipitation. In warm climates, the buildings are in heat surplus, thus the roof is required to play a more complex role of reducing solar gain during the day and but also promoting cooling particularly at night. A closer examination of thermodynamics of warm climate roof form reveals the significance of both geometry and the materiality. Hence Professor Woods speaks of the importance of the building section in determining response. The vertical section shows the relationship between sectional roof geometry, airflow, openings and thus ventilation.

The basis of the discussion of roof strategies is therefore on types of roof geometry. The tactical decisions about the deployment of materials for these geometry's raise a second set of issues. The following sectional roof strategies are examined:

- skillions (mono-pitch), duo-pitch and vaults
- attics
- parasol and free form
- trafficable
- shading, rain screening and ceiling reflectors
- roofing accessories

It should also be noted that the roof sectional geometry is specific to the climate. In areas where there is a low rainfall, flat roofs are common, the converse is true in areas of high rainfall where a steep pitch is used. In recent years, with the greater awareness of environmental issues and resource conservation, the roof is seen as a major element for harvesting natural resources from the climate. The roof has become a collector of rainwater and a

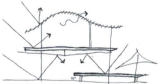

6.1 *Roofing types:*
top: single layer skillion and vaults with sectional geometry for ventilation
middle: attics reduce section height and provide heat sinks if not ventilated
middle: trafficable roofs pose materiality problems
bottom: shading roofs provide layers of defence

6.2 *The roof as the defensive element is shown in these colonial bungalows in Singapore. The predominance of roof to shade and protect the walls, allowing skin cooling through the use of lightweight materials. With large overhangs windows can be left open when it is rain to allowing ventilation at all times except in storms*

platform for mounting additional technology to harvest the energy sources provided by the climate. The technologies such as solar hot-water systems and photovoltaics, have added complexity to the design and are increasingly redefining the form and construction of the roof. The importance of appropriate roof accessories to the technical resolution of the roof add further complexity to the issues of geometry and materiality. With respect to this new function both the inclination and orientation of the roof is a major design factor for the efficiency of these technologies.

6.3 *The elements of roof acting in climate defence*
- material and surface
- structure
- ceiling

6.2 The defensive element

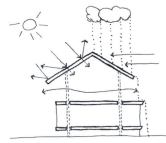

The roof in warm climates is often poorly designed and has led to the common perception that it is the main heating element in the house.[2] Furthermore, the role of the roof structure in these climates is often underestimated and misunderstood. In this study the roof is defined as consisting of three elements. First, the roof surface facing the sky that provides a defence against sun and precipitation, second, a structural system that supports or is integrated with the roof, and finally a ceiling system which is supported by or integrated with the structural system. It is the combination and positioning of these elements that creates the climatic response of the building.

The roof's primary functions are to acts to resist wind loads and precipitation as well as defend against solar gain. The magnitude of this latter problem can be seen from the weather data for warm climates. Solar radiation can provide a heat load of up to 1000 W m^{-2} on the roof surface. Unless the heat is dissipated quickly, performance problems ensue. This is primarily a materiality issue, the selection of strategies to prevent heat gain.

Another point of confusion is the role of the ceiling under the roof surface. For example in a truss roof the space between the roof and the ceiling can form a heat sink trapping heat. The stored heat can radiate through the ceiling to the space below and only compounds cooling problems. Thus adequate ceiling height and ventilation become crucial to removing this heat. The absence of the attic space provides a single layer roof which can be used in various forms. Each gives different sectional advantages for ventilation. Hot air will rise up and exhaust at high points therefore the strategy is to select a geometry that fits airflow and functional requirements of the building design.

The high volume of rain sustained over short periods also compounds the problems of climate defence; the use of internal gutters with this volume of water can cause local flooding if these are undersized or become blocked. In addition, high wind loads (due to cyclone conditions) found in some of the warm climate zones affect the aspect ratio of the roof, reducing inclination and thus volume within the roof space. Finally, roof geometry is used to protect other elements of the building; the common use of overhanging eaves

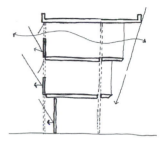

6.4 *Roof dominant versus wall dominant, the designer's choice*

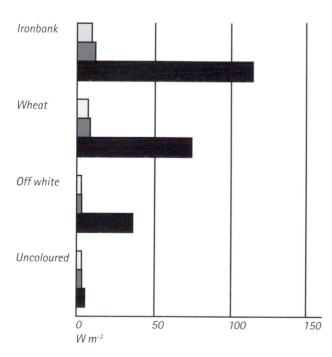

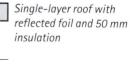

Single-layer roof with reflected foil and 50 mm insulation

Single-layer roof with reflected foil

Single-layer roof

6.5 *Comparison of the thermal performance of coloured metal roofs, the use of insulation under the surface is required with dark colours*

that protect walls and allows skin cooling is crucial to the overall performance of the building.

A distinction should be made between roof-dominant strategies and wall-dominant strategies. Designers have a choice as to the extent to which the roof becomes a feature of the building form. The geometry and form of the roof are arranged dependent on this role.

Therefore, for single-storey buildings in hot humid climates the common strategy is to use steeply pitched roof, with overhanging eaves to reduce wind-blown rain penetration and solar access. As the building increases in height the effect of the roof has to be extended. This can be achieved by setting walls back or by adding jack roofs or verandas. This form of building response can be called roof-dominant as the major feature is the roof element.

With tall buildings the proportion of roof to wall decreases and thus the roof is a minor player. This can be called a wall-dominant building. The technology of the wall fabric becomes critical to prevent heat gain to the interior spaces and also has to accommodate more exposure presenting a durability problem. In this case additional responses are used to shade the interior spaces, through balconies and shading. The challenge for the designer is therefore to optimize the roof design to meet the defensive climate requirements.

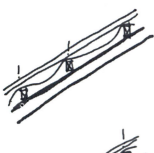

6.6 *Construction of roofs using double-sided reflective foil laminates*

6.3 Skillions, duo-pitch and vaults

The typical roof geometry for domestic buildings is to use a skillion (mono-pitch), duo-pitch or vaulted roof. These roofs can be used with or without a ceiling, depending on the construction and structural systems used. The inclusion of the ceiling directly below the roof surface does not create a large

6.7 *Roof form in the Malay house showing environmental shading and a single layer insulation-active roof system. The roof utilizes gable vents to promote cooling. The modern approach is shown below*

air space; in some cases, though, a ceiling is used to form an attic space. (Different thermal responses are found with this attic space: the thermal performance of this type of space is discussed in the next section.)

The modern form of construction without the attic is common practice in many warm climate countries in traditional buildings and for use in single-layer lightweight roofing systems as a low-cost form of roof construction. Materials such as corrugated iron and fibre-reinforced cement are used. The problem appears to be less with the thickness of the material than with the colour. Dark colour materials will reflect less and absorb more heat than a light coloured roof. A reflective surface reduces solar heating. Dark surface colours can increase internal temperatures to 30 degrees C above the external temperature.[3]

More detailed research compared the thermal performance of different coloured roofs where the solar radiation is 850 W m^{-2} and an air temperature is 30 degrees C. This shows that where light reflective materials are used there is little radiant heat gain. On the other hand, with dark roofs 15 per cent of the external heat is transferred through the roof.[4]

The strategy therefore to is to minimize this problem by using a white or highly reflective material, but where for aesthetic or other reasons darker materials are required the problem of heat gain should be addressed. Heat transfer through the roof is primarily by radiation. As the solar gain heats the surface of the roof it is back radiated from the roof surface to the inner space. The solution to the problem is to use a membrane of double-sided reflective foil laminate with low emittance. This can be hung below the roof sheeting, 50-75 mm, to provide an air gap to further improve performance. The thermal performance can be further improved by using additional bulk insulation, thus cutting the heat gain by convection, but this may also reduce the ability of the roof to lose heat at night unless ventilated. Thus in skin-cooled buildings, where the intention is to use systems to promote cool, optimum performance should be achieved by using light coloured reflective roofs. These types of roofs can be defined as insulation–active, as the principle method of defence is the insulation quality of the design through bulk or membranes.

The thermal performance of the roof is also related to its geometry and the provision of ventilation to the underside of the roof and to the external environment. Examination of the traditional Malay house illustrates this well. The house is essentially a rural agricultural building; sited in a Kampong (village) setting. The skin is created from shorter life elements, woven bamboo screens and 'attap' roof made of woven palm leaves.

The key advantage of the attap is that it is water-resistant and acts as a good insulator. Neither the full force of a tropical storm nor the heat of the mid-day sun on the surface of the roof penetrates through the roof. The construction of the attap roof provides the main defence by the use of small leaves are woven around rattan sticks and bound together to form a 'tile'. These are double-lapped to create a watertight envelope. The loose layering of the palm means that it traps air between the leaves reducing solar gain in a similar way to synthetic cellular insulation. The shiny surface of the palm

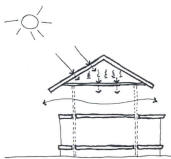

6.8 *Thermal dynamics in an attic roof: back radiation from the roof surface heats the attic air which is radiated via the ceiling to the internal air below*

leaves provides water resistance and therefore the lapping of leaves gives a watertight structure. Finally, the palm leaves have very little thermal mass; they do not accumulate large amounts of heat during the day and so do not radiate heat back into the building at night. Other features of the roof are seen in this example.

First, solar gain on the roof is minimized through the use of environmental shading. The landscape elements found in the Kampong setting act as a buffer to the roof. Palms, such as the Penang and coconut palms, provide a parasol over the roof, breaking the solar access yet still providing ventilation and breeze below.

Second, with the duo-pitch form of the roof, heat build-up under the roof is also a problem. Heat can be trapped under the roof and stratify into a number of layers with the hottest area below the roof. The mezzanine space directly under the roof is therefore uncomfortable. In the house this space is used for sleeping and therefore under-roof ventilation is provided by the use of end-gables vents.

In this example we begin to see that the design of the roof element is a resolution of four main factors. These are:

- minimizing solar gain
- minimizing heat storage
- provision of under roof ventilation
- provide environmental shading

6.4 Attics

The strategy of providing a ceiling below the roof presents another kind of problem in warm climates. Back-radiation from the roof may cause heat gain in the interstitial space between the roof and the ceiling, heating the ceiling and radiating heat into the occupied space below.

In a house with an external temperature of 30 degrees C, the temperature in the roof space can be 55 degrees C. Heat in the interstitial roof space is then transferred to the ceiling and re-radiated into the occupied space. The

6.9 *The use of bulk ceiling insulation is beneficial for attic spaces in moderate climates as can be seen.*
right: in summer, heat gain due to heat build-up is reduced. It is important that the internal spaces are well ventilated otherwise the insulation can trap heat at night
left: in winter heat loss from the internal spaces is reduced

Table 6.1 Effects of roof ventilation rates and insulation on the heating and cooling energy in a moderate climate

Insulation		Ventilation	Cooling energy		Heating energy	
Walls	Ceiling		$MJ\,m^{-2}\,y^{-1}$	Percentage	$MJ\,m^{-2}\,y^{-1}$	Percentage
Nil	Nil	10 air changes per hour	137.3	0.0	87.3	0.0
Nil	Nil	20 air changes per hour	127.2	7.4	96.1	10.1
DSRF	R1.5	50 air changes per hour	117.9	14.1	105	20.3
DSRF	R1.5	10 air changes per hour	63.9	0.0	21.5	0.0
DSRF	R1.5	20 air changes per hour	57.3	10.3	21.8	1.4

DSRF: double sided reflected foil

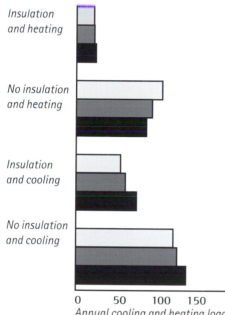

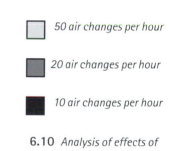

6.10 Analysis of effects of roof ventilation on energy use for a moderate climate

effect is to create temperatures of 40 degrees C below the roof and an average temperature of 31–32 degrees C.[5] The reduction of the transfer of solar heat gain can be achieved by three main mechanisms:

- use of reflective surfaces
- use of ventilation to the roof space
- insulation to the ceiling

First, surfaces are used that are highly reflective and have high emissivity. Tiles that are light in colour and are glazed tend to reflect more heat than darker mat finished materials. Second, the use of ventilation removes the heated air in the roof space thus preventing high heat loads on the ceiling.

Third, the use of insulation on the ceiling isolates the air below the ceiling from the charged air in the roof space.

The use of these three mechanisms has a significant effect on the internal temperature of the typical house. Back-radiation of heat from the ceiling is reduced, so the internal temperatures can be as low as 28 degrees C, depending on external temperatures and ventilation. The effects of heat gain can be overcome by other design responses; the use of higher ceilings and greater room ventilation can remove the excess heat and distance occupants from the effects of back radiation. In the case where ventilation is not present, the house can become uncomfortable. The alternative is to air-condition the house but with no insulation and little ventilation the proportion of heat gain through the roof increases – 45 per cent of heat gain will be through the roof, 20 per cent through glazing, 30 per cent through walls and 5 per cent through infiltration. This will increase energy costs and have wider environmental consequences.

The effectiveness of roof ventilation and insulation to attic spaces has been assessed through a computer simulation study as shown in Table 6.1.[6]

The analysis of this data shows that without insulation and with increased ventilation, summer performance is improved by approximately 14 per cent but winter performance is reduced by approximately 20 per cent. Adding

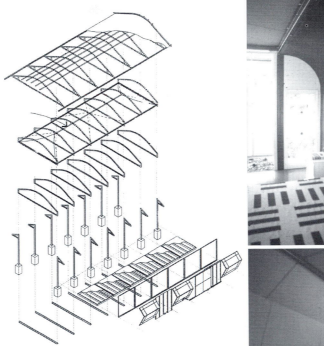

6.11 *Tent house by Gabriel Poole, 1994:*
Above: plan, section and elevations
right: portal frame system supports a light fabric roof system and retractable wall system. Details of canvas inner skin used in the bedroom bay and inner roof in the living room

6.12 *Queensland School System, roof cooling is used to reduce the high casual gains from pupils and staff*

insulation reduces heating requirements by approximately 75 per cent and minimizes the ventilation effects. Furthermore, adding insulation halves the cooling energy required and the increased ventilation reduces this load again by approximately 20 per cent.

The optimum performance for attic spaces for moderate climates where there is a season shift in heating and cooling requirements suggests a number of possible alternatives. This depends on the inclination of the roof, methods of ventilation and insulation (techniques for roof venting systems are dealt with in roof equipment). The types of construction used in hot and humid climates presents a different problem since the heating problem is absent, the argument for the parasol roof is persuasive.

6.5 Parasol roof and free-form roofs

The roof in hot humid climates is clearly different; the desired response is to use the roof for cooling. In this kind of configuration the roof acts as a parasol to simply protect the inner spaces from sun and rain as well as maximizing ventilation below the parasol. One of the main strategies is to use lightweight construction that is reflective and has little thermal mass so the roof fabric can cool rapidly.

The Tent house by Gabriel Poole is an example of this approach. The house was produced in a kit form that follows a linear plan with a portal frame structure is used to support a fabric roof. This roof surface is made of white PVC that is stretched across the roof frame. An inner tent of canvas is used to provide a ceiling. Air movement can be found through the double-roof system to provide cooling.

The potential for using more conventional construction is found in the case of the Queensland School System. This building system has a number of characteristics such as a deeper plan-form, low ceilings and open attic space. The plan form is rectangular with ventilation along the long axis. Extensive shading is provided to reduce solar gain.

The buildings in the hot humid tropics are free running, that is there is no air-conditioningsystems to provide cooling. The problem found is with the high casual gains from the staff and pupils, which raise temperatures above external temperatures. The reduction of this heat load has to be accommodated to give thermal comfort. Cross-ventilation is provided to the class space.

Studies of temperatures in the roof show that improved ventilation to the attic space can assist with the cooling of the occupied space. The construction of the roof and ceiling is crucial to this response.

The roof surface is insulated through blanket and double foil laminates. This strategy minimizes back-radiation to the attic space by solar radiation. Furthermore, as temperatures increase in the classroom spaces due to casual gains to above ambient, heat is lost to the attic space due to the radiant cooling through the ceiling. The heat in the roof space is removed by ventilation through eaves and gable vents. Given that the ceiling area of the space is as large or even larger than the perimeter area for ventilation, this provides a very useful cooling strategy.

6.6 Low-inclination and trafficable roofs

These types of roof are mainly low-inclination to facilitate pedestrian traffic and are made of heavyweight or lightweight construction. The construction types address the different design needs and technical requirements, and they provide different climate responses.

Design needs, technical requirements and climatic response

At the top of the building the designer has a number of ways of resolving the roofing problem. The normal form of construction is to use a lightweight system as this is the most efficient structurally (lightweight systems have reduced dead load and therefore can more effectively span roof space). The selection of heavyweight construction systems is guided by the need for the roof to act as a floor to provide for pedestrian and other functions such as storage. There are clearly exceptions to this approach where lightweight systems can be used. With heavyweight systems there are a number of technical requirements. The thermal mass of the roof is particularly important if the roof is made of concrete then it will act very much like the ground; high levels of solar radiation will produce temperatures that will remain equivalent to the upper levels of air temperature because of its thermal mass. Two strategies are found relating to the thickness of material of the slab used in the low-inclination roof.

One strategy is to use thermal mass to insulate the space. If the concrete is thick enough, so that there is sufficient mass to absorb solar radiation during the day and not radiate the heat inside, then the inner surface will remain cooler than the outer surface. Thickness of mass insulation also relates to the time taken for the roof to absorb heat, that is the time interval between the shift in temperature of the outer surface of the roof and that of the inner surface or ceiling. This is interval is called the thermal lag in the roof. As a general principle, the thicker and denser the slab the longer the thermal lag. This thermal lag would seem to be beneficial as it would seem to suggest that heat gain is through insulation of the slab. Unfortunately this is not so; thermal lag only delays the time taken to heat the inner surface of the slab. Also, heat stored in the slab can be re-radiated into the space after the sun has set, raising temperatures. It is therefore not recommended to use mass for insulation, particularly in spaces such as bedrooms that are used at night.[7]

The second strategy is therefore to control the heat flows in the slab by insulation. The aim is to prevent the mass of the slab from being charged by solar radiation. There are a number of ways to achieve this.

Water cooled roofs and mass roofs

The roof can be formed into a shallow tank of water called a roof pond. The high specific heat of the water means that it can act as an insulator. The water will remain at the lower levels of air temperature thus keeping the roof cool. Water sprays are similar to the roof pond, water can be sprayed onto the surface of the roof which evaporates and thereby cools the roof.[8] The problems with the use of water as a spray or a pond is that it may give further technical problems due to water leakage. Moreover, the additional structural requirements to support the pond may increase cost. The technical complexity of such a strategy may outweigh the climate benefits.

The technical complexity is reduced to some degree by using earth as a roofing element. This provides a layer of massive material to insulate the building. The needs for water proofing and additional structural loads are similar to that of the roof pond.

Double-roof

The roof surface can be split into two layers, the external surface and the ceiling can form a cavity. The air in the cavity and the use of ventilation removes unwanted heat. The separation prevents re-radiation of heat and also allows ventilation in the cavity. Variations on this can be found: Fry and Drew recommend that the slab should be raked so that heat penetrating the first roof heats the air which will rise up the slope of the cavity and be vented at the ridge. This thermal siphoning effect can keep the inner roof or ceiling cool.[9]

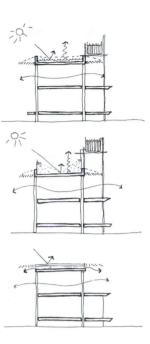

6.13 *Low inclination solid roof strategies:*
top: water pond
middle: water spray
bottom: double solid roof

Insulated and 'inverted' roof

The final alternative to preventing the slab from charging with heat is to place an insulating layer above the slab. The waterproofing layer is then placed below the insulating layer hence it is named the 'inverted' roof. The result is that the insulating layer protects the waterproofing layer and also reduces heat gain to the slab. A crude method to achieve this is to place concrete blocks above the slab. More sophisticated methods use flat concrete slabs supported on insulation.[10]

This type of inverted roof is useful in laboratories. In these building the roof can be used for additional space for experimental purposes houses and animal storage. In this case the increased loading was accommodated by pre-stressing the slab; this type of structural system also increases the water resistance of the concrete, thus overcoming problems of potential leakage through cracks. A waterproof membrane can be used over the slab to enhance the weather protection. A wearing surface is then formed by the use of concrete paving slabs set on pads. This provides insulation from solar gain and separates the membrane from the effects of the concrete.

The designer should examine each of these methods in turn to assess which is appropriate. The first methods tend to be least cost-effective and technically difficult to achieve. The disadvantage of roof ponds is that in solving the cooling they create further technical problems such leaking roofs and the removal of water due to evaporation. The last methods, of using some form of double roof or 'Inverted' roof are more cost-effective. Essentially these latter approaches seek to interrupt the solar rays before they can effect heat gain. These elements heat up and dissipate their heat like the fins of a motorbike cylinder head.

An alternative to these kinds of systems is to use lightweight construction which has low thermal mass and is insulated to reduce gain. In this type of

6.14 *Architects: Donovan and Hill Architects, 1998: Collaborative Design Laboratory, The University of Queensland:*
far right: section through the Laboratory showing the trafficable roof and timber substrate
left: elevation of the Laboratory showing the interaction of building and the landscape
(drawings Donovan and Hill Architects)

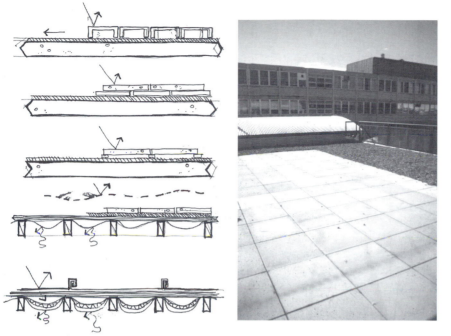

6.15 *Alternative low inclination roof configurations:*
left: typical roofing layers
top: double roof, concrete substrate, membrane, concrete blocks
next: inverted roof, concrete substrate, membrane, insulation, paving
next: as above but pads substituted for insulation to give air gap
next: timber substrate, polymer membrane, bonded paving
bottom: insulation, plywood substrate, moisture barrier, metal
right: inverted roof system

construction system there is a choice in the use of waterproofing material, steel versus synthetic membrane.

With a steel roof, interlocking sheets can be used to provide the waterproof layer to an angle of inclination as low as 5 degrees. The problem is how to achieve a trafficable surface above the roof. Where membranes are used a trafficable roof can be provided but then there is problem of where to place the insulation.

Two cases illustrate the problems. In the first case the position and form of the roof caused an interesting design problem. The building form is in a

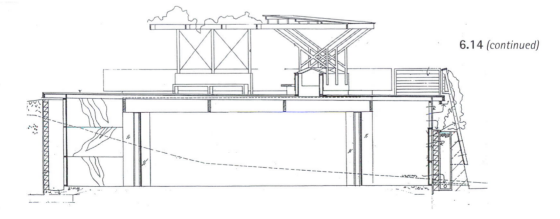

6.14 *(continued)*

6.16 *A low-inclination metal roof using a zinc and aluminium alloy with upstanding joints. This roof is highly visible to adjacent taller buildings, grey zinc reduces reflected glare to adjacent buildings. Note the deep parapet gutter to prevent blockage, this sits outside the line of enclosure to avoid internal flooding*

crescent shaped around the entrance foyer. This led to a radiating geometry and complications in the roof construction. In addition, the roof is over-looked from adjacent buildings and therefore needed to accommodate an aesthetic as well as technical function. A low-inclination metal roof was used, made of a composite zinc, aluminium and zinc alloy. This could be cold-formed on site, using a break-press, in tapering sections to accommo-date the radius of the roof. Metal ties are used to connect the metal deck to a plywood substrate. The main issue with this type of roof is the position and form of insulation. In moderate climates, the night sky radiation can reduce the surface temperatures of the metal deck to 7 or 8 degrees C.[11] Interstitial condensation can form on the underside of the metal deck from warm air moving up through the building. This will form into distilled water that can corrode the underside of the metal deck and fixings. The solution is to use a vapour barrier and insulation on the warm side of the metal deck.

The second case requires a trafficable roof for another laboratory build-ing. Concrete systems are not applicable for acoustic and aesthetic reasons; strategies appropriate for this roof is to either use a loose-laid or bonded system of roof construction. The advantage of the loose-laid system is that metal soakers can be installed between the joists and the paving set on pads. This provides a heat-screen approach, which rejects heat but allows water to drain through the paving to the roof and be caught by a metal membrane below. Heat is dissipated through the air gap between the paving and soakers. The paving system can be retracted for maintenance.

The advantage of the bonded system is that it is a simple system of bond-ing the paving warring surface to the plywood substrate with mastic. The disadvantages are from the durability and thermal performance standpoints. Insulation is required and the only place for this is below the plywood substrate. Yet the most effective position for the insulation is on the external surface of the insulation so that solar gain can be prevented from heating up the slab. In this case this is not possible and the insulation has to be placed below the timber deck. This is less effective, as the deck has little thermal resistance and enough heat will flow through the insulation to heat the air below the ceiling.[13]

Therefore the heat flows are higher with this configuration than with the exterior insulation. In this case light coloured paving is used to reflect heat and an external shading system is used above the roof, is used to provide shading. In this way high heat gain from solar radiation is reduced and thus

6.17 *A prototype lightweight trafficable metal roof system designed by the students the Department of Architecture, The University of Queensland. This innovative loose laid system addresses moisture movement that occurs to fully bonded systems*[12]

reduces the need for insulation. In addition the reduction of heat gain to the roof will help minimize the movement of timber and the paving system through expansion and contraction.

6.18 *This shading entrance porch to a plantation house in Penang, Malasiya, provides a transparency whilst also providing rain protection. For the time it was built a high tech. solution to the problem. Tinted glass segments set in lead soakers are used to create the curved form to echo the main lead roof*

6.7 Shading roofs, surface-diffusers and surface reflectors

In the previous case, heat load to low inclination roofs can be reduced by using a form of sun-breaker system. This is designed to alternately block and admit light thus reducing the amount of radiation reaching the roof below. The strategy used in the sun-breaker system can be applied in a number ways but essentially there is a separation in the sun-shading function of the roof from the water-resistance function. A further strategy is to change the surface material so that it can act as a roof diffuser and reflector of light into the interior spaces.

The first case examines the use of use of the roof as a sunbreaker. In the 'Roof-roof' house by Ken Yeang, concrete blades are used to form a shade over a concrete deck area.[14] The orientation of these blades is crucial to the effectiveness of the breaker system and to the cooling and ventilation of the space below. The blades are angled specifically to diffuse the sun at particular times of the day.

The blade system for shading roofs has been complemented by additional forms of shade structure using membranes and lightweight translucent sheets. These materials function as light diffusers, reducing and transforming the solar energy. The membrane materials can be made of Teflon-coated fibreglass or, alternatively, PVC-tension fabric and provide various degrees of shading from 10-20 per cent light transmission.

Polycarbonate and fibreglass sheets can also be used, various body tints are used to reduce heat gain. Two examples demonstrate this approach. The first is at The John Oxley Centre in Brisbane. A fibreglass roof is supported on a space frame structural system to provide an atrium. The light diffuses

6.19 *The 'roof-roof' house by Ken Yeang, 1989: The use of two roofs for different climate response, the shading parasol used angled louvres to reduce solar gain to the trafficable flat concrete roof below. This expressive icon of climate generated architecture is indicative of the work of this architect*

through the translucent roof providing 500 lux at the ground plane with an external illumination of 8000 lux.[15]

At Kingfisher Bay Resort, both membranes and sheet materials are used for both aesthetic and functional reasons. The sheet material is used in the roof above the bracing towers. The function of the towers is to assist with the structural stability of the building but they also provide an opportunity to provide landscaping and additional daylighting. A number of translucent panels are used in the roof surface which provide pools of light for the landscaping. Timber battens are used below the sheeting to provide a sun-breaking and diffusing functions to prevent glare. Over the dance floor area,

6.20 *A fibreglass shading roof used over a south facing semi-enclosed courtyard, Brisbane, Queensland. The use of a light space frame structure in combination with the diffusing roof assists with shading the glazing providing a buffering effect*

membranes are used with more timber diffusers below the membrane. This gives a further reduction in the light levels in this space.

Heat gain does occur by back-radiation from these roof lights but distance and ventilation accommodate it. The apertures located over three metres away from occupants so the radiated effect of heat is not felt. In addition, heat gain from the roof lights stratifies at the higher level and contributes to the natural ventilation strategy of the building. In this strategy, the air directly under the roof acts as a heat collector and, through thermal syphoning, rises drawing more hot air from the building which is exhausted through clerestory windows.[16] This also draws in cooler air at the lower level.

One further issue with these light-diffusing membranes is thermal performance. The lack of insulation causes problems of heat gain and heat loss. In the external areas at Kingfisher Bay the sky radiation, particularly in winter, reducing the surface temperature of the sheets causing condensation. This produces mould growth as well as discolouring to the surface. This effect can be visually intrusive if maintenance is not available.

6.21 Use of light diffusing properties of membranes to shade roof at Kingfisher Bay Resort, Fraser Island, Queensland

6.8 Roof accessories

Roof equipment includes a range of equipment for servicing the water run-off, catchment and storage. Hydraulic systems in buildings operate primarily by passive means using gravitational forces acting on the liquids and solids suspended or dissolved in that liquid. Water cannot flow up hill unless it is pumped by an 'active' energy-based system. Rainwater is delivered to the building by both gravitational forces and wind.

The roof design has to respect and accommodate the daily and seasonal

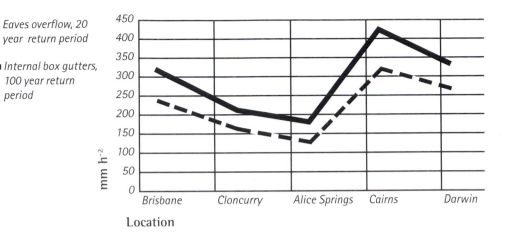

- - - Eaves overflow, 20 year return period

—— Internal box gutters, 100 year return period

6.22 *Rain intensity for the moderate and hot humid climates of Australia*[17]

variations in rainfall and wind forces. Warm climates are characterized by areas that have little rainfall and with pronounced dry seasons. Other areas have monsoon conditions in the wet season with days when large quantities of rain fall in short periods of time. In Equatorial regions the monsoon has a similar pattern, in fact there can be two monsoons with much shorter dry seasons. Singapore is a good example, a monsoon in December brings large quantities of rain which then gives way to drier weather in January. A second monsoon of lesser strength in July is also likely to occur. These monsoon changes are related to the passage of the Equatorial convergence zone over Singapore.[18] In December, drier winds from the north push down south and bring clear drier air from Siberia, forcing the moist tropical air south. The convergence of these two air masses causes the activity of the monsoon front and results in the large amounts of water that are deposited in these periods. The December monsoon is more active as it is a cold front i.e. colder, drier air displacing hotter, moist air. The colder air creeps under the warmer air forcing it to rise resulting in rain. The high water content of the tropical air means that this kind of displacement generates large quantities of rain. The July monsoon has the colder air retreating and the displacement of air is less active giving rise to less rain.

These types of rain conditions have a significant impact on roof design. In particular, the hydraulic design of roof pitch and overhang, gutter design

Table 6.2 Design guidelines for maximum roof run-off[19]

Deck Type	Roof slope	Rainfall Intensity	Maximum length, m
Corrugated iron	10 degrees	200	25
Corrugated iron	5 degrees	200	20
Profile steel	5 degrees	250	30
Profile steel	3 degrees	250	25
Interlocking	1 degree	400	35

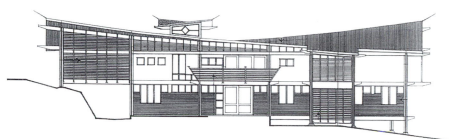

and down water pipes have to accommodate both the quantity of rain and the rain intensity, the large quantities of rain over a period of time. There are less obvious factors that should be considered; such issues as organic growth on roofs and in gutters, deposition or organic matter on roofs and collection in gutters are real design problems that have to be solved if longevity of the roof is to be provided. Finally, particularly in climates that have a long dry season or where water is imported (e.g. Singapore and Australia) storage of water from the roof is becoming a major issue.

This water is classified as drinkable, grey and black water; the latter two are unsuitable for drinking and are waste. The grey water can be treated to be suitable for the many household uses where drinking water is not required. The utilization of water makes the building more self-sustaining and less reliant on the external support infrastructure.

The hydraulic design of the roof is concerned first with roof pitch, overhang and water storage and second with gutter and down pipe design.

Roof inclination and overhang

In the past, distinctions between flat and pitched roofs have been made with regard to the types of construction materials. This definition is confusing; no roof can be truly flat since water has to be drained. Roof inclination is a more appropriate term as roofs can be described in terms of the angle of inclination, that is in turn related to the type of materials and construction systems. Materials that provide only water resistance should be steeply inclined while materials that provide waterproofing can be used with low inclination. The aim of the roof design should be self-cleansing, that is it should be designed so that the water will flush away organic matter and leave no pools of water to collect dirt and organic growth. This is easier said than done and requires establishing clear design goals at the beginning of the design project with regard to roof design. A useful example of this is the Habitat environmental home, Brisbane, Australia. The iron roof is steeply inclined and twisted in a hypar form to direct water catchment to different ends of the building. This is taken to tanks under the building.

In another project by Libby Watson-Brown the roof of a beach house is used to catch water. This steep inclination is designed to create a changing

6.24 *Beach house, architect, Libby Watson-Brown use of roof for collection and shading (photos Libby Watson-Brown)*

internal volume. within the building The interesting feature of the roof is that it overhangs the walls in an asymmetrical manner and thereby shades and protects walls and windows as required. Finally, the water from the roof drains into a water butt to one side of the living area. This creates a visual element in the garden.

In both these cases the use of the roof for shading and use of a clear strategy for integrating the climatic and technical requirements of the roof into the design strategy at an early stage is an important contribution to the success of this design.

6.25 *Design graph to assist with determining gutter sizes for catchment area per downpipe:*[20]
top: 200 m²
next: 100 m²
next: 50 m²
next: 20 m²
bottom: 10 m²

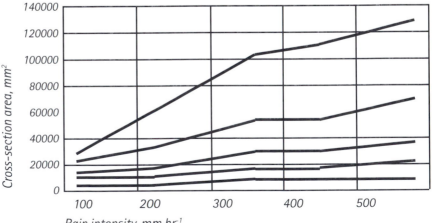

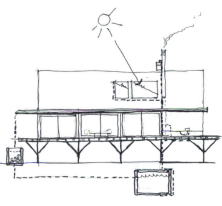

6.26 *The Mapleton house, Richard Leplastrier: the water collection system uses a monopitch roof linked to a large gutter, this discharges to a collection tank, filtered and then by gravity into a holding tank under the house. Solar power is used to pump to water to the areas in the house as it is required*

Gutter and rainwater pipe design

Key issues are related to the amount of water and velocity of water the roof delivers to the gutters, whether these are shallow or steeply inclined roofs. Steeply inclined roofs will deliver water faster to the gutter and in times of monsoon can overflow. Change of inclination as the water approaches the gutter reduces flow rate and thus helps prevent overflowing.

Roof gutters can be divided into two types; edge gutters and box gutters. Edge gutters as the name implies can be used on verges and eaves to direct water at the perimeter. Box gutters are used for low-inclination roofs or where two roofs intersect.

Edge gutters

Edge gutters are used to catch water from the roof and direct the water to a drain, soak-away or collection point by way of a down pipe or other devise. Roofs without edge gutters are often thought a desired design aim as it avoids overflows, keeps the edge of the building visually light as possible and avoids the clutter of down pipes. This approach can be achieved but the designer still has to consider providing water removal at some point, either back from the edge of the roof in a hidden gutter or at the ground in the form of a monsoon or spoon (open) drain. The latter is a good choice providing sufficient overhang can be provided to prevent wind-blown rain from falling on the building walls. These are likely to have open windows for ventilation, so avoiding splashing and wind-blown rain is important. Furthermore, with this strategy it is advantageous for the roof to be as close to the ground as possible. The higher the fall the farther the water can be blown. The water has to be directed and received at the ground plane, so some drain or metal grating or gravel is ideal.

Where gutters are used for water collection these can be oversized to maximize the amount of rain collected. An excellent example is to be found at the Mapleton house by Richard Leplastrier. A 'U' shaped gutter is used made of corrugated iron that accepts water from a mono-pitch roof. This is directed to a catchment area and then to an underground tank. No rainwater pipes are used and the filtering of the water is achieved at the catchment area.

Box gutters

Box gutters need a large cross section to carry water and to prevent blockage, a rule of thumb in Australia is to make them big enough to accommodate a dead possum. This is a small mammal up to 300 mm in length that inhabits roofs and invariably a dead one will block your box gutter, hence the dead possum rule.

In case of blockage, overflow spigots should be used below a point where water can access the roof and leak into the building. A minimum of two down pipes is important. Think about minimizing the risk of gutter failure by overflow and blockage, the more alternative routes for water, the less likely the gutters are to overflow into the building

The size of gutters and down pipes is dictated by fall and flow rate. A simplified design methodology for gutter and down pipe design can follow a few basic principles. Down pipes can be either internal or external or integrated with structural systems. Good design practice suggests keeping the rainwater pipes external to the building envelope and not integrated with structure. The

6.27 *Glen Murcutt, Kempsey Museum, 1990: Box gutter systems are used to join pavilions, these have a large width and depth and are open-ended to accept large peak flows thus avoiding blockage and flooding; the collection points have articulated hopper heads*

reasons for this are both practical and aesthetic; maintenance is far easier from the exterior, and if a blockage occurs it will only affect areas outside the skin. Integration of rainwater pipes within structural columns can be achieved but it requires coordination of a number of trades and so brings another layer of complexity into the construction process. Again, access for maintenance is limited. Aesthetically expressing rainwater pipes gives the building a further means of demonstrating an engagement of the building with climate.

A number of architects have taken the design of gutters and down pipes as foci in their building. Glen Murcutt at the Kempsey Museum uses large box gutters as small roofs that link the main pavilions. These are likened to a dry creek bed which periodically floods thus the gutters are continuous and continued down the front of the building as vertical elements. Down pipes are oversized and exaggerated to allow leaves to pass through which are collected in grills below. The technical problems with these gutters involves segmenting the long sections and connecting them on site so that they remain watertight. Also this watertight seal should withstand continual thermal expansion and contraction.[21]

References

1. Discussions with Professor Peter Woods, 1994.
2. B. Givoni, Man, *Man, Climate and Architecture*, Van Nostrand Reinhold, 1969, p. 156.
3. Givoni, op. cit., p. 158.
4. BHP, *Roofing and Walling Manual*, John Lysaght (Australia), Sydney, pp. 38-39.
5. *Design and Building of Energy Efficient Housing*, papers presented at a seminar sponsored by the Energy Management Sub-program of the Queensland Department of Resource Industries, internal publication, Queensland State Government, Brisbane, 1992.
6 National Energy Research Unit, *Roof Insulation Saves Cooling Energy, Research Bulletin*, Solarch, the Univerity of New South Wales, Sydney, 1998.
7. K. Harman, ed. *Environmental Design Guide*, Royal Australian Institute of Architects, Canberra, 1997, Pro7, p. 3.
8. Givoni, op. cit., p. 378.
9. J. R. Goulding, ed., et al, *Energy Conscious Design, A primer for Architects*, Department for Education, Architects and Building Division, HMSO, London, 1992, p. 65.
10. M. Fry and J. Drew, *Tropical Architecture in the Humid Zone*, Batsford, London, 1956, p. 56.
11. Discussion with Professor R. Aynsley, *Principles and Practice Conference*, Australian and New Zealand Architectural Science Association, 1998.

12. Fourth year student project, Department of Architecture, The University of Queensland.
13. Givoni, op. cit., p. 153.
14. R. Powell, *K. Yeang. The Rethinking the Environmental Filter*, Landmark Books, Singapore, 1989, p.15.
15. Spot measurements by the author.
16. Department of Education, *Passive Design of Schools*, HMSO, London,1994, p. 32.
17. Lysaght Building Industries, *The Referee*, BHP, Sydney, 1988, p.73.
18. O. H. Koenigsberger et al, *Manual of Tropical Housing*, Longmans, 19, p. 199.
19. Lysaght Building Industries, op. cit., p. 72.
20. Ibid., p. 74.
21. P. Drew, *Leaves of Iron. Glen Murcutt, pioneer of an Australian architectural form,* Sydney: Law Book, 1985.

The external wall

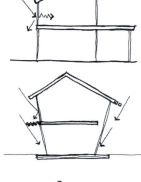

CHAPTER 7

'Architecture in the humid tropics is a collaboration with nature to establish a new order in which human beings may live in harmony with their surroundings', Maxwell Fry and Jane Drew.[1]

7.1 Introduction

The design of the wall element is of critical importance if a harmony with nature is to be achieved. The climatic forces of rain, sun and wind mean that the wall element has to be considered in terms of how it regulates these forces. A number of strategies can be identified which encourage collaboration between nature, the occupants and building skin to achieve a harmonious relationship. The metaphor of the external wall as a skin is commonly used as it perhaps best represents the interaction that is found in the skin of many organisms. It is the boundary between the inside and outside and moderates the inputs and outputs to the organism. The problem is that in warm climates this boundary serves an entirely different function to that in a cool climate with regard to heat, air and light. In the warm climate heat is rejected whilst light and air are admitted provided the air can cool and the light is diffuse. In the cool climate light and heat is retained whilst air is not required for cooling. The boundary in a warm climate building could follow a number of types; the first four deal with the problem of preventing heat gain, the last examines a more interactive approach resembling the metaphor of the building skin as an environmental filter:

- thin skins
- inclined skins
- thick skins
- buffering
- valve effects

7.2 The flexible element

The external wall is perhaps the most complex of elements to design from the climate point of view because of the number of relationships that require consideration. A useful concept for defining the external wall is to think of it as the flexible element.

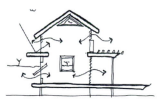

7.1 External wall types and strategies:
top: thin building skins mainly using materials
next: inclined skins using inclination of form
next: thick building skins using depth of form
next: buffering through depth of form and environment
bottom: valve effects through the use of mechanisms

7.2 *Climate responsive zoning shown in section; the environmental zone is defined as the area from which the building harvests the available natural energy, the buffer zone is adjacent to the line of enclosure on the exterior, the enclosure zone is an area of about 1-2 m in depth inside the line of enclosure, the passive zone is that which lies adjacent to the line of enclosure which receives a contribution from the exterior in terms of climate modification, the active zone receives little passive contribution*

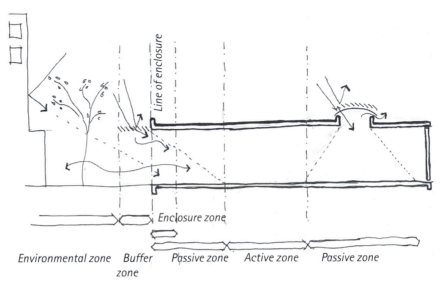

Environmental zone   Buffer zone   Passive zone   Active zone   Passive zone

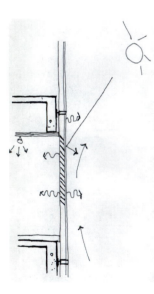

7.3 Section through a thin skin façade constructed of solar glass; back-radiation in particular from low-angle sun, is shielded by blinds; the consequence of using blinds and high shading coefficients of solar glass reduces daylight to the interior of the building

The rationale for this is that the external wall is the main element that controls and modifies the climate for activities immediately adjacent to the wall. As activities and the external climate change so too must the wall, by admitting or excluding sunlight, moderating ventilation, excluding rain and optimizing the internal climate. The designer may begin to consider the wall in terms of the degree of flexibility it offers in controlling the climatic forces. Furthermore, the design and configuration of the wall play an important part in enriching our experience of climate, so not only should the wall provide for our basic needs of comfort but also enhance and capture the nature of climate.

From this point of view it is possible to examine the wall not as a single defensive layer but as a series of layers or zones, for convenience called the 'climate responsive zones'. The conditions of the building orientation, site and climate can be analysed in terms of these zones and the appropriate strategy developed.[2]

Climate responsive zoning

The external wall is mainly defined in the building context as the line of enclosure. The normal definition of this part of the building skin is the point at which the interior is separated from the exterior by an air and moisture barrier. The problem with this definition is the meaning of barrier. In warm climate for free-running buildings the barrier need not necessarily be air-tight to maintain comfort. Yet with air-conditioned buildings the need for air- and moisture-tight barriers is crucial for energy efficiency. Hence the term filter is used conveying the notion of selective barriers at the line of enclosure.

From the line of enclosure different zones can be found which affect the

7.4 *Thin skin strategies rely on the use of materials to control solar heat gain, in particular the proportion of glass to solid materials, this is commonly called the glazing ratio:*
left: in these office buildings a combination of solid and opaque surfaces is used with a 50 per cent glazing ratio, this is the minimum to provide passive contributions to reduce energy use
middle: in the façade of this hotel the glazing ratio is reduced to less than 50 per cent as the plan depth is much less than office
right: with solar glass façade heat gain is reduced by the shading coefficient of the glass, usually additional systems are needed such as internal blinds to reduce radiation from the surfaces

climatic response of the building. These zones extend inwards and outwards from the line of enclosure. The inward zones comprise the main active and passive zones. The passive zone is defined in terms of the degree to which the external environmental affects the internal environment without the use of energy systems. Factors affecting the extent of the passive zone are complex but mainly related to transparency and opacity of the wall, as well as ceiling height.[3] As a rule of thumb the passive zone can be thought to extend internally to a point equal to twice the ceiling height, given high levels of transparency and opacity in the line of enclosure. The openings in the roof extend the passive zone, through the provision of light and ventilation. The notion of the passive zone and active zone is more commonly applied to air-conditioned building where the passive zone is used to moderate energy consumption but can be applied to free running buildings. The main parameters for calculation of the extent of the passive zone is related to the exclusion of heat, degree of opacity and transparency as well as the amount of casual heat gains from occupants and equipment.[4] Thus the concept of the passive zone requires careful application and critique in the context of warm climate free-running buildings.[5] It might be that the buildings defined as passively cooled may not provide constant performance and therefore the extent of the performance limitations should be articulated through a defined period of overheating. This may or may not be acceptable to clients and therefore the alternative strategies should be considered.

Within the passive zone a further subdivision is found, that of the enclosure zone, immediately adjacent to the line of enclosure.[6] This zone is approximately one to two metres in depth and is the zone most exposed to the external climate dependent on transparency of the line of enclosure. The

7.5 *Façade of the Federal Law Courts, Brisbane, this wall faces west and there is a need to provide views from the judges' chambers behind the façade; a number of strategies are used, first the glazing ratio is reduced, second, openings to west are shaded with solar glass to maintain views and third some openings are rotated to the south to give a better solar orientation*

active zone is the area of the building not influenced by the environmental effects of the external wall or openings in the roof, normally conditioned by active systems.

Moving out from the line of enclosure two zones are defined, the buffer zone and the environmental zone. The buffer zone is that immediately adjacent to the line of enclosure. This zone gives a level of protection to the line of enclosure dependent on depth and transparency. Effects of adjacent buildings and landscape can also effect the response of the wall, this is area can be defined as the environmental zone.

The design challenge is to understand the effects of these zones on the design and response of the wall. The climate design objective is to minimize heat gain from solar access whilst also providing maximum daylight by diffused light. Direct sunlight will increase heat gain and glare, diffused light provides light without the heat of direct sunlight. In addition, the minimization of rain penetration yet still providing ventilation is an additional objective. These performance requirements can be met by a number of wall types, the conceptually simplest type is the thin skin.

7.3 Thin skins

Thin skins are wall elements that essentially rely on the materials rather than buffering to shade the building to effect climate modification. Solar gain to the interior in transparent elements is accommodated through the glazing technology, whilst with the opaque elements different methods of insulation are used to prevent heat gain.

Opaque elements

The main performance requirements to walls depends on the method of cooling used in the building. The wall construction will have some generic characteristics to prevent heat gain but also specific characteristics to accommodate the temperature differences that occur between inside and out. With passive systems, which rely on ventilation for cooling, the best that can be achieved is to keep the internal air at ambient. The wall works primarily to resist heat gain rather than maintain a temperature difference between inside and out. Hence, to prevent moisture penetration, without shading to walls, the main strategy is to reflect heat and to reduce transmission through the wall. The key tactics for free-running buildings are as follows:

7.6 *Thin skin strategies used in tall buildings to minimize solar gain also reduces daylight penetration causing energy inefficiencies*

- use highly reflective and light coloured materials which reflect heat from the building and reduce surface temperatures
- use interstitial insulation, in particular the use of double-sided reflective foil, bulk insulation can be used but it may resist cooling at night if there is little insulation
- use bulk insulation in solar exposed areas such as west and east walls to prevent peak heat gain from low-angle sun

In air-conditioned buildings the opaque elements have to resist not only heat gain but also maintain temperature and humidity control between inside as well as provide for a level of energy efficiency. In addition to the above requirements the following should be considered:[8]

- the need for bulk insulation with a thermal rating of R 3. This will reduce the rate of heat transfer into the building
- a vapour barrier to be installed on the warm side of the wall to prevent interstitial condensation and vapour movement from outside to in. The vapour pressure difference caused by the set point is problematic. The set point temperature of the air-conditioned air is likely to be 55 per cent humidity and 24 degrees C for internal air temperature which is well below the ambient conditions for warm climates
- provision of air seals in windows and vapour barriers to prevent condensation points and air infiltration. Cold bridge can occur where cool parts of the building meet warm air causing internal 'rain' which reduces the efficiency of insulation and the deterioration of services as well as interior finishes. Similar problems occur with transparent elements but the problem is more complex as these elements requires the admittance of light without heat

Transparent elements

With transparent elements a number of issues are found which affect the design of the external wall. The main issue is related to the optical properties of glass and the trapping of heat inside a space due to the 'greenhouse effect'. Glass will admit the shortwave radiation but is opaque to longwave radiation and ultraviolet. There are two components to the 'greenhouse effect,' the radiant and convection component.[9] The shortwave component of light will pass through glass, be absorbed by internal objects and re-radiated. The longwave radiation is trapped by the glass and thus the temperatures will rise. This will increase unless convection of heat occurs which removes the excess heat. This radiant heat trap is a benefit in cool climates but problematic in warm climates. The result has been to beat the radiant trap by increasing the reflectance and reducing the transmission of glass through the use of specialized solar glasses.[10]

In recent years a common strategy has been to take advantage of the technical development in solar glass and the framing systems that have been advanced to support them in a thin skin system. The all too familiar mirror glass tower has become a feature of the city. The use of these types of glass has come about due to their shading efficiency. Three main types of solar glass are commonly used:

- heat absorbing
- heat reflecting
- hybrids which use composite layers of absorbing and reflecting glasses as well as coatings of low emissivity glasses (i.e. glass that have little re-radiation to the interior spaces)

The efficiency of these types of glass is dependent on the angle of solar radiation. This is called the angular dependency. For high-altitude sun, the rays are oblique to the vertical surface of the glass and thus more heat is reflected whilst with low angles the sun is normal to the glass giving less reflection and more transmission. In these lower angles of incidence the absorption of the glass is critical to the reducing heat gain.

There are two issues that are important with solar glass, first the shading coefficient and the light transmission. The shading coefficient is relative to the solar heat gain for a particular glass. It is possible to attain shading coefficients with these types of glass from manufacturers and assess the relative performance for solar heat gain. The lower the coefficient the better the performance, thus absorption glasses achieve shading coefficients of 0.70 to 0.60 as compared to 0.98 for clear float glass. The hybrids and reflective glasses are better in the range of 0.26 to 0.56. Yet the concern is that the shading of the glass also reduces the amount of light available for daylighting. Thus the reflecting glasses reduce light transmittance to 20–50 per cent whilst the absorbing glasses only reduce transmission by 60–80 per cent. If the need for daylighting is included, in theory it is possible to use smaller areas of absorbing glass and still achieve the same performance as larger areas of reflecting glass.

Alternatively the hybrid forms of glasses are used particularly in air-conditioned buildings in a double glazed assembly. In hot humid climates there is a tendency for single glazing to have condensation on the outside of the glass due to low surface temperatures. Two panes of glass are used, an outer pain of solar control glass with low emissivity coat on the inside surface. This re-radiates heat absorbed by the glass. The inner glass plane and the cavity prevent heat transfer from the cool interior pane thus keeping the outside pane at a temperature below the dew point. The increased technical complexity of these glasses increases the U-value of the glazed area and gives improved thermal performance.[12]

Finally, in recent years the development of 'smart' glasses which have the potential to offer variable shading effects due to changeable properties of the glass itself are being developed. Thus, the transmission of the glass can be varied dependent on the solar conditions.[13]

There have been a number of arguments for and against the use of solar glass. First, one of the main advantages comes from the economic and planning efficiency. In commercial buildings where the economic return is based on the lettable floor area maximum return is gained form building the maximum volume. Therefore, where there are planning controls that require specific setbacks and volume boundary constraints the use of a thin skin can achieve considerable savings in floor area. Arguments against the issue of thin skins comes from the resulting environment and building servicing issues associated with this kind of technology.

Environmental effects of thin skins

The environmental conditions inside a building can be defined as the resulting from both internal air temperatures and radiant heat gains from the outside. This is particularly important in offices where there are large areas

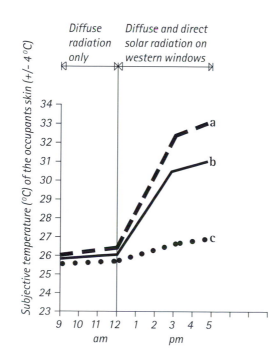

7.7 *A study of the effects of radiant heat on mean radiant internal temperatues in a Sydney office during the summer, after Harkness:*

a exposed to direct solar radiation through unshaded clear glass

b exposed to direct solar radiation through unshaded green, heat-absorbent glass;

c clear glass shaded from direct solar radiation

of glass and thus transparency. The radiation heat gains in this condition is important, particularly for occupants adjacent to the glass who can experience the radiant heating effect.

One concept that is useful in describing these phenomena is the term environmental temperature. Harkness has defined environmental temperature as the effective temperature felt by an individual in a space. [14] This results from the following:

- air temperature
- rate of air movement
- radiation effects

The first two factors are commonly associated with the designing of buildings but the effect of radiation is often ignored as it is difficult to quantify. This problem is particularly acute in high-rise office buildings where there is economic pressure to use space efficiently. In this case occupants of office buildings who sit directly next to windows that admit direct sunlight perceive a higher temperature than those sitting in other parts of the building away from the windows. This effect is caused even if solar glass is used to control admittance. With these types of glass there is still a radiation effect from the glass surface. This is independent of air-conditioning used since this controls air temperature but cannot alter radiation effects.

The reason for this is the way radiant heat strikes the skin and the consequent subjective experience of temperature felt by individuals. A useful way of measuring this is to combine the psychological effects of radiation with the Sol-air temperature. The Sol-air temperature is derived from combining air temperature with an equivalent-air-temperature-effect of the solar energy incident on the building. In this way, in an air-conditioned building, a reduction in air temperatures can be made to offset radiant heat gains to occupants.

Studies have been made of the implications of this on the design of different types of wall element and the likely effect on subjective skin temperatures. This indicated that for a December day in Sydney, solar radiation level on clear glass gave a subjective skin temperature of 33 degrees C. With green heat absorbing glass a slight reduction to 31 degrees C was found and for shaded clear glass, nearly 27 degrees C. Clearly, these temperatures exceeded the thermal comfort level and suggest that in order to reduce subjective skin temperatures air-conditioning temperatures have to be reduced further. Yet, it has been argued that air-conditioning cannot effectively control radiant gains and also reducing air-conditioned air temperatures influences cooling plant size and energy use. [15]

The solution is to shade against the direct component of solar radiation although it should be noted that diffuse radiation may still give a subjective temperature to the skin higher than the internal air temperature. To gain optimum performance, the configuration of the wall form is dependent on its solar orientation and the degree to which it is shaded from both rain and sun and the materials of its construction. The designer has considerable opportunity to manipulate these aspects to optimize the thermal performance of the building and provide a durable building fabric. Yet this is not an easy task. High levels of solar exposure and rain induce wear to the fabric of wall. Also there is a large solar heat gain in the mass of the wall which can be transmitted to the interior spaces.

This form of wall is by definition simply a skin of material that acts as a climatic filter. It is the most difficult to design technically and climatically because of its exposure. The materials of its construction, its joints and openings all have to take the full force of the climate. As discussed earlier it is difficult to use this type of wall in the poorest solar aspect, east or west. One solution is to simply make these walls opaque or use vertical sun breakers with limited views and insulate the opaque components to prevent heat gain. The greater challenge is to use some form of vision panel in the wall to break the mass and to provide glimpses out of the building. This approach is taken with the Federal Law Courts in Brisbane. The building faces south with views to the west across the Brisbane River. Views from the judicial quarters are provided through west-facing vision panels. A reduction of heat gain is required in the form of vertical louvres yet if these were to be made opaque this would limit the view. Using double-glazed windows and external shading of vertical solar glass achieve a compromise. Internal louvres are also used to assist with solar control.

Precast concrete panels are used with a cavity to improve resistance to heat transmission. Lightweight construction is used for interior walls thus giving a buffer effect to solar gain and minimizing the heat load for air-conditioning.

7.4 Inclined and orientated skins

The wall element can be inclined and orientated independent of the building

7.8 *Inclined walls in the Malay house to promote ventilation and reduce sky glare in roof mezanines*

7.9 *Incline glazing can be used as a shading facility but it also can cause unwanted reflections:*
left: reflections from this awning cause spectral reflections
right: this building receives the reflection although a veranda is used to control solar gain

7.10 *Incline glazing is used in this car show room:*
left: the façade is orientated west and thus receives low-angle sun. A combination of shading devices are used including inclined glazing, a large parasol roof and horizontal shades are used
right: reflections from the inclined glazing can also interrupt vision to the interior

structure. The inclination of the wall can be tilted away from the vertical or rotated horizontally to improve the thermal performance. This has the beneficial effect of improving performance for the wall, providing ventilation and providing views from the building. Three cases are examined, the first concerns the use of opaque materials and the other two the use of transparent materials.

In the Malay house the building structure comprises a post and beam frame. The roof is supported from the frame and is steely pitched to create an attic space under the roof. Large gables are placed at each end of the attic space. Ventilation to the attic space is provided through the gable walls. These walls are split into segments which are inclining and displaced. Openings are created that give the effect of a horizontal slit ventilator. This has two functions, first, preventing low-angle sun from penetrating the attic and second, providing ventilation. The horizontal slit ventilators also allow views from the attic down into the open space surrounding the building. This downward direction of view reduces sky glare. Hot air from inside the attic can diffuse out through the horizontal openings whilst rain cannot penetrate into the attic, thus giving to permanent ventilation into the building.[16]

In the next case the same approach is taken but with transparent glazing as a method of shading and controlling heat gain. This is based on the principle of increasing the reflectance of the glass by increasing the slope of the

glass plane away from the sun. Where the sun's rays are at 80 degrees to the glass then there will be little reflection, where it is oblique there is a large degree of reflectance. The resulting angularity reduces the angle incidence of the sun's rays and thus increases the reflectance. This forms a transparent shading device. The important feature of this strategy is that the angle of inclination of the glazing is not an arbitrary decision but specific to the solar geometry of a particular latitude and to the location on the façade of the building. Thus, like opaque shading, to optimize the shading effect the vertical sun angles should be used to determine angles of the glazing and the relative efficiency of the shading.

As was seen in the earlier discussion of the effects of glazing the amount of reflection is not a linear relationship to the angle of incidence. The use of reflection is only specific to high angles of incidence. For example with clear float glass and an angle of incidence of 80 degrees, 52 per cent is reflected, 6 per cent absorbed and 42 per cent transmitted. On the other hand, with an angle of incidence of 30 per cent, absorption is the same but reflection is reduced to 8 per cent whilst transmission is 86 per cent. This gives an 80/50 rule, below 80 degrees reflection drops in favour of transmission.[16] This suggests that for warm climates where there are high sun angles, this approach can be used to promote shading.

The application of this strategy requires the consideration of a number of factors. First, the calculation of the degrees of inclination needed to the glass for the particular orientation of the façade. Second, the selection of solar glasses which have a lower shading coefficient thus increasing daylight. Third, the consideration of the effects of reflection from the glass such as mirror and spectral effects. Therefore, reflections of this kind may cause visual glare and problems of vision through the glass.

The application of this approach for a north-facing façade in Brisbane three conditions can be compared, summer and winter solstice, and the equinox. The effective solar angle can be obtained by adding the angle of inclination of the glass to the solar angle. From this a qualitative analysis of efficiency can be made by comparing to the 80/50 rule. An application of this approach is found in the Concourse building in Singapore. This is a 41 storey office tower which uses tilted glass to minimize solar radiation. The angle of inclination of the glass is approximately 30 degrees which gives a shading efficiency of 60 per cent.[17] Also, like the Malay house, this directs the view downwards and reduces glare.

This approach has also been used in Brisbane at the Audi Car Showrooms. In this case a large shading roof provides an awning for cars, but the building is orientated north-west. This causes problems of low angled sun in the afternoon. A combination of shading devices and angled glazing is designed to reduce the heat gain.

7.5 Thick skins

Thick skins are those which use depth in the façade and projections to achieve

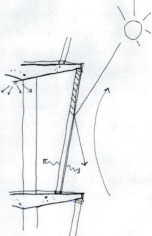

7.11 *Section through an inclined glazed façade, to achieve 50 per cent reflection the glazing should be inclined to an angle of incidence of 80 degrees*

7.12 *Grovenour Place, Sydney, Harry Seidler: the thick skin is formed by shading devices, the angle of these shades are varied around the façade depending on orientation*

7.13 *Deep skin façades use a buffering strategy:*
top: Menara Mesenaga building by Ken Yeang, Kuala Lumpur, the use of shading and shy courts for energy efficiency and providing amenity for office personnel at high level
right: the traditional recessing of windows and façades in this Victorian building
below: section through a deep skin façade showing the use of planting for buffering

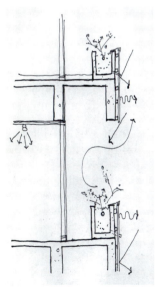

a shading effect from the sun. There are different methods which can be used to achieve this depending on orientation, thus for high sun angles horizontal shades are used whilst for low sun angles vertical shades are used. The principle method of protecting the interior spaces from high sun angles that is for the north-south orientation, is to buffer the glazed areas. These glazed areas are called vision panels, as their main purpose is to provide light and view out from the building.

Protection to the vision panels can be achieved by thrusting sun breakers out from the wall or recessing the panel back from the wall. Harry Seidler uses the former in the Riverside high-rise office building in Brisbane. The sun breakers are made of aluminium in a foil shape and are held away from the building on brackets. The angle of the foil is such that it achieves optimum direct shading to the vision panels and maximum daylight penetration to the space inside the building. The angle of these foils, that is the pitch, also changes with the face of the building thus ensuring equal protection to all office spaces.

An alternative to using sun breakers is to recess the vision panel. An extreme case of this is found in the Menara Boustard high-rise office building in Kuala Lumpur designed by Ken Yeang. The plan of the building is designed according to optimum orientation. The core of the building is placed to the west to block sun from the poorest solar aspect. Flush curtain walling is placed to the north where the solar aspect is best, in the remaining parts of the plan glazing is recessed to form a balcony this is planted. The use of recessed glazing forms a buffer zone but instead of using sunshades the balcony creates the shading effect. This is achieved by planting and by the use of opaque balcony walls. These are used like fins on a motor bike cylinder head to dissipate heat that strikes the surface of the balcony.

A number of thermodynamic principles are used here. A heat sink effect is used to insulate the building. As sunlight strikes the surfaces it is absorbed by the balcony. It is of sufficient mass to absorb all radiation during the day without transferring heat to the interior of the building. During the night heat is radiated back to the atmosphere. This heat transfer is assisted by the free flow of air around the balcony which also draws heat out of the thermal mass. Finally, plants contribute to the heat loss, the evaporation from the plants causes cooling. The effectiveness of this is difficult to gauge, although studies have shown that the evaporative cooling from plants does affect cooling loads on buildings. The recessing of glazing in this way seems to have a considerable advantage not only in terms of thermal dynamics but also as it creates an external space at high level that Yeang argues has many advantages to office users, providing them with considerable amenity.

The final type of wall element is to create a perforated wall as a boundary between inside and out. This can be designed as the only form of enclosure or a secondary element built in front of the line of enclosure. The function of this type of wall is similar to that of the recessed glazing. The main aim is to break the direct force of the sun and in this way only a proportion of the sunlight will penetrate. The contrast between the light and dark. The designer has two options here, to focus on the shape and pattern of the screen or on the kind of pattern that this creates on the floor or surface of the wall.

One application where the designer has focused on the pattern of the wall is in the external walls of the Diabumi building in Kuala Lumpur. In this case an aluminium screen is formed into Islamic motifs which provide the sunshade to the curtain wall behind. Views out and the admittance of daylight are filtered by the screen. Even so the use of the perforated wall as an architectural device and for sunshade is well integrated in this case.

Shading types, lighting and cooling load

As seen in the foregoing discussion, the configuration and construction of the wall contributes to reducing cooling load in the building and consequently the amount of ventilation or the size of air-conditioning plant required. With a glazing ratio 50 per cent and higher, the major heat load will

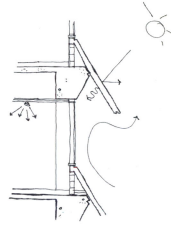

7.14 *200 Mary Street, Brisbane, Geoffry Pie, Architect and Planners, 1984. The section shows the heat sink shading made of reinforced concrete panels. The panels and concrete floor act as a heat sink absorbing solar radiation during the day and radiating to the exterior at night. The high levels of shading require the use of artificial light inside the building*

7.15 *Diabumi building, Kuala Lumpur, Malaysia, the use of the perforated wall to act as a sun screen*

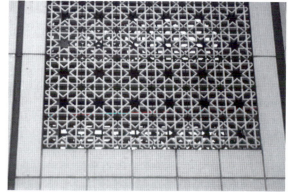

7.16 *This section shows methods of using shading to diffuse and direct light. This type of light guiding system offers a way to reduce the demand of artificial light. In this case the artificial lights are directed upwards and use the ceiling as a luminair, thus complementing the daylighting. The added technical complexity of the system can add cost to the skin and with the present low cost of energy, this works against these more innovative energy saving systems. In addition this type of system is orientation dependent*

7.17 *Problems of daylighting to office buildings is seen by comparing the deep skin of 200 Mary Street, Brisbane, with Waterfront Place, a thin skin building which uses solar glass. In both cases the high shading effects necessitate artificial lighting. The irony is that daylighting levels to the exterior of the building are abundant yet this resource appears not to be used*

come from the solar load and is the dominant load for cooling. Yet the problem is that the cooling load from the skin will vary with different orientation and time of the day. For an Equator-facing façade which is designed effectively it can be only a small part of the cooling load, contribution to about one-quarter of the overall cooling load. This is less than for the temperate climate as solar angles are higher.[18]

The important question is the amount of shade that is needed and design of the shading system. From the quantitative point of view there are many design tools that can establish the geometric properties of the shading device based on the solar angles for the climate.[19] These are designed to minimize direct solar radiation. Some research has pointed to the need to design shades not just from the point of view of solar gain control but also according to other criteria. These criteria include the need for maximizing daylight to reduce the need for artificial light but also to allow for greater user control of the environmentally systems.[20]

This research has begun to identified different types of shading device and the extent to which a contribution is made to reducing solar gain and enhancing natural light.[21]

1. Solar blocking devices
2. Solar and light blocking
3. Solar blocking and light enhancing systems

The first type simply blocks solar penetration. An example of this is the use of blinds. These can provide a useful device that has user control. They can be removed in cloudy conditions and applied when there is solar access. This gives the potential to provide a shading system that is flexible for the periodic heat gain and give users a level of control over the environmental systems to provide natural light. The installation of this kind can provide a 40 per cent shading from solar gain. The system is usually installed internally which is less effective as sunlight is allowed into the building and the heat is trapped. Alternatively, the blinds can be installed in a glass cavity to minimize this problem.[22]

The second type reduces solar gain and blocks sunlight to give full shad-

ing. Highly reflective solar glasses with low transmission rates are examples of this type. The low levels of light transmission means that they are very similar to opaque walls. These devices do not contribute effectively to the natural lighting of the building.

The third type, on the other hand, provides a solution. The shade can be formed into a light-guiding device which reduces the excess illumination at the window and gives a more even distribution across the room. This approach has potential in warm climates where high angles of sun can be diffused by the light shelf and directed to the interior. The saving in energy from the reduction of electric light from this type of system is an added advantage.[23] The application of these types of system depends on orientation and solar geometry. Yet the use of light guiding systems for low-angle sun may be problematic as there is insufficient solar heat control. Thus, the use of the second type of vertical shade which is a blocking system may be the only alternative. It is therefore necessary to use these methods of shading not as stereotype solutions but as strategies which the designer can test and, through the process of design, judiciously apply.

7. 6 Optimum orientation, environmental and building buffering

An early step in the design of the wall element is to examine the building context. It is useful to assess the effects of environmental shading of the wall and reflection to the building from other buildings and the extent to which buffering can be used to minimize solar access.

Solar access is the term given to the degree of solar penetration in a building. In cool climates this is often seen as a considerable advantage to provide winter heating. In moderate climates this can also be an advantage;

7.18 *Office with a plan depth of 10 m of open space from the skin, provide problems of view and lighting to the interior areas. The lighting levels are high at the edge at the skin and low in the interior giving a large variation. This combined with the shading systems increases rather than decreases the passive zone thus increasing energy use. Light shelves can more evenly distribute light across these larger plan depths and increase the passive zone*

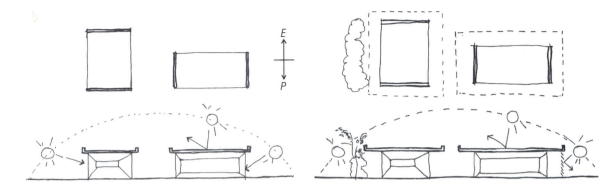

7.19 *Diagram of the effects of minimizing solar access by using optimum orientation:*
left: use of thin plan with shorter opaque walls facing east and west,
right: use of roof overhangs and environmental shading through landscape to minimize solar access

in the winter months heating in the early morning or late afternoon may be required, but in summer there is a need to prevent solar access. In hot climates that are in heat surplus all year round, walls in combination with the roof seek to prevent solar access. A number of strategies can be found to achieve this goal.

Optimum orientation

The first strategy is to establish a direct relationship between the wall and the sun that minimizes solar access by using optimum orientation. Fry and Drew point out that a wall unexposed to the sun remains at shade temperature which is the lowest possible temperature.[24] Furthermore, by not receiving solar heat gain, the wall will not transmit heat to internal spaces.

The use of optimum orientation is a planning strategy that seeks to manipulate the building shape and form to minimize the area of wall surface

7.20 *Plan of the Kempsey Museum showing optimum orientation*

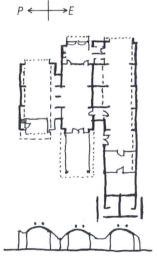

exposed to the sun. The premise is that a wall element that is orientated to the low-altitude sun, east or west is more exposed than a wall that is orientated to the north or to the south. This is due to the angle of incidence of the sun's rays; these rays are lower striking the wall closer to right angles. This proportionally generates more heat than the latter where the rays are more oblique to the surface of the wall. Placing shorter opaque walls to the east and west (maximum solar heating) and longer transparent walls to the north and south (minimum solar heating) is an optimum strategy.

Buffering and environmental shading

In addition the transparency in walls will require shading, this is where a further strategy is used that is by buffering and environmental shading. This involves placing a screening system of building elements or landscaping around the building to create shade. Thus the use of trees and adjacent buildings can effectively shade or shadow parts or all of the building. In urban areas the use of tall buildings to shade the site can be an advantage in summer but also prevent winter heating. Yet it can be argued that buffering of this kind incurs a cost penalty and it is suggested that optimum orientation of the building is a better strategy to minimize exposure of the walls to the adverse solar aspects.

These two strategies of optimum orientation and use of environmental and building shading are used at the Kempsey Museum by Glen Murcutt. The building, a small rural museum, is located in a farming town on the New South Wales coast.[25] It is designed as a series of linked rectangular pavilions with their long sides facing north and south. These pavilions provide a museum space and a tourist centre. The north-south building section is symmetrical in structure, formed from a tubular steel frame with supporting brick bays. The building skin is made mainly of corrugated iron and glass and is supported by the frame. The wall element seems to blend with the roof, both are made of corrugated iron and it is difficult to see where one starts and the other finishes.

7.21 *Kempsey Museum, Australia, Glen Murcutt*
left: the east elevation receives low-angle sun, the glazing ratio is minimized
right: a small vision panel is used to provide views yet reduces heat gain, glare is reduced by increasing internal illumination through the high lights above the window

Kempsey lies in the moderate coastal zone on the eastern coast of Australia. There is a need for winter heating and summer cooling, and the building aims to achieve this by passive means through the flexibility of the wall. In this context flexibility means the use of static as well as movable elements in the building to achieve what Fry describes as a 'collaboration with nature'.[24] To this end the need for solar access is achieved by careful design of the polar- and Equator-facing section. The building planning is advantageous with the long axis east-west and long walls facing north and south with smaller walls facing east and west. This optimizes solar gain in winter yet minimizes the buildings exposure to the solar heat gain in summer.

In addition, it is placed in a forest setting thus providing environmental shading to the building. Furthermore, buffering is used in certain parts of the building plan. The public entrances are all recessed back from the roof to create porches. These are found on the southern edges of the building and also to the east. The main entrance to the east is a good example. The building structure comprises a steel frame and at the entrance one structural bay is clad only with roofing panels. This makes an ideal entrance porch and is deep enough to prevent easterly sun from penetrating the building. As a consequence the line of enclosure is only a single glass curtain, thus minimizing the distinction between inside and out.

For buffering to be effective, that is to provide a shaded space between inside and out, careful understanding of solar angles is required. The daily solar path and also off the effect of changes to that path over the course of the year should be examined. Ray tracing diagrams are required to mark the point of maximum solar penetration at the equinoxes. This kind of precise concern for the location of the sun in relation to the building is a major generator in the building design. In this sense the building becomes a sundial, it is precisely orientated to respond to buffering and environmental shading to accept or exclude sunlight at different times of the day.

7.22 *Kempsey Museum by Glen Murcutt showing the westerly elevation of the pavilion:*
left: the diffusing effect of lattice sun breaker
right: the lattice sun breaker reduces the amount of light and heat from the westerly sun

The building as a sun dial

The design premise here is that the designer needs to know where the sunlight will fall at various times of the day and the year for a given site. It does not necessarily mean using strategies of minimizing solar access or buffer zones to the building. Rather it suggests that the designer make precise judgements where the sun will be at a particular time of year, where it will fall on the wall or floor and openings, and what architectural and thermal effects this creates. Therefore the form and shape of the walls takes on the characteristic of a sundial, for each orientation a different configuration will be found. In this way the sun begins to animate the different faces of the building and can be allowed to penetrate into the spaces at different times of the day. The importance of this is that the building becomes a climatic reference point, which is experientially significant for the occupants.

At the Kempsey this idea will be seen more clearly. A detailed study of the east-west and the northwest sections is required. Each gable is treated differently and most form entrance or exit points to the building. Two gables admit light into the interior. To avoid large heat gains this is achieved by a number of techniques. In the first case a lattice screen is used on the exterior of a glazed wall, reducing the amount of westerly sun and also creating a grid silhouette inside the building. It is this feature that terminates the long gallery space of the main pavilion of the museum. One other pavilion has a gable facing east. In this case glazing is in strip form high up under the roof overhang so light is abruptly cut off. Additional glazing is reduced to a small picture window that provides views from the building. It is deep set and does not cause glare.

The strategies of using optimum orientation with shading can be used to selectively admit light into a building. These strategies of minimizing the solar aspect can be justified on functional and efficient planning grounds.

7.23 *Buffering effects used at the entrance to the building* [23]

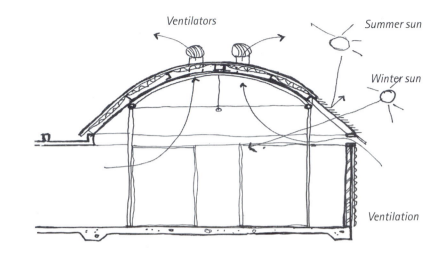

Ventilators

Summer sun

Winter sun

Ventilation

7.24 *Section through the Kempsey Museum showing valve effects for winter and summer mode*

Buffering can also be used but this has been criticized especially where a veranda is used around the occupied space thus equally shading all the walls and openings. This minimizes the need to consider appropriate solar orientation. The chief reasons for concern are the effects of lighting caused by the addition of the veranda. The veranda can cause dark and gloomy interior rooms and in addition, the function of the verandah is often not clearly defined, resulting in utilitarian functions such as storage.[25]

Yet the concept of buffer zoning is therefore, indicated by the use of architectural elements such as primary roofs or secondary roofs placed around the occupied space. The important technical significance is that it not only frees the wall from heat gain but also protects the wall from rain. This gives the designer considerable flexibility in the design and construction of the wall. Its function now becomes reduced to providing ventilation, security and defining the view. A less extensive form of buffering is found in thick skin systems.

7.7 Valve effects

The use of the wall element to control the internal environment can be likened to a valve, apertures in the skin can be opened and closed, filtered and directed to allow air and light to pass through. The valve effects are the nuances in wall design creating both thermal comfort and visual delight. There is usually a balance between static and dynamic elements.

In conventional wall design there is usually a static element, usually the wall, and an active element, usually the window. The window provides view, light and ventilation. Curtains moderate the penetration of light and improve the thermal efficiency of the window. The wall is opaque and is a thermal barrier. Improved response to the environment comes from a more precise use of these static and dynamic elements.

A closer examination of the Kempsey Museum illustrates this complex

relationship well. Roof lights on the Equator face selectively bring heat and daylight into the space. This is achieved through external diffusing horizontal fins. They are tuned to the solar angles to admit sunlight in winter but exclude and diffuse it in the summer. The effect in winter is to create a broken ribbon of sunlight onto the floor. This sun patch charges the air and the slab with heat providing the winter heating. The effect in summer is to exclude direct solar gain and to promote cooling through high level ventilation through air vents in the roof and walls. This configuration allows the wall to be used for display. Thermal siphoning of air removes environmental and internal heat gain through high level vents

The wall element as well as controlling the admittance of sun into the building also controls the infiltration of air. The purposeful infiltration of air is called 'ventilation.'

7.25 *Kempsey Museum, technology and detailing of the façade and shin to achieve the vale effects:*
left: ventilators on the roof remove unwanted heat
right: sunshades are angled to reflect sunlight in summer admit it in winter, ventilators at the eaves also allow for ventilation

References

1. M. Fry and J. Drew, *Tropical Architecture,* Batsford, 1954, p. 56.
2. J. R. Goulding (ed) et al, *Energy in Architecture. The European Passive Solar Handbook*, Commission of the European Community, The University of Dublin, 1993, p. 3.
3. N. Baker and T.C. Steemers, *LT Method version 2.0*, Cambridge Architectural Research, Martin Centre for Architectural and Urban Studies, University of Cambridge.
4. N. Baker et al, *Passive and Low Energy Design for Island Climates*, Commonwealth Science Council, London, 1987.
5. Baker and Steemers, op. cit. p. 5.
6. E.L. Harkness, *Precast Concrete Energy-Cost-Effective Building Façades*, Precast Concrete Manufacturers Association of New South Wales, Sydney, 1986, p. 2.

7.   Ibid.

8.   V. Keneally, 'An Introduction to Energy Efficiency in Air-conditioned Tropical Buildings', *Environmental Design Guide*, Royal Australian Institute of Architects, Canberra, 1997, Gen.14. p. 2.

9.   J. Greenland, *Foundations of Architectural Science*, University of Technology, Sydney, 1991, 3, p. 20.

10.   Ibid.

11.   D. Button and B. Pye et al, *Glass in Building*, Pilkington Glass and Butterworth, Oxford, 1993, p.160.

12.   Button and Pye et al, op. cit., p. 165.

13.   C. Kabre, 'Trends in Solar Glass Control in Contemporary Buildings,' in *Principles and Practice Conference*, Australian New Zealand Architectural Science Association, Department of Archicture, The University of Queensland, 1998, p. 18.

14.   Harkness, op. cit., p. 5

15.   Lim Jee Yuan, *The Malay House*, Institut Masyarakat, Pulau Penang, 1987, pp. 71 and 111.

16.   P. Holigan, 'Energy Loads in Buildings,' in *Asean-Australian, Energy Cooperation Program, Energy Conservation Program*, Energy Management Centre, Gas and Fuel Corporation of Victoria, 1985, p. 6.

17.   Kabre, op. cit., p. 22.

18.   Button and Pye, op. cit., p. 154

19.   B. Lim, 'Energy-efficient House Design, Natural Ventilation and Sun Protection' in *Design and Building of Energy-Efficient Houses*, papers presented at a seminar sponsored by the Energy Management Sub-program of the Queensland Department of Resource Industries, internal publication Queensland State Government, Brisbane, 1992.

20.   N. Baker and K. Steemers, 'Lt Method 3.0 – a Strategic Energy-Design Tool for Southern Europe.' in *Energy and buildings*, Vol. 23, 1996, pp. 254-255.

21.   Ibid.

22.   Button and Pye, op cit., p. 174.

23.   Baker and Steemers, op. cit., p. 255.

24.   Fry and Drew, op. cit.

25   See Chapter 6 for details of lighting in verandas.

Floors and internal walls CHAPTER 8

'Nest building is, in a way, a more advanced version of choosing a microclimate, An animal seeking out a rock crevice or hole in the earth as a place to rest and be cool is indeed seeking out a favourable microclimate. Digging the hole deeper and adding a bit of shed fur for insulation are simple improvements', Liza Heschong.[1]

8.1 Introduction

One of the basic ways of creating a favourable place to live is to use the structural and thermal stability of the earth. The qualities of thermal mass was known to the Egyptians who buried their kings and queens deep in 'super mass structures' where temperatures vary little over centuries. These structures replicate the thermal response of the earth. In this situation the floor elements and interior walls, as compared to the skin of a building, play a different role in the response of the building. Thus, a distinction can be made between the interior modifying as opposed to skin modifying buildings. In the interior modification process the construction and position of interior walls has a significant effect on moderating the building response. The objective for the designer is therefore to position interior elements such as floors and walls for maximum climatic effect. In addition the construction of these elements also has some bearing on the thermal response. Lighterweight elements such as timber floors or lightweight wall construction have less thermal mass and therefore are thought less efficient at heat storage.

Thus, the position of internal elements and the construction of the elements is one set of factors that should be considered in relation to the design and configuration of the floor. One other important factor is the relationship of floors to ground. The earth temperature has an effect on the temperature of the floors particularly those adjacent or connected to it. Earth has thermal mass; connecting floors to the earth means that floors behave thermally like the earth. In our archetypal temperate climate building, floors connected to the ground lose heat to the ground and represent a proportion of the heat lost from the skin.

Suspending the floor above the ground disconnects the floor from ground, but heat is still lost by ventilation depending on the insulation. In older buildings where this form of construction is common many will have witnessed the carpet rising from floor as the wind, forced through air vents, finds its way through cracks in the floorboards. The interconnection, there-

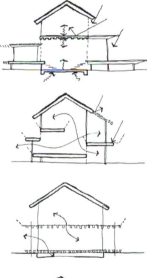

8.1 *Floor strategies:*
top: ground connected
high mass
low mass
middle: mezzanines
middle: perforated
bottom: integrated

8.2 *Floor as a separating element, the case of the thermally sensitive cat, moderate climates*

fore, between floor and ground, its construction in terms of position and ability to store heat, is a key factor. A number of floor strategies are identifiable:

- ground connected
- high mass
- low mass
- mezzanines
- perforated
- integrated

The first three strategies relate to the thermal performance issues concerned with the floor construction and position. The last three are related to the relationship between the floor and the comfort of occupants, and the way the floor and ceilings assist with lighting interior spaces. This response is illustrated by the work of Maxwell Fry. He made some useful observations in this respect,

'We had a cat in India that passed a lot of time under the shade of a proliferating green Koschia plant when the temperatures were over 100 degrees F, and she did that after a very thorough inspection of alternatives, and remained satisfied with her choice.'[2]

Clearly, if the Koschia plant is seen as the roof and the ground as the floor then a different architectural response to climate is found. At one level the cat is sheltering from the sun but it is also exposing its body to cool from the ground and from the breeze that travels over adjacent vegetation. The evaporative cooling from plants cools the breeze and thus optimizes the thermal environment. The tropical building can be viewed as providing a sheltering environment. The term sheltering here is used because it means the facility of the building to be proactive in relating occupants to climate rather than being reactive. Its function is to locate its occupants in space in such a

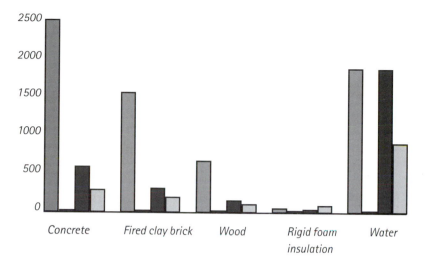

8.3 *Graphical representation of the factors concerning thermal performance of materials shown in Table 8.1: for each material the density, thermal conductivity, capacitance and thickness are shown. Note that concrete has high capacitance, high conductivity and high density which makes it ideal for thermal storage in floors and walls but less useful as an insulator. The converse is true for rigid foam*

Table 8.1 Thermal capacitance and thermal resistance

Material	Density, kg m²	Thermal conductivity, W mk (k)	Thermal capacitance, kJ m² k	Thickness, mm
Concrete	2400	2.1	576	240
Fired clay brick	1400	0.6	336	240
Wood	600	1.4	78	60
Rigid foam insulation	20	0.03	1.8	60
Water	1000	0.58	1008	240

way that it optimizes natural cooling, the key device in warm climate building is the floor. Thus, whereas in a temperate climate the floor is simply a functional response to activity and as a potential heat store, in a tropical climate it is a sophisticated and complex device that connects our bodies to the cooling influences of the climate.

The floor can therefore be defined as the positioning element that assists with location of occupants to maximize cooling.

8.2 The positioning element

In traditional buildings in warm climates the floors can usefully be conceived as platforms. Platforms comprise the floor surface on which we walk, when observed from below as the ceiling. We appreciate the ceiling visually but the floor has both a visual and tactile effect, particularly so if one walks on the floor barefoot. Conduction from the bare feet to the floor is a pleasurable part of living in the tropics and also serves to draw heat from the body. Subjectively, stone or ceramic feels cooler to the touch than timber. Often the materials are actually different in temperature. Stone, ceramics and concrete have larger thermal mass and so they often react more slowly to changes in temperature and therefore are and feel cooler than timber that is of a lower mass.

A useful example of a building that is conceived of as a series of platforms is the Inch house in Batu Pahat, Malaysia. It is built using a rationalized form of construction based on the traditional architecture of Malaysia but is designed on the basis of a series of platforms on three levels. The building is orientated north-south so that the major axis faces west and to the sea. The advantage is that the breezes flow in from the sea and across the platforms creating an appropriate thermal environment. This building will be examined in detail in this chapter as it exploits the floor platform principle in its various form.

8.4 *Inch house, c. 1990, the platform principles used to maximize thermal comfort by locating building occupants in positions to maximize access to breeze. The semi-outside sleeping area and the use of mezzanines within a large enclosure are useful strategies*

8.3 Ground-connected buildings

The relationship between the building and the ground plane occurs both within and outside the building.

Ground cover and landscape

The use of a timber deck on the ground plane is a useful device for reducing temperatures immediately around the building. Hard masonry surfaces retain heat and reflect it into buildings. Using other non-reflective materials is an answer. White gravel for example has a high surface area and also good reflectivity. Heat strikes these materials and is dispersed by reflection and convection. Timber is another useful material either in the form of slabs or as decks. At the Noble house, sleepers are used for paths and transition zones

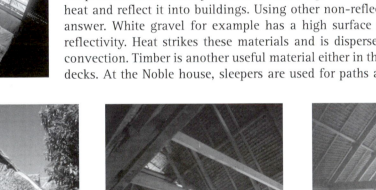

between the interior and the exterior.

The Clare house at Buderim, northern Queensland uses a series of timber ground decks for the entrance and to the northern side of the building. The thermal effect of this is discussed later. In this example the connection of the building to landscape must not be underestimated.

8.5 *Buderim house by Lynsey Clare: the house has a raised floor to provide ventilation under the building for cooling in summer*

Ground floor

The ground floor can either be suspended or engaged with the ground. The engaged effect with the ground is beneficial for a number of reasons. It means the floor temperature is related to ground temperature. For example, if the floor is shaded its surface temperature will be similar to the ground temperature, that is at or below the shade temperature. Raising the floor allows access to the breeze and makes the floor behave in correspondence

8.6 *High level platforms used in the Inche's house: dormer windows are used to provide view and ventilation*

8.7 *Noble house, non-reflective materials are used for the entrance path and in the surrounding landscape to reduce heat gain to the building*

with air temperature.

There is therefore a significant difference in the thermal performance of these two positions that is not appreciated. Often the floor systems are correlated to construction materials in terms of lightweight or heavyweight construction. As will be argued later, this approach to thinking can lead to a lack of understanding about how the building operates.

At the risk of overstating the obvious, the internal thermal environment of the building is a result of a number of factors but predominantly because of the external air temperature and solar radiation. The nature of this air in terms of its humidity and clarity is also critical. Dust in the wind of hot dry climates makes the use of the wind for ventilation difficult if not impossible whilst high humidity in the tropics can make it equally ineffective. Yet how does the building, particularly the floor, affect the thermal dynamics?

One of the key issues that dictates the thermal performance of the floor if not the building itself is its construction. A floor made of concrete will behave thermally in a different way to a floor made of timber. This is coupled with the degree to which it is exposed to direct solar gain and to the thermal regimes of the air and the ground surrounding or connecting to the floors. The understanding of this relationship is difficult without a holistic understanding of how elements respond in the prevailing thermal regime provided by the climate. First, though, what of the thermal behaviour of floor assemblies. The thermal behaviour of these assemblies is based on the thermal capacitance and thermal resistance. Resistance is used to denote the amount of heat flow through an assembly (m^{-2} K W), whilst capacitance describes the amount of heat stored or released (kJ m^{-2} K). Thus resistance is important where there are differences in temperature between floors and heat is transferred vertically through the section of the building. Capacitance is important where floors are used to absorb heat or release heat into spaces.

What is particularly interesting is that capacitance is related to the density of assemblies; the greater the density of the material the greater the capacitance. High-density assemblies such as masonry and concrete slabs

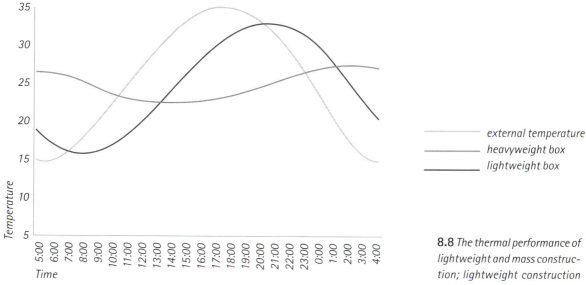

external temperature
heavyweight box
lightweight box

8.8 The thermal performance of lightweight and mass construction; lightweight construction with little insulation mirrors the outside temperature whilst the massive construction delays the heat gain and moderates internal temperatures

thus have greater capacitance. Since density is related to mass (kg m²), capacitance is therefore often called the 'thermal mass' of the assembly or building.[3]

Thermal mass

Thermal mass of a floor assembly is important because it is an important element that dictates the thermal response of the building and assists with ways of storing heat. An energy-efficient building employing solar design principles can use the sun's heat, taking advantage of the thermal mass to store heat and releasing this heat at night. Alternatively cooler temperatures at night can cool the thermal mass of the floor and assist with keeping the building cooler during the day. The main strategy with this approach is to manipulate the building structure to activate the high-density elements in the building in an appropriate manner to create an acceptable thermal regime. The term 'active thermal mass' is a more precise architectural term. If the thermal mass is not activated correctly it can have a reverse effect on the thermal regime.

Buildings in the hot humid tropics that are designed without appropriate climatic principles often do not activate mass properly. These buildings are usually made of reinforced concrete frame and masonry, thick concrete floors, and have low ceiling heights and small windows with little cross-ventilation. The high density of the structure of these buildings activates mass in the climatically wrong way, increasing temperatures and producing inappropriate architecture. Lack of ventilation at night means there is little opportunity for thermally discharging of heat in the structure so it does not cool. This creates high internal night temperatures and over time leads to a super-

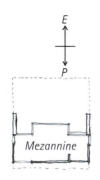

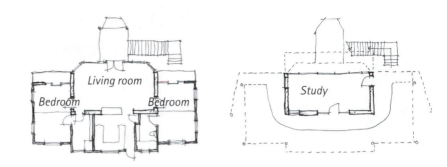

8.9 *Plans of Solar 1, by Peter Fries, designed by TVS partnership, Brisbane:*
right: ground floor
middle: first floor
left: second floor mezzanine
This building has a combination of mass and lightweight construction to suit the moderate climate; lightweight construction is used in the bedroom areas for summer cooling whilst more mass is used in the living and studio areas to moderate temperatures in winter

charged building particularly in the hot season.

To avoid these kinds of problems the floor should be used to position occupants to maximize cooling influences through ventilation or through activating thermal mass of the floor dependent on climatic opportunities. Decisions should be made with regard to thickness and density to control the amount of thermal capacity. In this respect floors can be used to influence the internal temperature. Designers should use either of two strategies:

- floors can act as thermal sinks by increasing density and thickness to adsorb or remove heat from the thermal regime, i.e. charging the floor with heat or coolth to moderate temperatures. The moderating effect usually results in a damping of temperature swings in the building
- floors can act as thermal diaphragms that, by decreasing density and reducing thickness, minimize the influence on the thermal regime inside the building. The consequence is that the floor does little to affect the fluctuations in temperature swings

8.4 Floors and walls as heat sinks

8.10 *The design of appropriate solar shading allows selective solar gain in moderate climates, sun is excluded in summer but accepted in winter allowing the charging of air*

Thermal damping is the influence of heat stored by an element in a building on its thermal regime. The element absorbs or loses heat when there is a temperature gradient between the element and the surrounding air. If the temperature is higher then the element will be 'charged' like a battery in a car but with heat rather than electricity. When the converse is found the element discharges heat to the surrounding air.[4]

Elements with high capacitance absorb quantities of heat which induces a lag in heat transfer and thus act partially to moderate heat gain. This process can be used as a form of insulation in walls to prevent heat gain but is not recommended as heat can be re-radiated at night to the interior structure. The process is more commonly used in floors as the input of heat into or extraction of heat from the element has a moderating effect on the internal thermal regime by reducing the variation in air temperatures.[5]

This process can be used effectively in subtropical buildings in winter. In

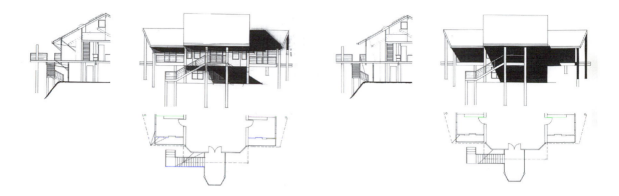

the following case study, Solar 1, a house has been designed to provide good solar access. The floor on the ground floor is concrete to provide thermal mass. This mass floor is charged when it receives direct solar gain in winter through north orientation and large areas of glass. Intermediate floors are made of timber and offer little insulation, thus heat can rise up through the building. Cross-walls of rammed earth are used to provide additional thermal mass.

The response of the building was examined for a seven-day period in the cool season, June to August. Measurements of temperatures at selected points across the section of the building were recorded automatically at intervals of 30 minutes The intention was to compare internal temperatures with shade temperatures to establish the building response. The results show that shade temperature gives highs of 20 degrees C at 14:00 hours with lows of 12 to 13 degrees C at around 05:00 hours. The prevailing weather pattern during this

8.11 *Solar 1, hybrid building containing both heavyweight and lightweight construction and located in a moderate climate; the shading study shows solar access:*
left: for winter, shading permits solar access for heating
right: for summer, shading prevents solar access for cooling

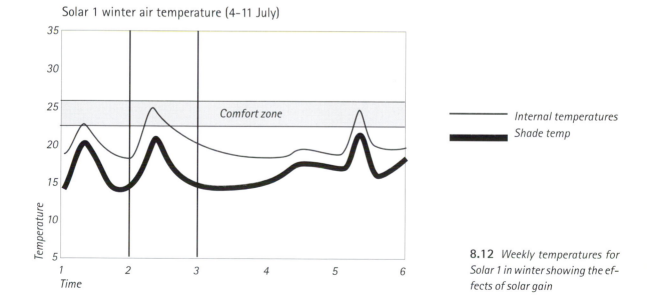

Solar 1 winter air temperature (4–11 July)

8.12 *Weekly temperatures for Solar 1 in winter showing the effects of solar gain*

Solar 1 winter air temperature

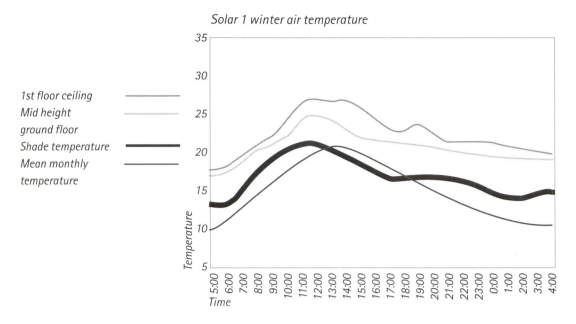

1st floor ceiling
Mid height ground floor
Shade temperature
Mean monthly temperature

8.13 *Solar 1: typical winter daily temperatures*

Winter wall surface temperatures day 2-3

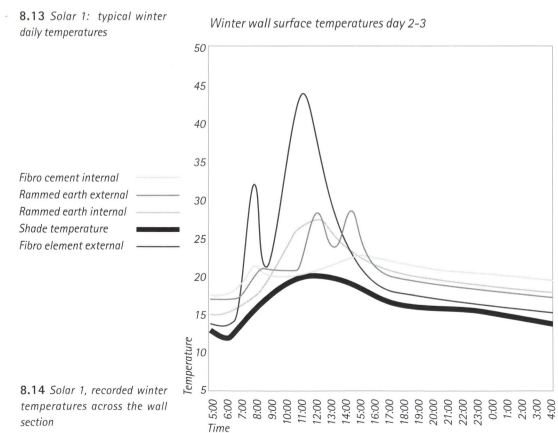

Fibro cement internal
Rammed earth external
Rammed earth internal
Shade temperature
Fibro element external

8.14 *Solar 1, recorded winter temperatures across the wall section*

period was clear sunny days and still cloudless nights. Much of the daily heat gain is re-radiated producing the cool or cold nights. The effect of solar gain on internal temperatures is seen by comparing the thermal signatures for days 1, 2, 5 and 6 which were clear and sunny, with days 3 and 4 that were cloudy. Even so, on cloudy days temperatures in the region of 18 degrees C were found, although shade temperatures were significantly lower.

In this case, the effect of thermal mass in the ground floor, in conjunction with the rammed earth walls, acts as a heat sink. The mass is 'charged' as it receives direct solar gain during the day. Heat can permeate vertically by conduction through the timber floor. It is interesting to note that there are specific times in the day when the building shifts from being interior to exterior dominant. During the day it is exterior dominant, receiving heat from the outside, whilst at night it is interior dominant using the effects of the storage of heat in interior elements. There are phase shift points, where the floor changes from discharging to charging and vice versa.

For a typical day these points are at 06:00 hours and 15:00 hours. Note the rapid acceleration of surface temperature of the ground floor and the

8.15 *Solar 1, ground floor slab and rammed earth walls are used as mass storage elements and are charged by direct solar gain and from the air*

8.16 *Solar 1, ection through Solar 1 showing the heat flow during the day and at night*

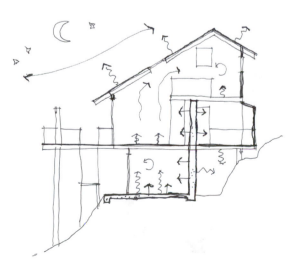

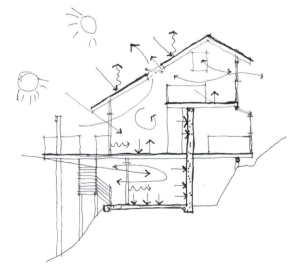

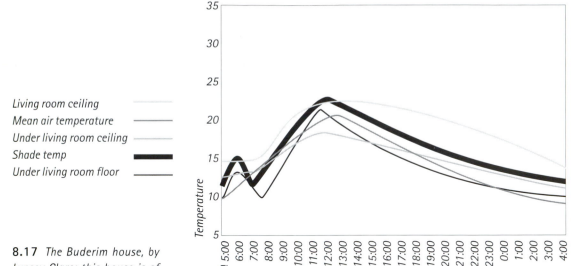

Living room ceiling

Mean air temperature

Under living room ceiling

Shade temp

Under living room floor

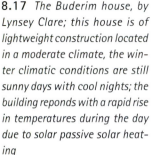

8.17 *The Buderim house, by Lynsey Clare; this house is of lightweight construction located in a moderate climate, the winter climatic conditions are still sunny days with cool nights; the building reponds with a rapid rise in temperatures during the day due to solar passive solar heating*

slower rate for the second-floor surface temperature. This is the result of less direct solar access to this floor. The daily thermal regime is influenced by solar gain until 14:30-15:00 hours, as the night regime sets in, the thermal mass starts to discharge heat into the space, keeping internal air temperatures at higher levels than external (shade) temperature.[6]

It is interesting to note that the effectiveness of mass storage relates to the amount of closure in the building and the containment of air. Where large areas of glass are used the heat loss through the skin can negate the heat gain from the mass. Also, if ventilation is present this will also negate the effect of the heat gain from the mass. Thus, there are also life style and behavioural consequences of using thermal storage to moderate temperatures. Occupants need to close the building to take full effect of the heat or coolth storage. This may be contrary to the conventional wisdom; while the convention is to close the building in cold weather, in warm weather the convention is to open the building to maximize ventilation. Thus to close the building to take advantage of the mass effect for cooling may be counter to the normal expectations and behavioural response of users.

6.5 Floors as thermal diaphragms

Floors that do not have thermal mass respond differently to temperature swings in the building. Rather than damping temperatures through absorbing or releasing heat they mirror the temperature swing. Thus we can see they act like a diaphragm, responding to temperature changes rather like the diaphragm in the ear which resonates to sound and enables us to hear.

The importance of thermal diaphragms is not often appreciated as ther-

mal mass is thought to be the most important aspect of moderating temperatures in buildings. The advantage of low-mass floors is that there is a resonance with the climate that allows buildings to rapidly increase temperatures
in winter.

A case study illustrates this well. This case study is of a house in Buderim,
Sunshine Coast, Australia. It was built in 1992 and won the House of the
Year award in Australia. The house is constructed using timber construction
with hardwood floors and corrugated iron for roofing and cladding to the
north and south walls. The interesting part of the building is orientation and
section. The building takes advantage of the good solar aspect by having the
long side facing to the northeast. This northeast face has a veranda attached
which acts as a buffer between inside and out. In winter direct sunlight is
prevented from entering the building; instead it strikes the timber deck and
is re-radiated into the house. The effect is to produce internal temperatures
4-5 degrees C warmer than shade temperature in winter.

These temperature profiles illustrate another effect of low thermal mass.
A characteristic of winter climates in Brisbane is the low night temperatures
but then sharp acceleration in temperature as the sun rises. With structures
that allow solar gain and have low mass, the internal temperatures begin to
follow the sharp acceleration in temperature. Thus, between dawn and 09:00
and 09:30 hours, the temperatures can rise by as much as 5-8 degrees C,
which gives an adequate internal temperature. A comparison of the house to
a normal timber frame house illustrates this point well. The normal timber-
framed house would also mirror the temperature swing, but if there is no
solar access temperatures will not accelerate in this way, and even the little
thermal mass will delay the internal heat gains.

The influence therefore of selective solar access in moderate climates is
important, the influence on floors with low-mass of temperature allows acceleration of daily temperatures. It should be noted that the low mass also
means that the floors mirror the drop in temperatures at night giving lower
temperatures.[7]

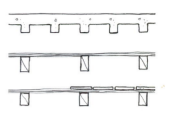

8.18 *Details of different floor
constructions:*

*top: heavyweight construction
using concrete, increasing the
surface area of the element improves its capacity to act as heat
sink*

*next: lightweight construction
using timber floors and joists has
little capacity to act as a heat
sink*

*bottom: lightweight construc-
tion with tiles, this creates a
composite construction*

Floor construction types

Two main construction types are found, heavyweight and lightweight. Heavyweight construction is formed from high density materials, usually earth
based such as concrete and masonry. These can be formed into floor assemblies such as vaults or plates or slabs. Most have high capacitance but low
resistance. The exception is aerated concrete which has both moderate capacitance and resistance. This form of concrete is common for walling elements. It is also used in a pre-cast form for floors and is becoming popular
with steel frame construction for office buildings. Spans of up to six metres
can be achieved. The thermal response of this type of concrete in air-conditioned office buildings is ideal as it provides good vertical acoustic insulation between tenanted areas as well has providing thermal mass.

Lightweight construction, as the name implies, consists of building elements with small thermal mass. This normally means materials which have low density such as softwood timber but higher density materials such as steel can be used to form light strong elements, i.e. have a high strength to weight ratio. Common elements are steel studs, plasterboard, plywood, timber studs. These elements when combined together to form walls and floors have little thermal mass.

Floor constructions are internal elements and therefore tend not to be climatically specific. Exceptions occur where the floor breaks the edge of the building to form decks or meets the ground. In these situations the generic form of construction should be detailed to respect the climate. Thus, in the hot humid climate, floors that meet the ground have to be detailed to accommodate high rainfall and prevent termite infestation. In hot dry climates thermal breaks are advisable to prevent thermal transfer to slabs. These forms of construction are significantly different from temperate climate solutions.

It should be noted that the details are only illustrations of principles and are not seen as solutions to detail design problems. Each detail in a project is best related to or designed from first principles to ensure satisfactory performance rather than simple copying the standard pattern. The rational for this that every detail is in a unique position. Different locations and positions of details mean that each detail has to be context specific and thus designed accordingly if failure is to be avoided.

8.6 Mezzanines

The relation of the floor to ground is important as are the condition of the ground and natural vegetation. As with Maxwell's cat, vegetation is an important shading device to the floor and the vegetation cools the breezes. What is also important is the relationship of the floor positions in space. An analysis of the ways floors are used in warm climate buildings established a number of key issues. Two types of floor platform are found;

- the main horizontal separating elements which subdivide the building
- intermediate floors called mezzanines which sit above or in between the main horizontal floors

A common characteristic of warm climate buildings is that the building is less cellular to promote ventilation. In a cool climate building the aim is to contain heat and to use interior walls to compartmentalize space and reduce heat loss. Heating can in this way be concentrated and energy efficiency achieved. The converse is found in the warm climate buildings, the building is less effective as a closed section since this reduces the potential of cooling through the roof, hence in many cases in warm climate buildings the openness of the section is important. This necessitates an interconnection of space between floors, also the introduction of mezzanines within the volume of the skin.

8.19 *Radcliff house, plans and section; note the open section creates a high ceiling to collect heat from stack effect*

8.20 *Radford house, measured temperature gradient for the cool season of a moderate climate taken at midday in the living room*

The open section

The chief conceptual difference between a tropical building and a temperate climate building is that the latter should be considered more as a volume rather than as a series of rooms. In the temperate climates it can be argued that the cellular configuration of buildings is appropriate. It conserves heat in spaces, allows space to be shut off and heated as required and also minimizes air movement. Economics dictate as small a space as possible to conserve heat. Air movement is restricted in the winter mode as it produces drafts. The floors can therefore be used to shut down the section, closing it off to vertical air movement. The sense of stacking spaces vertically and using separating floors is seen in many farmhouses in Austria. Animals are housed under the building and the heat generated rises vertically into the house through the lightweight timber floors. In the above case the tempera-

8.21 *Buderim house by Lynsey Clare, the building has voids in the first floor to promote cooling by stack effect*

ture gradient generated by the building is taken as an advantage for the heating it.

In warm climate buildings the use of open sections is a strategy for minimizing the effects of temperature gradients. It is of critical importance as it facilitates the shedding of heat rather than conserving heat as in the temperate climate building. The characteristics of the open section are as follows:

- cathedral (raked high) ceilings
- floors as mezzanines
- vertical connecting spaces
- horizontal connecting spaces
- high ceilings

A number of typical floor positions can be suggested which are appropriate for a house design and thermal advantages. As with temperate climate buildings the temperature gradient across the building section is marked by higher temperature under the roof and ceiling below.

A good example is seen in the living room with raked ceiling. This room is located in a single-storey building with a suspended floor in a moderate climate. The temperature gradient from underfloor temperature to the high level below the ceiling was found to vary by 5 degrees. This temperature variation occurs where there is no ventilation.

With this in mind some design principles can be developed for spaces

8.22 *Buderim house by Lynsey Clare, section showing air movement in the open section*

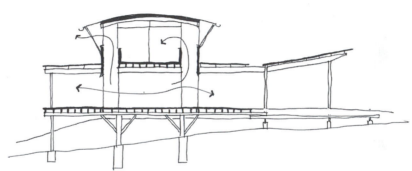

produced by different floor levels. One of the critical issues is to position floors so that they are comfortable for sleeping. In tropical climates this a major issue, temperatures over 30 degrees make sleeping difficult even if supplementary ventilation is provided through ceiling fans.

8.23 *Noble house by Donovan Hill Architects, use of mezzanines provide sleeping areas in this building*

Mezzanines and attic spaces

Mezzanines and attic spaces are those that are high up in the volume of the roof. In the Malay house the section of the house is open. Air can pass under

8.24 *Noble house by Donovan Hill Architects, exterior view of the building showing the raked roof to accommodate mezzanine spaces*

8.25 *This traditional house from Sarawak uses a combination of lightweight materials to insulate and ventilate the building, in particular the floor is made perforated to allow air movement*

a suspended timber floor and ventilation to the inner sleeping areas is provided by the windows. The space under the roof is the sleeping area for daughters of the family and one would think it to be an uncomfortable place. It is made habitable by gables that are ventilated to allow the breeze to flow through and hot air to escape.

Intermediate floors

Intermediate floors that sit between ceiling and ground floor can be used to protrude into the volume of the space. Careful arrangement of openings for ventilation can have a beneficial effect in making these spaces and provide comfortable sleeping areas. The Noble house on Stradbroke Island is good example of how intermediate floors can be designed for the subtropical coastal climate of Australia. The sleeping areas are designed at each end of a linear plan. The height and openness of the section provide volume for ventilation.

The master bedroom is orientated east, and is located at one end of the building. It is taller than its width and as high as it is long. This tube allows air to move in and up through the space. Guest accommodation is provided in bunk areas on mezzanines that are both inside and outside the building. One room for summer sleeping is made in a tower structure above the building whilst winter bunk space is provide in an intermediate floor above the living room. The bed is placed in a window alcove with fixed plate glass on two sides and ventilation on either side. The bed niche is also adjacent to the chimney to provide additional heat in the cool season.

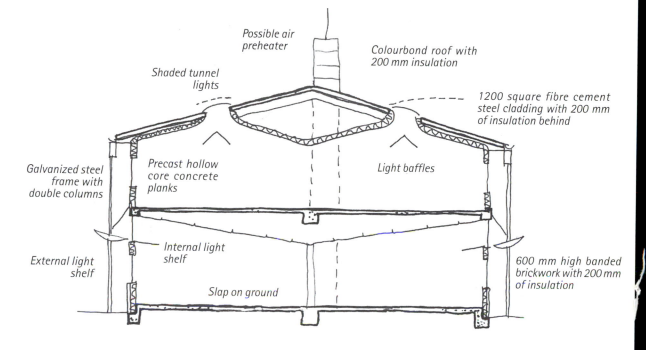

Possible air
preheater

Colourbond roof with
200 mm insulation

Shaded tunnel
lights

1200 square fibre cement
steel cladding with 200 mm
of insulation behind

Galvanized steel
frame with
double columns

Precast hollow
core concrete
planks

Light baffles

External light
shelf

Internal light
shelf

600 mm high banded
brickwork with 200 mm
of insulation

Slap on ground

8.7 Perforated floors

In this process a first key decision is the location of floors. Floors are the permanent part of the tropical building. Since we walk on them it is difficult for them to become retractable, although it is possible to make them perforated where this does not compromise function. For example in the Sarawak long house the floor is made of bamboo with small gaps between the pieces. This allows the building to become a permeable structure with ventilation through the floor. Also, it is a very useful device for cleaning since dirt can be swept through the gaps.

8.8 Integrated floors and ceilings

One of the crucial relationships in the climatic design of the building is the relationship between floor and ceiling. The distance between floors has a bearing on the overall construction cost, the ventilation to the floor, and admittance of daylight. The use of the floor and the ceiling for reflective purposes is an important consideration in the daylighting of buildings. To promote the admittance of daylight, the ceiling can become a luminaire to accept and direct daylight. The important consideration of this issue is found in a case study proposal for an environmental office in Canberra.[8] In this respect an integration of the roles of the wall and floor and ceiling is found in providing an appropriate climate response.

8.26 *Demonstration energy efficient building in Canberra, Australia; this uses light shelves and ceilings as luminaires to evenly distribute daylight and reduce the need for electric light*

References

1. L. Heschong, *Thermal Delight in Architecture*, MIT Press, 1979, p. 7.

2. M. Fry and J. Drew, *Tropical Architecture in the Hot Humid Zone*, Batsford, London, 1958, p. 58.

3. A.E. Delsante, 'Building Materials: Heavyweight or Lightweight?' in *the Design and Building of Energy Efficient Houses*, papers presented at a seminar sponsored by the Energy Management Sub-program of the Queensland Department of Resource Industries, internal publication Queensland State Government, Brisbane, 1992.

4. J.R. Goulding (ed) et al, *Energy in Architecture. The European Passive Solar Handbook*, Commission of the European Community, 1993, p. 78

5. Energy Victoria, 'Thermal Insulation in Domestic Buildings for Temperate Climates: An Introduction,' *Environmental Design Guide*,1996, Pro 7, p. 3

6. R.A. Hyde and M. Docherty, 'Climatic Design in the Hot Humid Tropics: A study of housing in the "Top End" of Australia', in *Proceedings of the 30th Conference of the Australian and New Zealand Architectural Science Association Conference*, The Chinese University of Hong Kong, July 1996, pp. 41-50.

7. R.A. Hyde, 'Thermal Performance of Innovative Lightweight Construction Systems: "Building Response in the Queensland Climate", in *Proceedings, Ecological Perspectives and Teaching Architectural Science*, ANZAScA Conference, Canberra, Australia, 1995, pp. 171-179.
   R.A. Hyde, 'Thermal Performance of Innovative Lightweight Construction Systems: Performance of Solar One', in *Proceedings of the Solar 95 Conference*, Tasmania, Australia, 1995, pp. 219-232

8. ERDAC Final Study Report, *Tropical Buildings Innovation Program: Phase 1*, Energy Research and Development Corporation, Canberra, 1997.

The veranda

'The Arabic veranda adjoining the inward looking courtyard was a place of reception which protected the private realm of the house from the univited. The Australian tradition of treating the veranda as a place of reception for the univited perpetuated the Arabic attitude. The essence of the veranda is expressed by lattice. It conveys better than anything the fundamental character of the traditional veranda, that of a filter between inside and out. Because it was a place of coolness, "the place where one drinks", it continued to signify, if only unconsciously, a place of physical and spiritual refreshment', Philip Drew.[1]

9.1 Introduction

Early records show that the veranda was used in Egyptian times. Its main climatic function appears to be that it should catch the breeze as well as provide an orientation to the exterior landscape and to views from the building. These distinctive climatic and experiential features characterize many of these types of veranda structure today.[2] The purpose of this chapter is to examine some of the developments in the form of the veranda and its wider relation to the surroundings. From this analysis it is clear that the underlying climate responsive strategy is to provide a thermal refuge and a place of transition from the inside to outside. In some cases it is functionless except to escape from the extremes of both the internal and external environment. In other cases the strategy used is to design the veranda as a connecting element between the interior and exterior.

9.2 The connecting element

A modern definition of a veranda is an open roofed platform along the side of a house. A historical definition of the word meant a latticed room opening of an internal courtyard,[3] but since these early times the climatic purpose of the veranda has evolved, giving a wider variety of options to the designer. In particular, less attention has been placed on the form of the veranda per se and more on the way it connects with the main building and in some situations forms the main building. Indeed the veranda can be called a 'servant' space. The veranda is used to serve the main building through its function. It has become a multi-functional space used for circulation, eating, sleeping,

9.1 *Veranda types:*
top: balconies, bays and decks
next: shade verandas
next: breezeway verandas
next: veranda houses
bottom: external rooms and
'sleep-outs'

relaxing, entertaining as well as being a sheltering and shading space.

It is argued here that examining this functional and spatial complexity is important in understanding the dialogue between the enclosure of the parent structure and the openness of the veranda. Moreover, further important relationships are established between the connecting element of the veranda, the wider landscape and the climate. The veranda is in a sense an intermediate zone between building and climate. In creating this zone, the veranda has a clear spatial role. Space is implied rather than defined due to the lack of walls. The exploration of types of veranda examines this spatial role in relation to the climatic factors.

Specific types of connecting space can be identified to aid this discussion:

- balconies, bays and decks
- shade verandas
- breezeway verandas
- veranda houses
- external rooms and 'sleep-outs'

9.3 Balconies, bays and decks

Balconies, bays and decks jutting out from the building serve a similar function to the veranda. The principal difference is the size of the space and the degree of enclosure. Balconies tend to be smaller less enclosed spaces, decks mostly open to the elements and bays more enclosed.

Balconies

9.2 'Illegal' balcony 'veranda' in Hong Kong, used for buffering, landscaping and additional space

Balconies are usually uncovered platforms that are located at high level and adjacent to a window or door. Often these structures form a platform and additional external space. This allows one to move out from the interior space to appraise the street, to enjoy the breeze and to provide small seating

areas. The function of these types of space is often confused. For example Equator facing decks often lead to climate-related performance problems in summer due to overheating. This makes the space difficult to use. Therefore because of the lack of enclosure of these unprotected spaces, a clear under-standing of the orientation and buffering to these spaces is required make them more workable. Often these spaces are balconies and decks acting as verandas. In areas where land is densely occupied, the balcony takes on the function of a veranda.

The balcony verandas of Hong Kong are renowned spaces that typically make use of the veranda concept for climatic purposes. The light-steel struc-tures are added illegally to apartments and flats in Hong Kong. There are three main reasons for the use of this type of space. First, there is a shortage of space at high level; the apartment buildings are efficiently planned and have little surplus space. Second, the balconies are used to increase the depth of the façade to buffer interior space. This is not only for privacy but also to reduce solar gain. Third, the balcony provides an opportunity for landscap-ing. The plants are used to assist with the buffering process.

9.3 The Inche's house, Batu Pahat, Malaysia; the use of large decks provides an external vantage point from the house, during the day it is an inhospitable place due to height levels of solar radiation but it is pleasant at night as it receives radiant cooling from clear night skies and sea breezes

Decks

Decks, on the other hand, are larger raised platforms without the roof of the veranda. In this case the greater exposure to the elements provides a highly contrasting space. It neither shades in the sun nor shelters in the rain. The lack of enclosure has a number of advantages that are often not appreciated. A self-evident feature of the deck is that it maximizes the access of breeze that promotes cooling to people using it. A less evident feature is the func-tion of the deck at night. The lack of the roof gives access to the clear night sky. Users of the deck can experience significant cooling through radiation to the sky. Temperatures on the deck will be at ambient therefore cooler than internal spaces, thus giving opportunity to utilize the space for sleeping in extreme conditions of high night temperatures. The very advantages of the deck are also its disadvantages. The vulnerability the deck makes its use dependent on careful orientation and landscaping. The building can be used as a shield to the sun and the landscape as a buffer.

The Inche house on the West Coast of Malaysia near Batu Pahat provides an interesting use of the open deck. The plan form of the deck is an of a typical 'umbrage' veranda; a particular plan arrangement where the rooms of the house follow the long side of the deck and with bedrooms on the ends. This approach was typical of the early Anglo-Indian bungalow style,[4] the deck is primarily a night space for circulation to bedrooms and for allowing greater openness in walls to promote ventilation. The deck is not useable during the day due to high solar radiation and glare during the heat of the day. The deck does, however, act as a pergola and provides a shaded undercroft to lower-level living rooms and kitchen.

To allow the open deck to function during the day it must be orientated to minimize solar access and should be integrated with landscaping elements. The Mapleton house by Richard Leplastrier provides a useful example.

Situated on 27 acres of rainforest on the Sunshine Coast in Queensland, the timber veranda house has large sliding doors opening onto an Equator facing deck. The site for the house is a clearing in the rainforest. Humidity in this type of location is a particular problem; first, for the thermal comfort of the occupants, second, for the durability of the fabric of the building and third, because of the lack of daylight. The lack of sunlight can lead to mould growth and deterioration of the structure. The clearing is therefore large enough to allow solar access to the deck in both winter and summer, a feature that is not normally desirable in summer for a moderate climate.

Additional strategies are used to address the problem of humidity. A veranda roof was proposed for the building, but this was deleted to facilitate solar access for heating in winter and to allow daylight into the building. Also a slow combustion stove is also kept alight during the year to further reduce humidity.

In this way the forest acts as a buffer and permits the use of the deck without excessive sun exposure. The large overhanging eaves and gutter provide sufficient shade so that one can sit behind the line of solar access

9.4 *The Mapleton house, Richard Leplastrier; the deck is Equator-facing with buffering through the use of landscape elements to minimize solar gain during the day*

and still appreciate the deck. The surrounding trees reduce the levels of solar radiation and shade from low-altitude solar gain both to the east and west. Tree ferns and medium height vegetation grow up from the ground level to provide sufficient shade without precluding views. The prospect and view to the clearing is enhanced through the detailing of the edge of the deck. No handrails are used only an increase in the spacing of the decking boards indicates the edge; the minimalist platform increases the connection with climate and place. In the Mapleton house the design of the deck has responded to both climate and context.

9.5 *Veranda bays used in this traditional Queensland house. These bays can be used as stove alcoves and as seating alcoves*

Bays

The investigation of the use of bays is seen in the integration of the veranda into vernacular buildings in Australia. This is achieved by a fusion of

9.5 *(continued) Bays in a traditional Queenslander: left: bays created by closing in the veranda right: bay window extends the room*

climate, function, technological and experiential qualities. The regional pre-war domestic architecture found in Queensland demonstrates this integration. The use of the veranda in these buildings has led to a number of climate responsive features. The house type commonly built in this period is the 'Queenslander.' In this house type the verandas are found to the front, side and back of the house and are characterized by an iron sheeted roof, sloping away following the main roof line of the house supported by posts. This has practical repercussions of reducing the solar aperture and thus decreasing solar access. This shade and protection relieves the wall of many of its thermal and weather-proofing functions. The veranda wall is often made of single skin construction with structural diagonal bracing to resist wind loads.

The veranda takes on many forms depending on orientation to the street, particularly in urban areas. The size and use becomes constrained due to setbacks and adjacent property lines. The front verandas are used as porches and semi-public spaces. The side and rear verandas are the more private and secluded spaces. A form of veranda, the bay or small enclosed side veranda, has evolved in these constrained conditions. In many cases the distance between adjacent properties is 3 m or less with a distance of 1.5 m to the property line.

The bay cantilevers from the main house into this constrained space between the two buildings. This positioning of the bay takes advantage of the opportunities of breeze between buildings. The extension of the bay out from the façade increases surface area and thus potential for cooling the space. Additional openings in these bays provide the ventilation, the size and nature of these openings depends on privacy issues. The main functions of the bays are to form niches for sitting and cooking.

In the sitting niche the charm and climatic rationale behind these smaller veranda bays is simple. By providing a secondary space to the main space of the room, the room perceptually appears larger. A place is also provided for

9.6 *Veranda bays in a beach house on Stradbroke Island, Brisbane, by Gabriel Poole, the bays are used to provide additional storage and space*

enjoying the cooling breezes and increased daylighting. Operable windows wrap the niche, opaque glass is used in the panes for privacy.

The stove alcove is similar in structural design to the sitting niche but is constructed differently. The alcove is an extension of the mechanical system of the stove, located in a niche outside the envelope of the building, providing for the venting of excess heat without raising the temperature of the kitchen or the surrounding building. The non-combustible steel form of these niches is a sensible and practical strategy given the timber construction of the main building.

More recent examples of the veranda bay are provided by Gabriel Poole. In his beach houses and kit homes the veranda bay is used for a variety of purposes including storage and bed niches. The Clake House is a notable case.

9.4 Shade veranda

One of the main climatic negative aspects of warm climates is solar access. High levels of solar radiation, ambient radiation and glare contribute to levels of discomfort when looking from the building to the exterior. The purpose of the shade veranda is to act as a buffer space and reduce the effects of this climatic problem. There are a number of strategies used to incrase the effectiveness of the shade veranda. These are:

- minimal structural form to reduce thermal mass and promote cooling
- sloping skillion roof that is angled away from the main roof to reduce solar admittance
- veranda supports and columns that allow openness and transparency
- cladding elements such as lattices and screens are used to reduce glare and heat gain from low-altitude sun. These elements are designed to reduce solar admittance yet still promote ventilation
- optimum plan depth of about 3 m to provide for exterior functions such as sitting, eating and sleeping and to allow sufficient daylight to penetrate interior spaces. Increasing veranda depth reduces daylight and can give a gloomy interior, highly desirable for mosquitoes
- provision of diffuse daylight to interior spaces reducing ultraviolet radiation and heat gain
- use as an armature for vegetation to promote evaporative cooling
- elevation of the floor to provide a transition space between inside and out, removing dust from the feet and providing for a prospect to the surroundings

These basic strategies can be tuned to accommodate different orientations, microclimates and the line of enclosure and the interior spatial organization. The development of the early shade veranda principally explored the implications of the veranda on the line of enclosure. French doors were substituted for windows to provide access, the additional louvred doors and

9.7 *The Buderim house, Lynsey Clare Architects, this use of the shade veranda for a moderate climate; it provides passive solar heating in winter and facilitates cooling in summer; in winter the orientation of the veranda permits low-angle sun to strikes the deck which reflects heat into the building*

shutters were added to allow ventilation and privacy. Fanlights in walls provide permanent ventilation and are located at a high level to remove hotter air near the ceiling. Also a reduction in the amount of material in the skin is used to reduce thermal mass. 'Single-skin' construction provided a simple privacy screen with little capacity for thermal resistance. Yet the veranda was still a separating zone between the house and garden.[5] And a closer connection between veranda and interior space was yet to be defined.

An approach that strives to connect the house and the veranda as an integral climatic unit is used in the Buderim house. The house is located on the Sunshine Coast, Australia. The plans of the building show the building has a simple 'gun barrel' organization.[6]

On the ground floor are located the kitchen, dining and living areas which form one space. Connected to the north is the shade veranda whilst to the south are the utility spaces, separated from the main building by an entrance deck. Stairs and bathroom separate the master bedroom from the living spaces. On the first floor, another bathroom, stairs and a large family room separate the second and third bedroom. The climate design approach for the building follows accepted basic principles with few exceptions.

The first strategy is optimum orientation. In this case the longest axis of the building faces north-east, a desirable option for ventilation in summer (cooling breezes in summer come from the northeast, also warm winds in winter come from this direction). The northerly aspect gives good solar access in winter, the thin rectangular plan form with its shortest sides facing east and west minimizes the solar aspect for these walls. In this way area of wall exposed to the low-altitude sun, particularly in summer, is reduced thus reducing heating in the morning and evening. In addition the building takes advantage of microclimatic aspects of the site in this respect.

The second strategy is microclimate integration. The building juts out over a creek which helps funnel breeze into the building in summer. The hills to the south and west help protect the building from westerly sun and cool breezes in winter.

The third strategy is passive heating and cooling. This is achieved by the unusual spatial organization of linking the shade veranda to the northeast of the interior spaces and the open section which facilitates air movement by convection from the lower floors to the first floor family room, bedrooms and living areas. The line of enclosure is highly transparent in the area of the shade veranda. In winter heating is achieved through a solar charging process. The analysis of solar angles shows the building receives solar access up to 10:00 hours and after this the shade veranda provides a solar cutoff, the direct sunlight only strikes the deck after 10:00 hours. The interior is heated in three ways, through direct solar gain, indirect solar gain through reflected light from the deck and through convection, air moving across the solar heated deck to the interior. The line of enclosure has large areas of louvres and doors to allow ventilation. Thermal performance studies show that the building rapidly heats up, the heated air is moved by convection to other parts of the building through openings in the first-floor.[7]

The fourth strategy relates to daylighting, the shade veranda provides sufficient shade to the building to allow large glazing ratios and indirect light. This reduces glare and the harmful effects of direct sunlight on interior fixtures and finishes. In addition reflected light from the roof provides addition daylighting to the first-floor spaces. In summer the shade veranda plays a more traditional role, providing an exterior room and facilitating cross-ventilation to the interior spaces.

9.5 Breezeway veranda

A breezeway is a space that is aligned to catch prevailing wind directions. Normally it is an open passage through a building or between adjacent buildings. The passageway produces a 'duct' through which the breeze can be channelled. The breezeway veranda is a variety of this type of building

9.8 *Breezeway veranda uses the elevation of the deck to collect summer breezes. The deck is partially covered to provide different spaces for varying climatic conditions; on summer nights the roofless part provides exposure to clear skies by radiant cooling, during the day the roof provides a shaded area*

response. These verandas are designed to address the effects of breeze through funnelling and other pressure effects. Two examples illustrate this approach, the first is a side veranda extension for a residence; the second a large veranda to a public building.

Side veranda, domestic residence

In this case an existing carport roof to a residence is found to have a favourable microclimate in summer. The location of the building on the side of a ridge orientated to the prevailing cooling summer breezes provides the ideal opportunity to utilize this building response. The breeze funnels between the two existing buildings and across the roof providing the potential for a summer cooling space. The roof is required to assist with reducing solar gain and assisting with the funnelling effect. Construction of a veranda in this location posed a number of problems:

- privacy for the existing building
- glare from adjacent roofs
- windblown rain
- building control setbacks

In the design the setback conditions prevent the deck from being built closer than 1.5 m to the boundary. The roof could only be built to within 2 m to the boundary. This posed problems of function and structure. Posts to the roof would reduce the usable area of the deck. The solution used was to cantilever the roof from the existing structure and to prop at the gutter line. The props intrude slightly into the deck space but are angled back to the wall

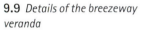

9.9 *Details of the breezeway veranda*
left: the pitch of veranda roofs is angled up rather than down to increase breeze. Glare is reduced by the use of plants
right: the roof line is set back form the deck to comply with council setback requirements

line, thus keeping the floor of the deck clear of posts. The roof is raked away from the building and upwards at 7 degrees to allow breeze and view.

The use of the side veranda and the cantilever roof posed problems of glare control and privacy. The reflection of sunlight from the adjacent reflective metal roof provides discomfort to the occupants of the veranda. Also problems of visual and acoustic privacy are found for the occupants of the adjacent property. Solutions to these problems are best addressed at source. On the adjacent property horizontal blinds can be attached to the existing sun-hoods to provide privacy and ventilation, a low-sheen reflective paint is used on the roof to prevent glare. Yet these solutions were not used in this case. A strategy, therefore, of using both landscaping and handrail design were used to maximize privacy and minimize glare.

Visual privacy is addressed by directing the view to the sky and distant views. In this way the tendency to look down is avoided and the problems of glare are reduced by the use of sun breakers. The semi-permeable nature of this screening device is critical.

Acoustic privacy still remains a problem. The use of high density hardwood and the sensible use of space are critical for this type of veranda to function. The side veranda in this case is a more private domain and is used as an external dining and reading area. Different parts of the deck are used at different times of the day for the dining function. The western end is used for breakfast as it is sheltered from the early morning sun by the roof. The open eastern end, which is not roofed, is used for evening eating in dry weather. This area catches the breeze and is open to the sky thus taking advantage of radiant cooling in clear night sky conditions. The careful zoning of the veranda and the use of plants suited to the conditions are important aspects of the climatic design of these type of structure.

In inclement weather the veranda is washed by rain. The deck furniture is protected by water-resistant covers, canvas chairs are used as these dry quickly, are light and are manoeuvrable. Rain penetration is problematic for the carport

9.9 *(continued)*
left: construction of the roof is by bearers cantilevered from the wall and propped struts right: the orientation and elevation of the deck proves access to views and to the prevailing cooling summer breezes

below the space. Dirt and tannin stain from the timber structure is washed through the deck and is caught by a suspended steel roof screwed to the timber joists. Water is collected in a gutter and directed to the landscaping for irrigation. The use of the steel roof in this location has further advantages. The reflective nature of the steel increases diffuse light into the bedroom below thus reducing the need for artificial light. Thus, careful design of the space can overcome one of the problems with the veranda, that is the reduction of daylight to the internal rooms.

Overall, the elevated breezeway use of the verandas as timber additions to the building for summer cooling can also buffer the line of enclosure allowing the use of non-solar glazing and improving transparency. The veranda in this case is an important passive low-energy feature in the design of the building, as well as providing a naturally ventilated walkway and reading area for summer use.

Entrance veranda and buffer space

In the case of the Sunshine Coast Library the breezeway veranda is used in a large public building. Architects, John Mainwaring and Lawrence Nield, make reference to a number of historical precedents and climate design features in the design of this building. The building addresses master planning issues and as a consequence becomes a focal transparent building. An axis is used to align the building resulting in a northeast orientation.

One of the concerns with the building is the high levels of transparency created by the use of a saw tooth roof, reminiscent of traditional wool stores. As with the early precedents the clerestory lighting is orientated south, polar facing. The transparency to the north Equator-facing windows is protected by the use of the veranda. In this way the intent of increasing the transpar-

9.10 *Sunshine Coast University College Library by architects Lawrence Nield and John Mainwairing, 1997, in this building the breezeway veranda is used in a larger buildings as a buffer space to the highly glazed external skin. This allows diffused light to enter the building without the heat load; the buffer space also provides opportunities for seating and shade*

9.11 *The Tent house by Gabriel Poole is development of a tropical version of the veranda house. The movable walls mean the interior of the building can be opened to the exterior to provide ventilation and access to views*

ency of the building to maximize natural light can be achieved without the negative effects of solar access such as glare, ultraviolet penetration, over heating and radiant heat from the glazing.

The veranda is also used as a breezeway. The veranda brings people from the entrance courtyard on the west to an entrance on the northeast corner on the first floor. The advantage of this strategy is that in summer this area attracts the northeast sea breeze. It sweeps across an open square and through the breezeway. In addition the space under the veranda also receives the breeze and is shaded making a shaded sitting area. Furthermore, the veranda provides a buffer space to the air-conditioned space of the library. This takes out the heat load on the glass and reduces glare. The buffering effect is achieved by using timber raked sunbreakers and inclined mono-pitched roof.

9.6 Veranda houses

The veranda house is a form of building that evolved from the traditional shade veranda. One of the first types of veranda house was developed by Australian architect Glen Murcutt. It was a departure from the nineteenth-century bungalow which was squarer in form and provided a deep plan building. In this type of building the veranda was located on three sides, wrapping the house. The Murcutt development, focusing on climate parameters, was used as a way of generating a place-making architecture,[8] and used a longer thinner plan to provide cross-ventilation in summer. A shallow veranda to the north (Equator facing) buffered the interior space, and adjustable louvres were used in the veranda wall to selectively admit or exclude sun and ventilation. This particular type of house was developed in the milder climates of southern Australia.

9.12 *The Malaysian Sarambie, this space provides an external room to the building. The climatic response of the space provides an ideal area for a wide range of social, and cultural activities*

The application of the veranda house to the warmer climates of Queensland has been carried out by local architect Gabriel Poole. He attempted to popularize a new system of housing using the veranda house strategy. Poole developed a housing system based on an experimental Tent house. The prototype used a linear plan form similar to the Murcutt buildings to provide optimum summer cooling. The innovation comes from the departure from traditional form of the veranda. The development of the technology in the line of enclosure so that the walls can be removed gives the potential for the

9.13 *Beach house by Gabriel Poole; use of the external room at the seaward side of the building for breeze and view*

whole room to become an external veranda-like space. The strategy in the Poole building is to limit the long, thin shallow space of the veranda to a number of free-standing pavilions with individual pyramid roofs. Fold-up walls provide a high degree of flexibility in rooms. The technology is similar to a fold-up garage door except that it is made of translucent material.

The climatic response of the space is different dependent on the position of the wall. With the wall open a veranda roof is provided, creating shade and openness in the room. With the wall closed the internal space is created. The flexibility offered by this radical approach is driven by economics as well as by climatic criteria. It enables a cost-effective steel system to be built with a minimum of architectural elements. This particular form of the veranda house emphasizes that the veranda derives its character and climate response from the degree of enclosure provided in the building. Indeed by manipulating enclosure and the relationship of the veranda to the enclosed building, new forms of veranda can be developed which have a variety of functions and provisions of thermal delight for the occupants.

9.7   External room and the 'sleep-out'

A number of veranda types that follow this development are represented by two extremes. First there is the external room, where the veranda is separated from the main building and thrust into the landscape to provide greater connection with the external space and greater ventilation. Often the external room uses the main building as a buffer against solar penetration and therefore provides a cool area to relax and entertain. The other is the enclosed veranda, often called a 'sleep-out,' which has a greater degree of enclosure to provide privacy for sleeping yet still provides ventilation. The

9.13 *continued*

edge location of the veranda makes a more comfortable area for sleeping in hot months.

Traditional Malay architecture demonstrates the use of the external room, the traditional shade veranda and the sleep-out. The Malay house is planned around a 'core' building, called the 'rumah ibu'. This main house is used for sleeping and for meetings. As space and accommodation are required, further spaces are added. This is usually in the form of two verandas that sit on either side of the main house. The 'serambi gantung' literally means 'hanging veranda' because its floor is lower than the main house. Its function is for entertaining guests and a place where children can sleep. The 'serambi samanaik' is on the same level as the main house and functionally similar to main house also used for praying.[9] The 'serambi gantung' is often extended forward from the main building to form an entrance porch. This also extends the veranda creating an external room. This space is often used for entertaining guests and as an entrance porch.

The interesting feature of these spaces is the scale and enclosure. The veranda roof is formed as a scillion under the main roof. This reduces the headroom and the scale of the space. Handrails are similarly scaled to allow occupants to sit on the floor and rest their arms on the rails in comfort. This anthropomorphic nature of the design and the thermal comfort provided by the location of the body close to the floor (which is the coolest part) demonstrates an excellent synthesis of climatic and human factors which is rarely found in equivalent modern buildings .

The use of the external room can also be related to specific orientation. In the case of a beach house by Gabriel Poole, an elevated first-floor platform is created on a ridge overlooking the ocean. At the ground floor, below the platform, are the storage and carparking spaces. The main living spaces are

9.13 *Residential renovation in Brisbane, Australia, architect Richard Hyde; the external room is used as a vertical circulation space as well as seating area saving space with in the building*

on the first-floor platform, with a mezzanine providing a bedroom space and galley looking over the living area. The veranda is used as an extension to the living room.

The building is orientated to the northeast and the ocean views. The microclimate conditions are reflected in the design of the longitudinal section. A raking curved roof is used to accommodate the changing volume of the house from the two-storey height of the mezzanine to the single-storey veranda. This reduces solar access and creates opportunities for breeze and ventilation at the veranda edge. Over the living area the volume is increased to give an open section with windows at high level. This provides opportunities for the removal of heat by the stack effect in calm conditions. In this house the main intention is to use a veranda on the east of the building as a buffer space reducing heat gain from the morning sun. External rooms can be used as buffer spaces to the west but should be used in conjunction with landscape and external shading systems.

In another example, an external room is used in the extension and renovation of a Post-War Austerity Model Queensland house. The house has been converted into a two-storey home through development of an undercroft space. The lack of interior space made it difficult to include an interior stair in the living room of the house. An external room is used as a remedy for this problem as well as providing additional cost-effective living space.

The room is located to the west of the main building, offering opportunities to protect the living space from the western sun in the summer. This is linked to the use of landscaping and a buffer of forest trees. The interesting feature of this landscape buffer is the way it has been precisely planted to optimize orientation. The external room is shielded in summer but in winter the sun is not excluded and provides warming. This permits solar access in the late afternoon heating the external room and the kitchen. The open plan arrangement of the house allows this air to circulate and heat the whole house. In this case the use of the external room as a buffer to low-angle sun can regulate the solar access to provide heating and cooling required.

With this kind of interrelation between the external room and the rest of

9.13 *(continued)*
right: plan shows the external stair and seating area. The external room allows doors to the westerly bedroom to be opened for ventilation
left: site section shows the landscape buffer which protects from room form the westerly sun

P

E

bedroom

dinning

external room

kitchen

the house adequate climatic control of adverse solar access can be achieved. The climate response is coupled with the integration of vertical circulation elements. Additional benefits are found with this approach; the stairs to the exterior of the room directs people to the external landscape and to the wider views to the hills. The prospect that this creates demonstrates the way the veranda can be adapted in many ways for climatic, experiential and functional advantages.

References

1   P. Drew, *Veranda Embracing Place,* Angus Robinson, Pymble, Australia, 1992, p. 4.
2   Drew, op. cit., p. 3.
3   Drew, op. cit., Appendix A.
4   Ibid., p. 47.
5   Ibid., p. 53.
6   'Rippled Soul', in *Steel Profile*, BHP Steel, Melbourne, No. 42, December, 1992, p. 14.
7   R.A. Hyde and M. Docherty, 'Thermal Performance of Housing in the Hot Humid Tropics of Australia', *Architectural Science Review*, 1997, Vol. 40, pp. 105-112.
8   Drew, op. cit. p. 216.
9   Lim Jee Yuan, *The Malay House*, Institute Masyarakat, Pulau Penang, 1987, p. 24.

Courtyards

'They provide a place to bask in the sun or a shady and airy place to be cool, while the houses are stuffy and either too cool from the night before or overheated by the afternoon sun,' Lisa Heschong.[1]

10.0 Introduction

The use of courtyards and plazas are common features in Mediterranean climates to provide a thermal refuge from the building. The affection that people have for these spaces is ignored. Also in densely built-up environments the need for natural light and ventilation becomes of primary concern. Without these natural aspects of climate control some form of active system is required to provide the physical comfort of building occupants. A courtyard is a method of providing these aspects. In this chapter the nature of courtyards is considered as a strategy for design. Detailed discussion is provided on the way these types of spaces can be created and evidence provided on their performance. At first glance the nature of a courtyard as a space seems to be well defined. It is usually considered to be a space that is bounded on all sides by buildings. From the climatic design standpoint, the size and degree of enclosure have a significant impact on its performance and on the performance of the building adjacent to the courtyard. If a courtyard becomes too large, it begins to lose its identity as such and becomes a square or larger external space such as a park. In this case the influence of buildings on the microclimate in the space becomes less, and the microclimate is dominated by the landscape and topography of the open space.

Similarly, if it is too small it can become a corridor, transforming it into a breezeway or to have the more selective function of an air and light shaft. In this case the courtyard provides both light and ventilation and admits rain, but the important factor is that the microclimate of the space becomes dominated more by the buildings. Other allied forms of space to the courtyard include re-entrant spaces, light wells and light shafts.

One form of courtyard is a re-entrant space. This space can be developed as a way of increasing the external wall surface area of the building through increasing the area of the external façade, thus improving the amount of light and ventilation to adjacent spaces. Smaller courtyards are called light or airshafts, depending on the function. These spaces allow light into internal spaces and facilitate air movement and ventilation to adjacent spaces. In

10.1 *Strategies for courtyard design*
top: fully-enclosed
middle: semi-enclosed
bottom: semi-open

10.2 *Semi-open courtyard at Raffles Hotel, Singapore. The courtyard as a penetrating element, creating the conceptual 'centre' and focus to the building*

this respect the shaft operates like a large duct that permits the penetration of light and air deep into the building. 'Light well' is another name given to these types of elements, but this name should not be used as it is often confusing with regard to the precise function of the well. Sometimes these wells are primarily for ventilation and bring little light, and sometimes there is little ventilation effect and more light distribution.

Further consideration should be given to the term 'atrium'. Both courtyards and atriums are spaces enclosed by buildings. The main difference between the two is that an atrium has a horizontal roof plane which can be opaque or transparent; in the case of a courtyard it is open to the sky. This definition is not mutually exclusive with regard to the nature of these spaces and means of enclosure. Clearly there are different forms which complicate the definition: courtyards with retractable roofs or vegetation enclosures to form roofs do not necessarily constitute an atrium, nor do atriums with roof areas that can be extensively opened become courtyards. Indeed the classical atrium had an opening to the sky for light and ventilation. It seems simpler to suggest that with the enclosure of the courtyard by a roof, a number of further issues must be considered, such as internal heat gain and ventilation.

Concept: the penetrating space

In this sense it is appropriate to consider the courtyard not as a single device but as an element that has a number of forms. The principle function of a courtyard varies; it can be conceptual, visual and functional and vary with the type of building. Its climatic function is more singular, primarily to bring light and ventilation into a building, but it can create a powerful microclimate when combined with different functions, wall types, building forms and landscaping. This can provide

10.3 *Airwell in a Malysian plantation house, note the recessed floor to prevent water penetration to the interior spaces*

a climatic and experiential centre to the building which transforms the architecture and provides a superb interstitial space.

In conceptual terms, therefore, the courtyard should be considered as a spatial element that is open to the sky and penetrates the mass of the building. The position, orientation, relation to other building elements and open space are important factors for the design of the courtyard and other semi-open spaces. Lack of concern for these factors in design can lead to under-performance of these spaces.

10.1 Courtyard types

Three strategies are worth examining which represent basic ways of utilizing courtyards in climatic design. In these strategies the courtyard can be examined with respect to the way the space is inserted into the building mass, the extent to which enclosure is formed either by buildings themselves or by walls, and the degree of openness in the enclosure. These strategies can be summarized as follows:

- fully enclosed courtyards, the use of open space in deep-plan buildings for light, air and visual amenity
- semi-enclosed courtyards, formed as residual spaces from the interlocking of buildings that provide privacy, shade and semi-enclosure
- semi-open courtyards, formed from a building by a minimum of enclosure. The courtyard space is normally open on one side, providing access for ventilation and opportunities or view

Fully enclosed courtyards

The enclosed courtyard is often used in deep plan terrace-type buildings to provide light and ventilation. The first case study, of the traditional merchants' houses found in Malacca, demonstrates the key factors in courtyard design. These houses respond to three main conditions; economic constraints, site orientation and macroclimatic airflow in urban areas

Malacca is located on the east coast of Malaysia. Historically it developed as a trading port similar to Penang and Singapore, thus its architecture is a result of a number of influences mixed with the indigenous Malay culture. The merchants were wealthy business people who had large extended families. The houses were therefore storage facilities and business premises but also living accommodation. Up to 200 people were often found living in these buildings. The length of the house could be up to 60 m long with one or two courtyards inserted into the building. The frontage was kept as narrow as possible because of economic factors. The colonial administration at the time imposed a tax based on the width of the house; the larger the width the greater the tax. Thus the front façade became an indicator of wealth and success of the family. Also, the larger the façade, the larger the courtyards and greater potential for ventilation.[2]

The form of the house comprises a number of linked two-storey terraced houses. In section the roofs slope into the courtyard, allowing the penetration of air, rainwater and light. To understand more fully how these houses perform, it is best to examine the building response to the macroclimate as well as microclimatic factors. The merchants' houses are located on the coastal

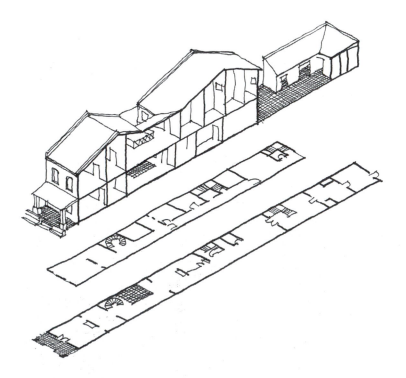

10.4 *Malacca courtyard houses, after Gurstein.*[2]

strip in a northwest orientation parallel to the coast. The houses are in a dense part of the city, but at the time of construction had connection to the sea to facilitate docking and storage. The orientation of the building provides access to the sea breeze and to the two monsoon wind directions, from the northeast and southwest.

This advantageous orientation is mitigated by the urban density of the surrounding town. How the building operates within this context is interesting. Givoni suggests that in hot humid climates the design of the building fabric in urban areas should provide optimum ventilation and shading. The main problem is that the high density of buildings reduces airflow at the ground plane as compared to that of a rural area. In general, in urban areas the wind is divided into an area of free-running air above the average building height and restricted airflow is found at the ground plain. In this way 'wind shadows' occur where wind is forced over buildings. In some cases, though, negative pressures behind buildings and differential heights in buildings can draw air from the free-running zone to the ground plane. This can be an advantage in providing additional ventilation and higher velocities to the ground plane.[3]

Examining this theory in relation to the merchants' houses, the prevailing winds are directed along the length of the building, across the courtyard. From observations in these buildings it appears that air is drawn from the free-running air stream to the ground plane. Pressure differences, in particular from the southwest monsoon, would create negative pressure within the courtyard. This would appear to be relieved by air brought in from above or through ground-floor openings. In this way the courtyard appears to be enhanced by the potential for ventilation from the higher-level breeze.

10.5 *Malacca merchant houses, façade and interior view of courtyard*

The magnitude of this ventilation effect is dependent on the type of ventilation provided, displacement, diffusion or cross-ventilation. Cross-ventilation is the condition where the pressure and suction sides of the building are connected, high pressure from one side drives the air to the other. Air movement can occur where there is no such connection but generally it is difficult as the external air has to displace the air inside the room. Thus, a

10.6 *Ventilation to the courtyard in the merchant's house, Malacca.*
+ negative pressure
- positive pressure

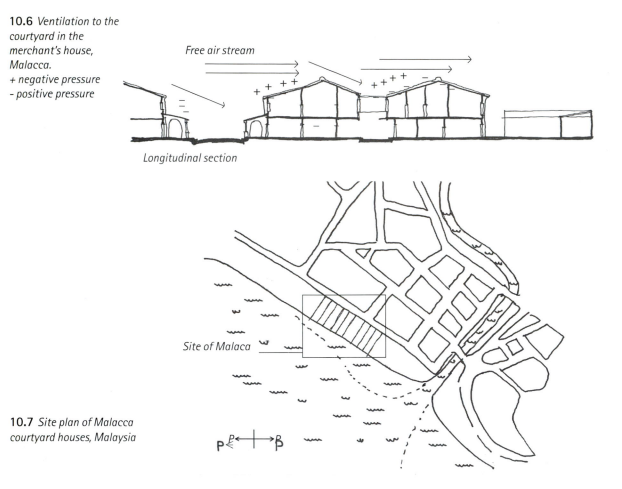

Free air stream

Longitudinal section

10.7 *Site plan of Malacca courtyard houses, Malaysia*

Site of Malaca

room which is ventilated on only one side, normally uses this type of displacement-ventilation.[4] The effect of these different types of ventilation on internal air movement can be gauged. The provision of cross-ventilation is found to give almost twice the velocity of internal air movement than with non-cross-ventilated spaces. The question arises as to whether courtyards can provide sufficient cross-ventilation given that these types of spaces are enclosed by buildings and usually in urban areas. Analysis of the window and glazing show that three main techniques are used to maximize ventilation.

First, from the street the elevation has approximately a 50 per cent ratio of opening to wall with operable and permanent ventilation. Normally, two doors are provided through the inner spaces to allow the movement of air down each side of the space and to the courtyard area. The walls adjacent to the courtyard on the ground plane are omitted, creating a semi-open space. A small step-down in the floor is provided to prevent water in the open area of the courtyard from spilling into the adjacent space. Operable timber screens can be used in some courtyards to shield the semi-open space from wind-

blown rain. It is interesting to note that in some cases the rainwater pipes drain into the courtyards and are featured as water elements enhancing the space. In drier periods of the year when the relative humidity is low, the courtyard provides the possibility of evaporative cooling from this kind of feature. It has a similar potential to that found in the Arabic courtyard.

Second, at the first-floor level, the perimeter is enclosed by a similar fenestration pattern as the façade but with 75 per cent operable windows. A solid panel below the windows provides privacy up to the window level. Operable louvres are used in the window area, whilst permanent ventilation is provided above these windows.

Finally, in smaller courtyards the proportion of the courtyard changes so that the height is greater than the floor plan. This has the effect of reducing the sky openings and thus provides shading to the courtyard. In addition the light into the courtyard is seen to be reflected light from side walls and into the adjacent spaces. These techniques of removing walls adjacent to the courtyard at the ground plane, using the largest number operable windows at the upper level promotes cross-ventilation and with smaller courtyards shading the ground plane providing reflected light to the adjacent spaces. The reflected light is diffused thus reducing heat gain from the light.

10.8 Interior Malacca courtyard showing ventilation techniques to the windows and at the ground plane

10.9 Street elevation of a 'shotgun' single-storey housing in New Orleans, circa 1800s

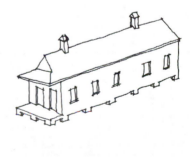

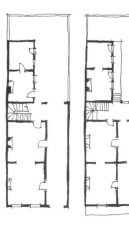

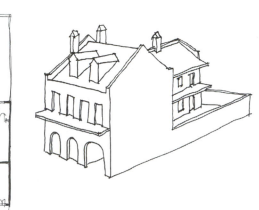

ground floor   *first floor*

10.10 *Plans of the Porte-Cochere townhouse and appropriated courtyard*

Semi-enclosed courtyards

These courtyards are formed from the interlocking of buildings or by the addition of walls to enclose open spaces for privacy and shade. The second case study focuses on this courtyard type. Many houses found in the French Quarter of subtropical New Orleans share these characteristics. The evolution of the courtyard space appears to come from an additive process as the density of the French Quarter increased.

Many of the early houses in New Orleans were of a single-storey design, called 'shotgun singles.' These houses are of timber construction, suspended timber floors and weatherboard cladding. The origin of these houses is unclear, but the design appears to have originated in other tropical climates such as Haiti or Africa. Features of the buildings reflect the tropical and subtropical climate. The plan is one room deep to maximize ventilation and is in a simple linear or 'gun barrel' form, so named as it allows inhabitants to fire a shotgun directly from one end of the building to the other.[5]

The connectivity of this type of building also allows ventilation longitudinally through the building. In addition the buildings are raised off the ground and sit on brick piers. Ventilation is provided to the subfloor areas through vents which are often ornate in design. Centrally spaced fireplaces are featured as heating devices in the cool season. In denser areas of the city the more interlocking building forms are found. Small utility spaces are added to the buildings as wings running away from the street.

Townhouse forms with cross-wall construction are also found. The effect of this kind of development is to form a courtyard space. The two-storey Porte-Cochere townhouse is an example of this type of building. These two-, three- or four-storey buildings are common in the Vieux Carre area. They were built from the 1800s and feature a carriage entrance at the ground floor which links both the street and the courtyard.

Comparing these courtyards to the Malaysian examples, there are some

major differences. First, the New Orleans courtyard is much larger, two or three times as large, and is thus more of an external space. Second, the opportunities for ventilation from the free-running layer seem to be less, due to the more dense urban fabric and the remoteness of the area from the ocean. In this case, therefore, the predominant cooling feature in summer is shading of the space from direct solar gain. This is achieved with a narrow courtyard space. Buildings form a U-shaped enclosure around the space with a small 2 m high dividing wall. The courtyard therefore is effectively twice the size, since the wall does little to separate the space. In addition, the use of elevated verandas as circulation routes and the use of vegetation through pergolas and arbours provides shading to the space. Further cooling of the

10.11 *Interior views of the courtyards to the Porte-Cochere townhouses, New Orleans*

10.12 *Inche house, front elevation from the east*

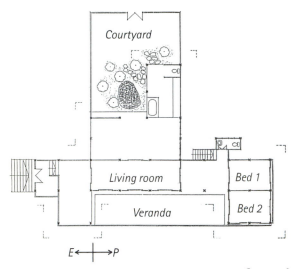

10.12 *(continued)*
right: plan of the Inche house
left: interior view of courtyard

space comes from other devices: flags and paving are used as surface materials in the courtyard, providing thermal mass for storing coolness during the day, and the use of vegetation and water features increases humidity, providing evaporative cooling in the drier seasons.

Semi-open courtyards

Semi-open courtyards differ from the preceding types again in the amount of enclosure. Courtyards need not be made by buildings but also by walls. These afford privacy as well as enclosure.

In the hot humid tropics this can be used to afford privacy for bathing. An example is found in the Inch residence at Batu Pahat, Malaysia. This

10.13 *Re-entrant spaces, public housing in Hong Kong*

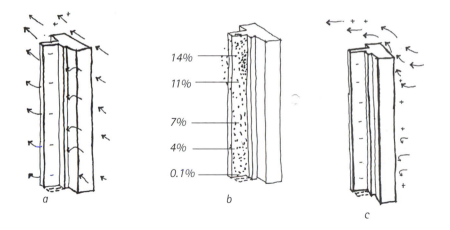

14%
11%
7%
4%
0.1%

17%
13%
8%
4%
0.1%

a   b   c   d

dwelling is an adaptation of the Malay Kampong house's long linear plan. The courtyard does not form a central space, but creates a secondary space adjacent to the bedroom area. This semi-enclosed space is partly roofed and partly open to the sky, providing a discrete bathing space.

10.14 *Computer fluid dynamics modelling of air quality in public housing in Hong Kong*
a. Velocity vectors of wind at right-angles to the re-entrant.
b. Velocity vectors of wind where the re-entrant is on the leeward side.
c. Concentration of cooking fumes where wind is at right-angles to the re-entrant.
d. Concentration of cooking fumes where the re-entrant is on the leeward side

10.2 Re-entrant spaces

The use of re-entrant space is a particularly useful strategy in warm climates as it enables increased light and ventilation to habitable and service spaces. Two examples are given which illustrate the differing roles that re-entrant spaces can play in the design of these kinds of spaces: for ventilation and light, or primarily just for light.

Re-entrant spaces for ventilation and light

In order to understand the role of the re-entrant space, one must trace its evolution. An example of this is the development of public housing in Hong Kong. Early research often presents this evolution as an architectural response to the problems of density and land shortage on the island.[6] In the early 1880s, there were densities of over 2000 people per hectare were found in the Chinese neighbourhoods, and now new communities are being planned with densities around 2500 per hectare. Recent research shows that the evolution of the flat design has responded not only to these significant social and planning constraints but also to the use of passive environmental control principles. Sullivan reports that three generations of flat design can be found. The first-generation flats (1950–60) are of a minimalist design with a service zone on the exterior edge. The second generation (1960–70) provided a similar layout but increased the number of rooms inside the flat. This gave the flat an 'interior orientation' which provided little or no direct light or ventilation to the living and sleeping areas. The third generation (1980 onwards) are the 'exterior orientated' flats, which provide light and ventilation to living and sleeping areas. This has been made possible by three factors.[7]

1. The use of the tower block form and the increase in living space of flats, from an area of 2.25 m² per person in the 1960s to 5–7 m² per person at present
2. The increase in the height of the tower block to 30-40 storeys
3. Shifting of services zones to the interior, accessed by re-entrant spaces

The nature of these re-entrant spaces is controlled by a number of form determinants. The minimum width is 2.3 m and is prescribed by a rectangular plane of 21 m². This creates an inner zone for the kitchen and bathroom at the end of the re-entrant space. Other spaces such as the living space access the re-entrant space for light and ventilation. Research has been carried out on the effectiveness of these re-entrant spaces in relation to air quality.

Using a computer-based fluid dynamics modelling technique has shown that given some wind directions, there could be an increase in pollution from kitchens, nine times greater than the odour threshold. This suggests that there should be greater interrelation between the planning determinants and the environmental determinants in the design of these types of buildings to prevent such problems.[8]

10.15 Queensland's Therapies and Anatomies Building

Re-entrant spaces for light

Re-entrant spaces can also be used to provide light into deep-plan buildings in a similar way to atriums and courtyards. An example of this is found at the University of Queensland's Therapies and Anatomies Building. The building, a research and teaching facility, is rectilinear and is orientated with its major façades facing the north and south. On the south side a re-entrant space is created with a large roof canopy over the space. There are a number of advantages to this approach:

- reduction of low-altitude solar gain
- reduction of high-altitude solar gain and diffused light

The location and climate of Brisbane provide some problems for façades in summer. In particular, south-facing glazing receives direct low-angle sun onto the face for about four hours in the morning and a similar period in the evening. This can create overheating to spaces where large areas of glass are used. The solution often used is to place a vertical sunshade on the façade to avoid this problem. Re-entrant spaces that have opaque transverse walls can therefore act as blocking devices to reduce access to low-angle sun. The use of the canopy over the re-entrant space also appears to have an advantage. It helps shade the space from direct sun and provides reflected light to the space. As a consequence, large areas of glazing can be used to increase natural light into the adjacent offices and teaching space. The solution in this way avoids the use of individual sunshades to each of the facades.

10.3 Light shafts

Light shafts are defined as small apertures in a roof for the admittance of natural light. These areas are usually glazed. These light shafts are particularly useful for providing natural light to spaces in a deep plan building. It is often assumed, though, that in tropical buildings light admittance should be avoided. This is because the high intensity of light in tropical climates provides a number of problems: the admission of direct sunlight into a building admits heat and high levels of ultraviolet radiation not only increasing heat gain in spaces, but also leading to bleaching to furnishings and fittings in the space. The latter problem can be addressed by using ultraviolet resistant glasses; the former can only be addressed by shading the aperture to the roof light or by reducing its size so that the amount of light is reduced. Some form of sun shading to the exterior of the glass can also be used to defuse the light.

10.4 Air wells, air shafts and thermal chimneys

'Air well' and 'thermal chimney' are similar terms for a mechanism that provides air into a building to provide ventilation, but a distinction should be made between these two terms.

Air wells differ in nature from a courtyard in terms of relative size and function; a courtyard is normally a larger open space, whereas air wells can be roofed or unroofed. Air shafts are often smaller spaces and act as natural air plenums or ducts through the building. In principle these shafts and wells rely on air pressure-induced ventilation and thermal siphonage to induce air movement. Thermal chimneys rely an induced form of air movement by heat.

10.16 *Mechanically assisted airshaft system for domestic scale buildings*

Air wells

Air wells are a common feature of terrace housing in countries such as Malaysia, where the deep plan nature of the building necessitates methods of improving ventilation. This is particularly important in tropical areas where ventilation is achieved by air pressure. In Malaysia the climate has a typical low outside wind speed of 1m s^{-1} to 1.2 m s^{-1}. In addition, the weather data shows periods of calm when there is little air movement; seasonally the low velocity is uniform with small diurnal ranges of temperature.

Since air movement is one of the key aspects of comfort in the tropics, developing an effective mechanism to induce and maximize the limited natural forces in this climate is crucial. Typical in a modern terraced house design is single-storey narrow frontage of 6 m, with a typical length of 18 m. The air well is placed in the back third of the building to provide ventilation to the kitchen, bathroom and bedrooms. In section the roof is left open to admit ventilation.

Some researchers have questioned the use of this approach with regard to the provision of the air wells for this purpose in these modern terraced house designs. The main problems are first security – intruders can gain access to

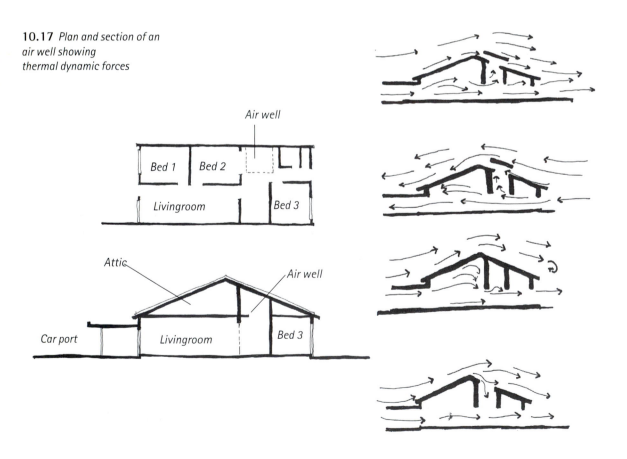

10.17 *Plan and section of an air well showing thermal dynamic forces*

the house through the roof. Second, air wells are modified to improve security which reduces efficiency. Third, lack of user awareness of the function of the air well often means that the function is compromised.[9]

Suggestions have been made to improve the design of these air wells by adding a built-up roof section. This, with clerestory openings to the side walls, provides security yet also provides ventilation. Research has shown that by increasing the side-wall ventilation to 1.2 m and providing a 1.2 m² aperture, the efficiency of through ventilation to the house is improved by a third. In addition the research pointed to lack of performance of the open air well as not promoting ventilation in the test house and concluded use of the clerestory pop-up roof in the terraced house has further potential to improve the wind flow.

The reasons for this are related to the way the additional roof element directs and regulates pressure at the roof level. As seen in earlier examples of courtyard design, air movement creates positive pressure at the windward side of the building and negative pressure at the leeward side. The operation of the air well as a ventilation system is related to how it is connected to these pressure areas. It seems that without a 'pop-up' roof the negative pressure induced to the leeward side of the pitched roof is not induced in the air well, thus reducing its efficiency. The pop-up roof form directs or induces negative pressure, thereby improving efficiency. Moreover, the improvement of the efficiency of the air well is also related to positioning and sizing of upwind openings.

Chimneys

The use of air shafts in buildings to provide ventilation is common, particularly in large complex buildings, but they are used in conjunction with active systems. A fan is usually attached to the shaft to enhance efficiency by

10.18 *Solar chimney proposed by S.P. Rao for apartments in Singapore. The ventilation system is driven by heat generated from solar thermal collectors located at the base of the stack:*

left: section through apartments showing central corridor and ducts

below: plan of a typical bay

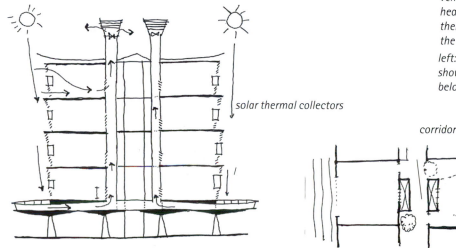

solar thermal collectors

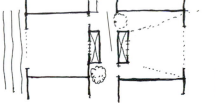

corridor with ducts

10.19 *Graphs showing the preliminary sizing of elements for a solar chimney to give ventilation:*
top: air changes per hours for a particular unit size given a 20 metre stack
bottom: air changes per hour for a unit size of 100 m³ related to stack height

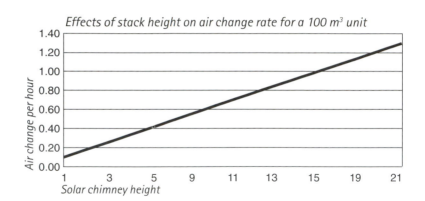

Effects of stack height on air change rate for a 100 m³ unit

Air change per hour (y-axis: 0.00, 0.20, 0.40, 0.60, 0.80, 1.00, 1.20, 1.40)

Solar chimney height (x-axis: 1, 3, 5, 9, 11, 13, 15, 19, 21)

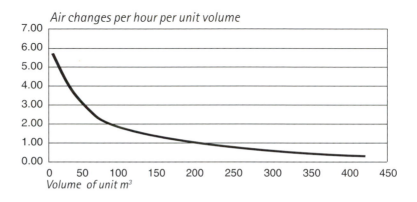

Air changes per hour per unit volume

(y-axis: 0.00, 1.00, 2.00, 3.00, 4.00, 5.00, 6.00, 7.00)

Volume of unit m³ (x-axis: 0, 50, 100, 150, 200, 250, 300, 350, 400, 450)

10.20 *MBF building, Penang, use of horizontal and vertical air shafts.*

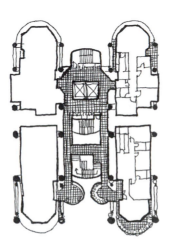

inducing air movement.

Without the use of active systems, pressure or thermally induced ventilation is required. The problem is that the cross-section area and friction losses in the shaft mean that high pressure differences are required to drive the air through the apertures and shaft. The size of the shaft is related to the capacity to ventilate, very similar to an air-conditioning duct. Roof ventilators are an example of how air shafts work.

Attempts to apply these principles in large buildings have been found in Hong Kong, Singapore, Malaysia and Queensland. In Hong Kong some of the post-war flat designs, air shafts were used to ventilate interior bathrooms. Observation of these spaces suggests that they were less than effective. More recently the use of these shafts has been attempted in high-rise buildings.

Research work in Singapore has investigated the use of chimneys to provide ventilation to high-rise buildings.

This ventilation is enhanced by using a solar heat gain. In this case a perimeter canopy is used to collect heat and induce ventilation in an air shaft by way of a stack effect. As with a traditional chimney to a fireplace, air heated at low level rises by way of its natural buoyancy over the surrounding colder air and rises to exhaust through a chimney. This sucks air in from the served spaces and from the outside, thus providing ventilation. This work is still at the conceptual stage and modelling studies have been carried out. The inherent problem is that while these systems work in theory, there is little empirical evidence to support general design principles.[10] Factors affecting the efficiency of the solar chimney are as follows

- height, the higher the chimney the better the draft (flow of air through the chimney

10.21 *MBF building, Penang, use of horizontal and vertical air shifts.*

- temperature difference of the internal air in the stack and the ambient air temperature
- resistances to airflow in the chimney, bends and surfaces resistance reduce the airflow
- the design of the inlet and exit openings of the chimney control the amount of air through the chimney, the problem is that wind pressure can affect the workings of the stack effect as the pressures from wind are likely to be higher than the stake effect

Careful alignment of the inlet and exits openings with respect to the prevailing winds is recommended. If this is not achieved then the chimney can work in reverse.[11] Questions arise as to the heat difference required between the input air and the external air to induce sufficient buoyancy in the air to overcome friction losses in the vertical shaft. In this sense, whilst architects may conceptually design and integrate air shafts into design strategies, their functionality is questionable. Here lies the conundrum for passive design: whilst there are clear strategies for utilizing these systems, without basic principles to work from there will be little use of the strategy in practice.

Other systems of providing air shafts can be found which take a different approach, rather than create special ducts in the building to promote ventilation the circulation spaces can be used as vertical and horizontal ducts for exhausting hot air from the building and promote air movement. A radical concept by Ken Yeang that uses this approach can be found in the MBF tower, Penang. In this building, four units per floor are supported between a concrete mega structure.[12] The circulation space between units not only provides a connection to a central core but also provides horizontal and vertical ducts for cross-ventilation of the units. This system is less reliant on solar gain to drive a stack system.

A project on the Gold Coast, Queensland, demonstrates a more modest approach to the use of air shafts. In a two- and three-story duplex design the stairways are used as air shafts. The plan for the building is deep with a distance of 12 m across the main living areas. Kitchens are located in a central position which is not typical for this type of moderate climate. On the lower floor an open plan arrangement of space is used. The stairs are adjacent to the kitchen so there is a potential to use them as air shafts so that excess heat from the kitchens drives the stack effect. The stairs are therefore open tread to allow maximum air movement. The stack is open to bedrooms at higher levels. Doors are 1.5 m wide with door heads taken to the ceiling. This facilitates air movement from the bedroom to the shaft. At the roof level rather, than use a 'pop-up' roof which is expensive to construct and detail, a centre pivot roof window is used. This sits in plane with the roof and is integrated with the roofing material. This gives a simple and effective construction. The windows can be set between trusses or bulkheads formed to create a larger space between the roof and the ceiling line. For ventilation the pivot window maximizes the opening size and can be automatically closed in inclement weather.

One other issue concerned with the design of air shafts or other forms of

open enclosed space which transfers air is that it will also reverberate sound. The lack of privacy and increase in the attenuation of sound through buildings should be addressed in the shaft design. In the Gold Coast example, perforated fibre-cement is used to line the stairway. This is combined with insulation in the wall cavity to act as a Holtz resonator and absorb sound. In this way the air movement is provided without the noise intrusion.

10.22 *Air shaft used in conjunction with the vertical circulation system*

References

1.   L. Heschong, *Thermal Delight in Architecture*, MIT Press. 1979, p. 45.
2   P. Gurstein, 'Traditional Shop Houses of Peninsular Malaysia,' *UIA International 6*, London 1984, pp. 21-22.
3.   B. Givoni, *Man, Climate and Architecture*, Van Nostrand Reinhold, 1976, p. 305.
4.   Givoni, op. cit., p. 294.
5.   L. Vogt, *New Orleans Houses*, Pelican Publishing, Gretena, Louisiana, 1992, pp. 22-23.
6.   B.Y. Sullivan, 'Living in Hong Kong: A Typological Study of Living Patterns in Small Flats', *Proceedings of the European Conference, American Collegiate Society of Architects*, London, May 1994, p.1.
7.   B.Y. Sullivan, 'Inhabiting Public Housing in Hong Kong', unpublished paper, Department of Architecture, Chinese University of Hong Kong, 1994, pp. 2-4.
8.   D. Cronin, 'Investigation into the Dynamics of Waste Air Dispersal from High-rise Residences', in *Proceedings of 30th Conference, Australian New Zealand, Architectural Science Conference*, The Chinese University of Hong Kong 1996, pp. 85-92.
9.   R. Salleh, 'Wind ventilation of terrace housing in Malaysia,' in *Proceedings of Towards Better Buildings in the Tropics*, Institute Sultan

Iskandar-Universiti Technologi Malaysia, Kuala Lumpur, 1994.

10. C. Able, 'Cool high-rise', *Architectural Review*, September 1994, pp. 23-29.

11. R. Aynesley, 'Natural Ventilation in Passive Design,' *Environmental Design Guide*, Royal Australian Institute of Architects, 1996, TEC 2: 5.

12. B. Lim, *Environmental Design Criteria of Tall Buildings*, Lehigh University Bethlehem, Pennsylvania 1994, p. 218.

Index